Confederate General
Lloyd Tilghman

Confederate General Lloyd Tilghman

A Biography

JAMES W. RAAB

McFarland & Company, Inc., Publishers
Jefferson, North Carolina, and London

ALSO BY JAMES W. RAAB

*J. Patton Anderson, Confederate General:
A Biography* (McFarland, 2004)

FRONTISPIECE: Brigadier General Lloyd Tilghman, 1816–1863, one of the most picturesque figures in the Confederate army and a strict disciplinarian. This photograph (1861) is taken from a carte de visite.

LIBRARY OF CONGRESS CATALOGUING-IN-PUBLICATION DATA

Raab, James W.
    Confederate General Lloyd Tilghman : a biography / James W. Raab.
      p.   cm.
    Includes bibliographical references and index.

    ISBN-13: 978-0-7864-2460-3
    ISBN-10: 0-7864-2460-5
    (softcover : 50# alkaline paper) ∞

    1. Tilghman, Lloyd, 1816–1863. 2. Generals—Confederate States of America—Biography. 3. Confederate States of America. Army—Biography. 4. United States—History—Civil War, 1861–1865—Campaigns. 5. Mississippi—History—Civil War, 1861–1865—Campaigns. I. Title.
E467.1.T55R33 2006
973.7'3092—dc22   2006020678
[B]

British Library cataloguing data are available

©2006 James W. Raab. All rights reserved

No part of this book may be reproduced or transmitted in any form or by any means, electronic or mechanical, including photocopying or recording, or by any information storage and retrieval system, without permission in writing from the publisher.

On the cover: General Lloyd Tilghman Memorial, Vicksburg National Military Park, Mississippi

Manufactured in the United States of America

*McFarland & Company, Inc., Publishers
  Box 611, Jefferson, North Carolina 28640
  www.mcfarlandpub.com*

Table of Contents

List of Maps	vii
Preface	1
Prologue	3
Profile: Tilghman's Lineage	5
1. West Point and the Mexican War	7
2. Panama, Railroading, and the Compromise of 1850	19
3. A Godsend, and Kentucky Service	26
4. Confederate Western War Department	37
5. A Trinity of Forts	47
6. Eve of Disaster	63
7. The Surrender of Fort Henry	77
8. Armageddon on the Cumberland, and the Surrender of Fort Donelson	92
9. A Prisoner of War at Fort Warren, Massachusetts	109
10. The Exchange Cartel, and the Attacks on Iuka and Corinth	120
11. The Skirmish at Coffeeville, Mississippi	133

12. Grenada: Winter Quarters, 1863	144
13. The Yazoo Pass Expedition	151
14. The Siege of Fort Pemberton	159
15. Grierson's Raid, Port Gibson, and the Grand Gulf Collapse	167
16. Champion Hill	178
17. In the Midst of Life There Is Death	194
Appendix: Staff of Brig. Gen. Lloyd Tilghman	199
Notes	201
Bibliography	209
Index	213

List of Maps

All maps by Jean Light Willis

Campaigns of the Mexican War	14
Panama railroad	20
The Western Theater, 1861–1862	38
Forts Heiman, Henry and Donelson	48
Fort Henry on the Tennessee River	67
Scope of the Confederate calamity at Fort Henry	73
Fort Donelson on the Cumberland River	97
Mississippi railroads	118
Battle for Corinth	124
The Yazoo Pass expedition	152
Union route to Fort Pemberton	154
Fort Pemberton at Greenwood, Mississippi	161
Grierson's Raid	169
Grand Gulf and Port Gibson	173
Confederate line of march — Champion Hill, May 16, 1863	184

Preface

Many Civil War books published during the past 20 years have had little to offer that is new, mainly because their authors have had to rewrite old references from previously used source material. The eastern battlefields of Virginia, Maryland, and Pennsylvania were the most prestigious to write about because of the abundance of heroes and spectacular battles.

The objective of this book is to inform the reader about the drama and battles that took place between the Appalachian Mountains and the Mississippi River. This western part of the conflict was loosely coordinated by an assortment of colorful, cavalier, and politically appointed generals who answered the call and served the cause to the end of the war.

Their disadvantages were many, including a geography of mountains, rivers, and trails hundreds of miles long; older, untrained volunteers who followed in the footsteps of younger, experienced militia that the Confederate states sent to Virginia at the beginning of the conflict; and inferior arms, clothing, and military supplies. Lastly, they faced off against superstar generals such as Ulysses S. Grant, George H. Thomas, William Tecumseh Sherman, and others.

I feature Lloyd Tilghman of Paducah, Kentucky, as one of these patriot generals. A wellborn Marylander, Tilghman had no particular economic reason to take arms against the North. Instead, he held a strong personal conviction that at certain critical moments the people of the land had the right to defend themselves against abuses of their government and to remedy their grievances. Tilghman believed in States' Rights as justification for rebelling against the Federal Union. A West Pointer, this chivalrous, courageous Southern gentleman of the antebellum period became one of the grandest embodiments of a gallant commander from the western theater of war. Like tens of thousands, he would fall upon a Civil War battlefield in his cherished South. Now, decades after his death, the flame of his respected life glimmers in the dusk of what is past.

I am indebted to Beth Mansbridge, of Mansbridge Editing and Transcription, who was generous with her time and expertise in editing the manuscript; and to Jean Light Willis, artist, who provided the fine maps for the book.

James W. Raab
St. Augustine, Florida

Prologue

The new Federation of States was not far into the 1800s when men on both sides of the Mason-Dixon Line became sharply aware of two distinct and differing socioeconomic systems evolving side by side in their respective sections of the country. The North was being thrust into the Industrial Revolution with its commerce, industry, and finance; slavery could simply no longer be accepted in this new age. Horace Greeley, editor and politician of the *New York Tribune*, who advocated immediate emancipation, said that if the cotton states were satisfied that they could do better out of the Union than in it, let them go in peace. In South Carolina, the *Charleston Mercury* argued that the North and South were two nations made by their institutions, customs, and habits as distinct as the English from the French. The South was predominantly agricultural, was doing very well for itself, and saw no need to surrender its way of life or its chattels.

By the summer of 1860, Southerners could see their national role in Washington slowly eroding and consequently their way of existence being threatened. They decided to exercise what they believed to be their Constitutional rights by peacefully withdrawing from the Union and resuming their sovereignty, proposing no war upon the government in Washington or upon any particular state. Conservative elements of both North and South made great efforts to bring about reconciliation, but were unsuccessful in closing the breach.

When Abraham Lincoln, who said he would take action to keep the

Union together, emerged victorious in 1860 as the new president, the South Carolina legislature voted unanimously for a sovereign convention for the purpose of dissolving South Carolina's ties to the Union. On December 20, the convention delegates voted for independence. This action of secession was followed closely by the states of Mississippi, Florida, Alabama, Georgia, Louisiana, and Texas, which summoned their own conventions to adopt ordinances of secession. These seceded states elected delegates to a convention in Montgomery, Alabama, in February, 1861, organizing a new republic called the Confederate States of America.

As the telegraph clicked off the news of the Confederate States, intense anger and excitement broke out in all sections of the country. At outset, the states of Delaware, Maryland, Missouri, and Kentucky were viewed as "border states" because of geographic position and questionable loyalty.

Lloyd Tilghman resided in Paducah, Kentucky. Distinctly Southern in character, he resented abolitionists and favored secession, but was divided in his sympathies, being attached to the North by strong blood ties. Governor Beriah Magoffin, believing Kentucky to be a buffer zone, refused Abraham Lincoln's call for Federal troops, declaring his state neutral. But his attempt proved futile as both Union and Confederate recruiters began operating in Kentucky, causing a serious dilemma for the Tilghmans. "Are you for the South, or are you for the North?" was a question not easily answered. Lloyd Tilghman cast his lot with the South and quickly discovered that misfortune never travels alone.

Profile: Tilghman's Lineage

The Tilghman name is prominently identified with early American history. Dr. Richard Tilghman, an eminent London surgeon in the 17th century and a descendant of John Gaunt, first Duke of Lancaster, emigrated from England for the American colonies, having obtained from the first Lord Baltimore a grant of 100 acres of land in the colony of Maryland. He became the original patentee and settler of Canterbury Manor, Talbot County, and the "Hermitage" in Queen Anne County, about 1662.[1] Subsequently, the Tilghmans became men of rank in Colonial times.

Richard Tilghman III was a member of the Lord Proprietor's Council and Chancellor of the Province; Matthew Tilghman was a member of the Continental Congress and president of the Constitutional Convention (1774–1775). Matthew Tilghman, styled as the patriarch of the Maryland colony, would have been a signer of the Declaration of Independence but for the fact that he was called to Annapolis in June to preside over the convention that framed the first constitution of the state of Maryland. William Tilghman, who studied law under Benjamin Chew before the Revolution, became Chief Justice of Pennsylvania. Lloyd's great-grandfather, Lieutenant Colonel Tench C. Tilghman (1774–1786), on the eve of the American Revolution, liquidated his business and became secretary and treasurer for the Continental Congress Commissioners to the Iroquois Indians. In July, 1776, he was commissioned captain of an independent militia that joined a Pennsylvania battalion, and he assumed the duties of military secretary to General George Washington. He took the news of Cornwallis's surrender at Yorktown to the Continental Congress in 1781. Tench served in the army until December 1783, when he entered business in Baltimore with Robert Morris, a prominent financier of the American Revolution. Unfortunately, Tench died a few months after his 41st birthday, death caused by "hardships encountered during the revolution."[2]

At the commencement of the Civil War, Lloyd Tilghman had three cousins who would serve the Confederacy. Captain Oswald Tilghman of Easton, Maryland, commanded a battery at Port Hudson, Louisiana, participated effectively in the defense of the fort, and survived the siege but became a prisoner of war, serving 23 months at Johnston's Island, Ohio. Captain John Leeds Tilghman of Oxford, Maryland, commanded the Huger Battery of Light Artillery of Norfolk, Virginia. He died of consumption at Augusta, Georgia, in 1863. The third cousin, Colonel Tench F. Tilghman, was one of the officers who formed the bodyguard of Jefferson Davis during his attempt to escape through Georgia to the Trans-Mississippi.[3]

Subsequent references to Tilghman genealogy will apply only to Lloyd Tilghman, unless otherwise noted. Lloyd Tilghman was born to James and Anne Caroline Shoemaker Tilghman at Rich Neck Manor, Queen Anne County, Maryland, on January 18, 1816. Lloyd was the fourth child and only son of the marriage. Without doubt, young Lloyd was of genteel blood, inheriting aristocratic traits of pride, condescension, arrogance, and family privilege. His tutors early saw 15-year-old Lloyd's merit, abilities, and forcefulness before his appointment to the United States Military Academy at West Point, New York.

1

West Point and the Mexican War

Early on, many earthen and wooden forts of defense had been erected by the Spanish, French, and English in their colonies, territories, and Indian country. At the conclusion of the American Revolution, the maintenance and occupation of these fortifications became the responsibility of the new nation's army.

In 1802, the United States Congress authorized the establishment of the U.S. Military Academy on a reservation on the Hudson River in southeastern New York State. The freshmen, or plebes, as they were called, were offered tactical training, weaponry, field maneuvers, military engineering, and, upon graduation, commissions in the United States Army. The superintendent at this time was Sylvanus Thayer, who received his commission in engineering and implemented many of the courses now intact. Thayer departed to engage in the construction of fortifications along the New England coast, principally at Boston Harbor. He later founded Dartmouth's Thayer School of Engineering.[1]

Succeeding Thayer was Lieutenant Dennis Hart Mahan, a New York native who graduated at the head of his class in 1824. Mahan studied under Napoleon's officers at a school in Metz, France, and returned to West Point, where he was appointed Professor of Military and Civil Engineering.[2] His teaching included general outlines for constructing forts, redoubts, carriers, entrenchments, bridges, and railroads, and regulating the attack and defense of such permanent works.[3]

A glimpse of Plebe Tilghman at West Point can be seen through a *New York Standard* article about the reporter's visit to West Point on July 4, 1831. The article was reprinted on the front page of the *Easton Gazette*, Talbot County, Maryland, on July 16, 1831.

> As has been our custom for several years past, we selected this delightful spot for a retreat with our family, from the din and bustle of the city on the 4th. The day was ushered in with the customary national salute, and the celebration of the Jubilee was characterized by the usual military display by the Cadets. At half past 11 o'clock, a civic and military procession was formed and proceeded to the Chapel where an impressive address was delivered by Cadet Tilghman of Maryland, the orator of the day, in the mingled feeling of hope and fear he could not but ejaculate the prayer that heaven would not favor the oppressor—"that principle would prevail over numbers in the fearful contest now raging for Polish freedom or Russian domination—that even the serfs of the Autocrat might breathe the spirit of Kosciusko* as they touch the soil of his birth—and breathing it might refuse to war against his countrymen."

Tilghman was an orator before he was sixteen years old, a great honor for the cadet.

The reporter finishes his story at West Point:

> The Chapel was decorated with wreaths of evergreens, and a superb eagle curiously wrought from laurel and other emblems of immortality, spread its broad wings about the stage, resting on a shield formed by the national flag, supported by the colors of the corps. A national salute was repeated at noon. At three o'clock the Cadets under the Presidency of Capt. Hitchcock, their accomplished commandant and acting commandant of the post, in the absence of Col. Thayer, sat down to an excellent dinner prepared with his usual taste by Mr. Cozzens, and were honoured by the presences of General Aaron Ward, member of Congress elect from Westchester, General Pierre Van Courtland, Philip Van Wyck, Esq. of Westchester, Lieut. Ogden of the Navy, Henry Carey, Esq. of Philadelphia, and the officers and professors of the Academy as invited guests.
> In the evening the Point was lighted up by thousands of rockets, darting like meteors in every direction through the heavens, and the shades of night closed upon a quiet and gratified camp.—*New York Standard*[4]

The youthful Tilghman was fortunate to be schooled under the Sylvanus Thayer and Dennis H. Mahan curriculum. He also learned the Academy Honor Code—a cadet will not lie, cheat, or steal—a moral self-discipline he adhered to throughout his life. He graduated from West

---

*Thaddeus Kosciusko, Polish general and patriot (1746–1817).

Point on July 1, 1836, 46th in a class of 49. Among his classmates was Lieutenant Richard A. Anderson of Fort Sumter, South Carolina, fame. Upon graduation Tilghman was a brevet second lieutenant, United States regiment Dragoons, and made a second lieutenant four days thereafter.

"Old Hickory," Andrew Jackson, the nation's seventh president, was in office at this time. The Jacksonian Democrats were concerned with defending slavery, capturing runaway slaves, and moving the eastern Indian tribes to western reservations. "The United States army at the time was far smaller in power than the nation it served. There were some seven thousand men and six hundred officers scattered about the country at small forts and army posts. The army called upon to do the job was led by officers now drawn mostly from West Point Military Academy, who thought of themselves as an elite few who fought for the honor and glory of their country."[5] The enlisted men they were to lead were at the opposite pole of society: uneducated, outcasts, dregs who drank heavily and went missing just as easily on five dollars a month.

America's Manifest Destiny traversed in any direction it pleased. In the new Florida territory it granted the white settlers freedom to clear and cultivate their cheap land grants at the expense of Creek and Seminole Indian tribes' lands. During the Second Seminole War, the U.S. Army, not properly trained for the Indian warfare that developed, spent seven years trying to move or eliminate these elusive Indians. Only by deceit, not defeat, could the government troopers obtain the removal of the majority of the Creeks to western reservations. The few thousand remaining Seminoles took to hiding in swampland in southern Florida, remaining there for years, to the frustration of the U.S. Army.

Lloyd Tilghman, born of genteel blood, wanted no part of the Indian war in Florida or to be garrisoned at some isolated fort in the West, so he resigned his commission on September 30, 1836.

As immigrants swarmed to join the new nation with its opportunities and freedoms, they automatically fostered and developed additional stages of Manifest Destiny. The nation of 35 million began an unprecedented sweep to the west with railroad construction. "Go West, young man" was the cry, sending millions westward to cheap government land. Soon thereafter came the railroads and the telegraph.

The nation had many opportunities for the well educated 20-year-old West Point graduate. In 1837 Tilghman accepted the position of division engineer with the Baltimore & Susquehanna Railroad.[6] He next associated himself in the survey of the Norfolk & Wilmington Canal, 1838; following this, he was an engineer for Eastern Shore Railroad of Maryland in 1839. Afterwards, he superintended public improvements for the City of Baltimore, Maryland.[7]

On May 26, 1843, Lloyd Tilghman married Augusta Murray Boyd, whose father, Joseph L. Boyd, had been first treasurer of the state of Maine; her aunt Elizabeth Southgate was married to Walter Browne, mayor of New York City. The affluent couple was married in Portland, Maine, with West Pointer Joseph Hooker as best man. "Fighting Joe" Hooker later became commanding officer of the Army of the Potomac during the coming conflict.[8]

Texas Manifest Destiny

On December 29, 1845, Texas accepted the terms of annexation to the United States, entering the Union as the 28th state. In addition the Texans asked President James K. Polk to protect them against any further attacks from Mexico. Mexico objected and ended diplomatic relations with the United States as disputes arose over the new boundary of Texas and Mexico.

As the press covered these historic events in early 1846, the news inevitably became a foreshadowing of war with Mexico. Across the states the militia was organized, drilled, and made ready to support the government.

Lloyd Tilghman had been free from army service for ten years. However, during the winter, his inherited chivalry, a Tilghman family tradition, spurred the 32-two-year-old West Pointer to rejoin the United States army as aide-de-camp to General David E. Twiggs.

Twiggs's family had long been famous in the military history of the country. His father, General John Twiggs, rendered services in the Revolutionary War of such importance as to gain him the title of "Saviour of Georgia."[9]

David Twiggs was born in Richmond County, Georgia, in 1790. A veteran officer, he joined the army at the beginning of the War of 1812 and became a regular officer fighting under Andrew Jackson in the Indian campaigns with Generals E. P. Gaines and Winfield Scott. At present he held the rank of colonel of the 2nd Regiment of Dragoons. Interestingly, not until after the Civil War did the West Point influence dominate the top ranks of the army. "At this time Scott, Twiggs, Taylor, Wool, Worth, and other officers in the military hierarchy seemed to support the Minutemen tradition against the growing notion that a man needed a formal military education to lead troops in battle. Nearly one-fourth of the officer corps had been drawn from civil life."[10] "Twiggs, for example, shaped the 2nd Dragoons to fit Professor Mahan's definition of the cavalryman as that epitome of military impudence — an image quite in contrast to that of the more dignified and methodical 1st Dragoons."[11] One of his peculiarities was his faculty of getting more work out of men in a given time than any other officer in the army. A quartermaster stood no chance; Twiggs's stentorian lungs drowned everyone's voice and his tone of command did not admit any question. "Speak to your mules, sir, and keep them going as long as they will. Drive slowly, a little way at a time, and let your mules blow."[12]

Major General David E. Twiggs (Massachusetts Commandery, Military Order of the Loyal Legion, U.S. Army Military History Institute).

As aide-de-camp (A.D.C.), Tilghman was a military officer acting as a secretary and confidential assistant to a superior officer.

> **aide-de-camp:** A confidential *ex officio* officer appointed by general officers to their staffs; an aide-de-camp reported directly to his commander and took orders only from him. In a position of great responsibility, an aide was required to write orders, deliver them personally if necessary, and

be thoroughly knowledgeable about troop positions, maneuvers, columns, orders of corps, routes, and the locations of officers' quarters. An aide also had to understand tactics and operations thoroughly enough to modify orders on the battlefield if new orders could not be issued by the commanding general. In wartime, a lieutenant general was permitted to appoint 4 aides, a major general 2, and a brigadier general 1.—PLF[13]

It was a good mix. Twiggs, a veteran of 32 years of service, some during wartime, was a disciplinarian who could outswear anyone. He was a good soldier, though rough in manner and speech. Twiggs personified the Frontier Regular Army. Tilghman, educated in West Point protocol, 20 years different in age, would attempt to temper the tiger on the way to Mexico.

Agreeable to instructions from President Polk, General Zachary Taylor, stationed at Fort Jessup, Louisiana, moved his small force of United States regulars to the north shore of the Gulf of Mexico, at Corpus Christi in eastern Texas in early 1846. This became the staging area for collection of United States volunteer forces. Joining General Taylor were many noteworthy officers. Colonel Jefferson Davis, Taylor's son-in-law, joined with the 1st Mississippi Rifles. Lieutenant U. S. Grant, Captain E. Kirby Smith, Major Sam Ringgold's flying artillery units, Colonel J. C. Hays, and Texas Rangers led by Captains Sam Walker and Ben McCulloch were present. General Twiggs, a.d.C. Lieutenant Tilghman, General William J. Worth, and his a.d.C., Lieutenant John C. Pemberton, joined up as well. Pemberton graduated from West Point a year later than Tilghman. He had continued his army career with nine years' service in garrison duty.

For the first time in the military history of the young nation, many of the junior officer corps such as Tilghman, Pemberton, and Grant were professionals, the product of the military academy at West Point.

Invasion

By the beginning of March, 61-year-old General Zachary Taylor had mustered an army of 3,000 volunteers and regulars, hundreds of horses, oxen, mules, 300 supply wagons, and cannon. On March 11, Taylor was ready to move his expeditionary force into territory claimed by Mexico and the United States, deploying his invading force toward the Rio

Grande. Pacing themselves, the columns of men wearing blue woolen uniforms were ordered out in four sections, separated by a day's march. It would be a difficult and hot 200-mile trek across the prairies and desert of south Texas. Men and animals suffered thirst due to the absence of suitable drinking water along the way. Dry wells and brackish water holes spoiled by salt made the 20-day advance across sun-baked Texas a severe experience for the volunteers, tormented also by the blazing sun. On this forward movement, Lieutenant Tilghman, commanding a small corps of volunteers, was on foot because no junior officers were permitted to ride a horse during the march.

Campaigns of the Mexican War

Taylor's advance Dragoons began sighting Mexican horsemen around the shallow Colorado River. As the Americans approached, the general received word from a Mexican officer stating that any attempt to cross over would be an act of war.[14]

Disregarding the warning, Taylor ordered his men forward, crossing the river under the protection of Lieutenant Braxton Bragg's artillery. The token Mexican cavalry disappeared as the Americans scrambled up the riverbank. Moving away from the coast, Taylor aimed his army toward the Rio Grande, arriving on March 28. He was now across the Rio Grande from the Mexican city of Matamoros. Raising the Stars and Stripes, Taylor ordered Tilghman to superintend the construction of a supply fort.[15] The fort had five sides and was built of earthen walls nine feet high and 15 feet thick.

Surprisingly, the Mexicans made no attempt to interfere with the threat. Day by day the fort rose, each corner holding a battery of cannon, an arrogant gesture on Mexican soil.[16] This would be the first of several famous forts that Tilghman would engineer during his military career.

The Mexicans were not a ragtag rabble of barefooted peasants. They were fully uniformed in blue or green tunics with white pants. They wore sandals, which were more suited to the sandy terrain than the heavy shoes worn by the Americans. Headgear: the leather tar-bucket shako of the French army. The infantry was armed with British tower muskets; the cavalry carried British carbines as well as formidable 10-foot, razor-sharp

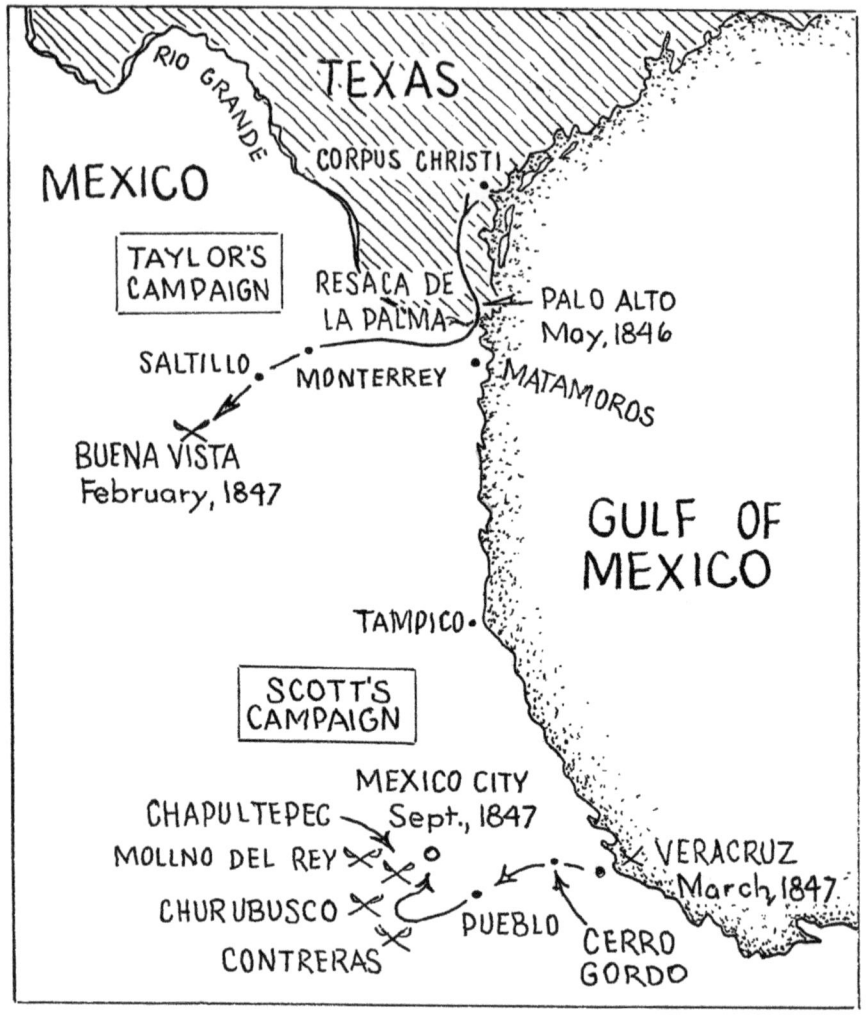

Campaigns of the Mexican War.

lances. Most troops had been battle-tried in the perennial Mexican civil wars or in the Texas fight for independence. Each regiment had its own band, besides trumpeters and buglers.[17]

General Taylor ordered the construction of a supply depot at Point Isabel, a tiny Mexican village on the Gulf coast. The 26-mile road linking Point Isabel and the supply fort at Matamoros became Taylor's lifeline for supplies and reinforcements. In May, Mexican General Mariano

Arista moved his army across the river, upstream from Matamoros towards Point Isabel, in an attempt to cut off Taylor's supply line.

To meet the challenge, Taylor, leaving 500 men at the earthen fort, moved quickly for Point Isabel. General Arista was waiting for him at Palo Alto with his army of 4,000 men. In a crucial battle for survival, Taylor's forces battered the Mexicans at Palo Alto. The next day at Resaca de la Palma, the Mexican resistance failed after a heated battle, and their army was routed, fleeing back toward the Rio Grande.

At the same time Mexican forces stationed across the river in Matamoros turned their attention to the American fort. On May 6, Mexican cavalry and infantry assumed assault positions, and at dawn a ferocious Mexican cannonade began. This lasted five days and nights without a break. General Taylor's dispatch: "It affords me peculiar pleasure to report that the field-work opposite to Matamoros has sustained itself handsomely during a cannonade and bombardment of one hundred and sixty hours. But the pleasure is allayed with profound regret at the loss of its heroic and indomitable commander, Major Jacob Brown, who died today from the effect of a shell."[18] Thereafter the supply fort was referred to as Fort Brown, at present-day Brownsville, Texas.

Taylor's dispatch added: "The Mexican forces are almost disorganized, and I shall lose no time investing Matamoros, and opening the navigation of the river."[19] Shortly thereafter, "Old Rough and Ready" Taylor appointed Twiggs governor of Matamoros.[20]

Brigadier General Twiggs had now advanced in rank. His 1st Division of the army consisted of the 2nd Dragoons, 1st, 2nd, 3rd, and 4th Regiments of Infantry, plus Bragg's and Ridgely's artillery. While Colonel Wilson demonstrated against enemy troops at Barita, General Twiggs and Lieutenant Tilghman were crossing over the river above the town, with the band playing *Yankee Doodle*.[21]

It was a succession of battles, sieges, marches, and skirmishes. The conflict lasted through a period of 19 months. This war was marked by so many incidents of individual courage and resourcefulness that every officer seemed to return a hero.

With Matamoros in American hands and the supply fort safe, Taylor's forces advanced on Camargo and Cerralvo and in September attacked the Citadel at Monterrey, the metropolis of northern Mexico. A body of mounted Texas Rangers under Ben McCulloch and Jack Hays scouted and spearheaded the march. "These men in outlandish dress, huge beards, looked almost like savages and kept the Mexicans in mortal terror. They were armed with rifles and Colt's five-shooters [and] mounted on tough and wiry prairie mustangs. They were probably the best irregular horsemen of their times and broke up all Mexican cavalry opposition by rifle and pistol fire. The Rangers were credited with originating the 'Rebel yell' during this fighting. It started with a low bass rumble and rose in a crescendo to a frenzied treble shriek which suggested a sort of berserk mania of blood lust. Hays's order for attack was to point at the Mexicans and shout, 'Give 'em Hell!' "[22]

The American forces entered Monterrey in short order, and they later occupied Saltillo, 65 miles away.

Author Charles Fenno Hoffman wrote of this hard-fought battle:

> We were not many, we who stood
> Before the iron fleet that day:
> Yet many a gallant spirit would
> Give half his years if but he could
> Have been with us at Monterrey.[23]

By this time Taylor's army was shrinking from battle casualties, malaria fever, and most of all, the expiration of the one-year enlistment period. President Polk then proposed uniting the army in Mexico with additional U.S. forces to be led by the ranking general of the U.S. Army, General Winfield Scott. Dubbed "Old Fuss and Feathers" for his meticulous dress and insistence on military protocol, General Scott was a veteran of every U.S. war since 1812.

"Old Rough and Ready" Taylor remained at Monterrey. He was reinforced by new volunteers. On February 22 and 23, 1847, near the ranch of Buena Vista, Taylor's forces of 5,000 defeated Antonio Lopez de Santa Anna's army of 20,000, thus establishing the United States' hold on northeastern Mexico.

General Twiggs, Tilghman, and other units joined General Scott's new army at Lobos Island, south of Tampico, Mexico. Once assembled, the American forces sailed to Veracruz, Mexico, in March, 1847, and captured the city in 23 days. Unopposed, General Twiggs led his force out of Veracruz in April, marching towards Jalapa, then inland to Cerro Gordo, where the Americans scored a victory on April 18. While other American forces took the National Highway to Mexico City, Twiggs's forces stayed at Ayotla to mask Scott's move. Aide-de-camp Lloyd Tilghman was at Twiggs's side throughout most of the war. Twiggs next moved on Mexico City at Churubusco, southern entrance, acting as a decoy while the main American force stormed the main gates of Mexico City.

Here Captain Robert E. Lee earned his notoriety by opening the route to Mexico City, finding a path through terrain the Mexicans considered impassable. His unit's bravery in attacking Chapultepec, a fortified hill guarding the city gates, carried them inside Mexico City. The Mexicans abandoned Mexico City on September 7, 1847, and sued for peace. Attempts after the fall of the city to instigate a treaty of peace were delayed for months; ultimately the Treaty of Guadalupe Hidalgo was signed by both sides on February 2, 1848.

"The treaty secured for the United States the vast territories of New Mexico, California, Western Texas, the Pacific Coast, together with the harbor of San Francisco, and internal navigation of the Colorado, Gila, and other rivers. Fifteen million dollars was paid to Mexico by the United States as compensation for part of this grant."[24] The treaty only aggravated the United States' internal political uncertainty, for the acquisition of New Mexico and California set off the momentous constitutional debate over slavery in the new territories and delayed for another three years the organization of a territorial government in the wake of the Compromise of 1850."[25]

By an article of the treaty, arrangements had been made for withdrawing all United States forces from Mexican territory within three months after the final ratifications. Earlier, Lieutenant Tilghman was advanced in rank to Captain of Maryland and District of Columbia Volunteer Artillery, commanded by Colonel George W. Hughes. In the early part of June, 1848, the greater part of the soldiers in the city of Mexico marched for Veracruz. They left the city by detachments, reached New Orleans about the middle of June, then proceeded by steamboat or railway towards their respective home bases. Tilghman's unit was disbanded on July 13, 1848.[26]

By now Tilghman had proved he was not one of those "wasp-waisted lieutenants of West Point, a mock word of contempt used to deride the national academy."[27] Emerging from the Mexican War as an extremely competent field officer, Captain Tilghman returned home to civilian life, resuming his civil engineering career. He had served his country well.

President James K. Polk favored annexation of Texas and had invaded the Republic at their request. But not everyone was in favor of the war. Abolitionists from New England found effective spokesmen to denounce "Polk's war." Horace Greeley, a leading abolitionist, condemned in his newspaper the slaughter on the southwestern battlefields and the endless rivers of blood. Former President John Quincy Adams openly opposed the annexation of Texas and voted against the declaration of war with Mexico. Whig Congressman Abraham Lincoln, U.S. Representative 1847–1849, opposed U.S. involvement in the Mexican War, supporting Whig measures blaming President Polk for starting the conflict. In the end, Lincoln supported appropriations to continue to supply the U.S. Army in Mexico as well as the candidacy of Zachary Taylor for president.[28]

Taylor, although a slaveholder, riding high on the coattails of victory in Mexico, won the election of 1848, becoming the twelfth President of the United States.

Among the many results of the Mexican War was an extremely competent officer corps for both sides' causes in the upcoming War Between the States. The earlier conflict was a practical training ground for a large number of junior officers, such as Tilghman and many others serving in combat for the first time. A point often overlooked was the American trait of volunteerism. It filled the army ranks for two years without a military draft or paid mercenaries from foreign shores. In many ways it duplicated the American Revolution forces, with a blend of English, French, Scots-Irish, Jewish, German, and freed black men, all citizens.

2

Panama, Railroading, and the Compromise of 1850

To travel to the west coast of the American continent from the east coast, a person had several options available. He could ride a Conestoga wagon, or prairie schooner along the Oregon Trail, a three-thousand-mile trip over the Continental Divide and South Pass. This would entail months of hardship, crossing the difficult mountain ranges through a maze of shortcuts and bypasses, experiencing prairie storms, rain, mud, Indians, snakes, and depending on a freight wagon for provisions.

Or a person could ignore the overland route, taking passage on a sailing ship from New York, Boston, or New Orleans. This route was a six-month trip and upwards of thirteen thousand miles of sea voyage around Cape Horn, the southernmost point in South America, to reach destinations on the west coast.

There was a third choice, the shortest distance between the Atlantic and the Pacific. This occurred at the narrow strip of land that connects North America and South America at the isthmus in Colombia. The distance between the oceans at this point was only fifty miles. Transportation through the jungles was by small riverboats, mule train, or on foot. Waiting on the western side of the isthmus, seagoing vessels would take the traveler to his destination. Regardless of inconvenience, the isthmus became the route of choice for thousands of travelers because it was quicker and cheaper.

Throughout most of the 1800s, Nicaragua provided this shortcut to

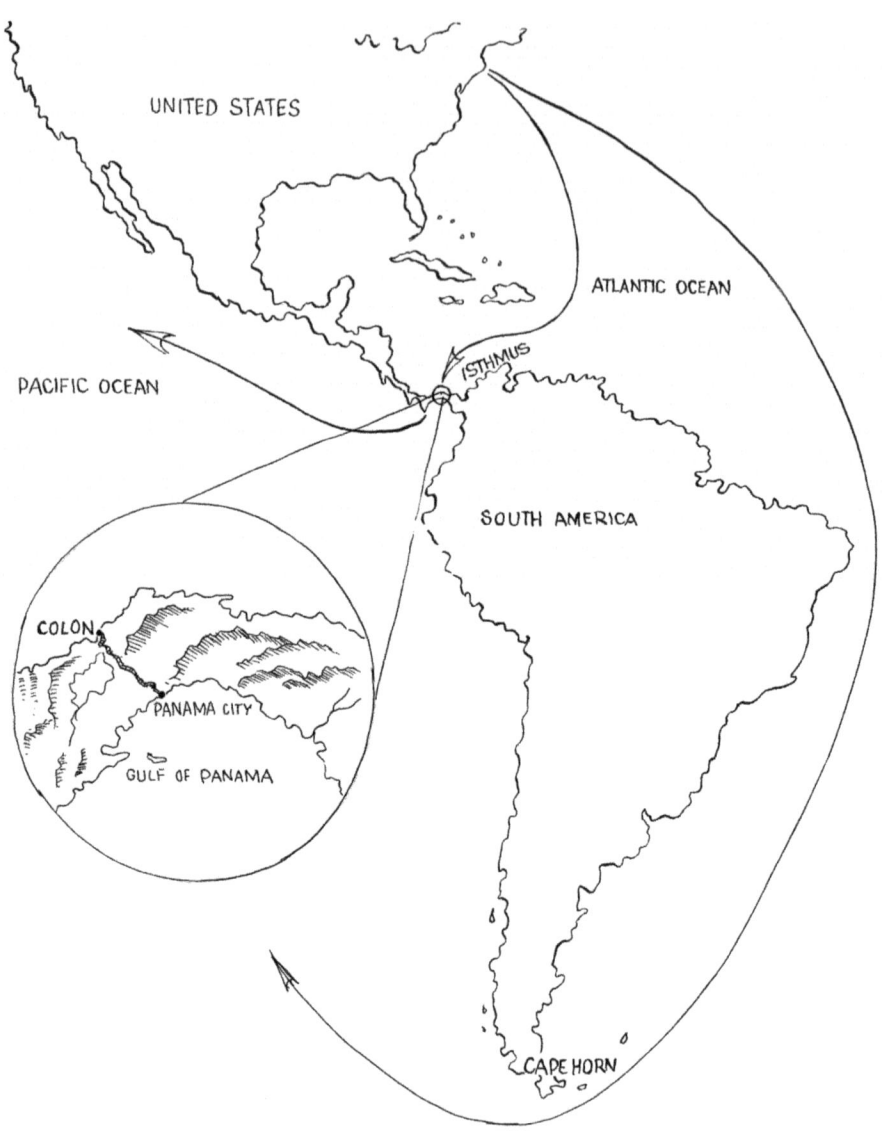

Panama railroad. The railroad provided a short route from Atlantic ports to Pacific ports.

the Pacific Ocean, and it became a chief center of plans to build a canal across the isthmus. During the 1840s, the U.S. and Great Britain almost went to war because of disputes over which one would control the proposed canal. In 1850, under the Clayton-Bulwer Treaty, both countries agreed to maintain the neutrality of such canal and the land on either side of it.[1]

2. Panama, Railroading, and the Compromise of 1850

At the same time, present-day Panama, a province of Colombia south of Nicaragua, presented the closest route to the Pacific. Colombia feared that Great Britain would try to seize Panama for use as their canal site. Therefore Colombia signed a treaty with the United States in 1846, which stated that the United States agreed to guard all trade routes across Panama to preserve its neutrality.[2] Certainly America's success in the Mexican War at this time hastened such an agreement.

The Mexican War was no sooner concluded in 1848 than the amazing discovery of gold at Sutter's Mill, California, created a great American gold craze in 1849. Panama and its possibilities became the focus of not only the gold diggers, but also their suppliers, as well as the U.S. Post Office and the army, which had new western territory to defend.

Excavating and construction of a canal would take capital and lots of time; therefore for the immediate future the Colombian government in 1850 granted permission to a group of businessmen from New York City to build a railroad across the isthmus to the Pacific Ocean, providing quick and safe egress through the jungle.

Lloyd Tilghman, a believer in Manifest Destiny and always ready for a new challenge that would pay well, accepted a position as principal assistant engineer of the Panama Division of the new Isthmus Railroad. The proposed route of the railroad would link Colon on the Atlantic side and the city of Panama on the Pacific side. The position required Lloyd to be both engineer and explorer at the same time. He would join tough-minded contractors, subcontractors, gang foremen, section gangs, and of course the railroad promoters.

Clearing brush, draining jungle swamps, cutting through hills and mountains consisting of soft volcanic material, would be a challenge. Far worse was the danger of yellow fever and malaria, the leading killers at that time. While laborers were Negroes and Indians from the British West Indies, most of the highly paid clerical and skilled workers came from the United States. Without careful surveys there was no guarantee that trains could follow where people had gone on foot or by mule train.

Lloyd's adventure of nearly two years in Panama is absent records in the form of letters or a diary. Research indicates he returned to the United States in 1852 to resume his railroad engineering opportunities. The Panama Railroad was completed in 1855 at a cost of $8 million.[3]

We don't know whether Tilghman was ever a stockholder. Many

such early deals had stock bonuses or stock options tied to the exploration. In 1878, Ferdinand Marie de Lesseps, who had directed the construction of the Suez Canal in Egypt, bought control of the Panama Railroad for $20 million. In 1899, the French company sold its Panama rights and property of the Panama Railroad for $40 million to the United States government, who changed the name to the Panama Canal Company.

Returning to the United States in 1852, Lloyd Tilghman moved his family to Paducah, Kentucky, located on the southern bank of the Ohio River at the confluence of the Tennessee River. Paducah was a growing cosmopolitan community of 3,000 residents. The affluent Tilghman had Robert O. Woolfolk construct a two-story brick home for his expanding family at Seventh and Kentucky Avenues. Despite Lloyd's nomadic army service in the Mexican War and employment with the Panama Railroad, the family was blessed with eight children, including three sons: Lloyd Jr., Sidell, and Frederick Boyd.

Lloyd Tilghman maintained five Negro slaves as house servants. For the next eight years the Tilghmans would be at home in Paducah. While away, Lloyd would continue his surveying and superintending the construction of southern railroads.

"Old Rough and Ready," President Zachary Taylor, died in office, and Millard Fillmore became the 13th President of the United States. The military had some worries about how well California could be defended, now that it was part of the Union and gold had been discovered there. Also, the Washington and Oregon Territory would need attention. These were daunting challenges for the new president. President Fillmore signed the first railroad land-grant act, giving 2.6 million acres to the Illinois Central Railroad and similar acreage to the railroad out of Mobile, Alabama. In the next ten years, up to the beginning of the Civil War, 20 million acres of public lands would be granted to the railroads. The nation was paying attention to its infrastructure, building seaports, roads, and turnpikes, but mostly railroads. It was unglamorous work, yet essential for a vital and growing country. The railroad was crucial to the economic underpinnings of the expanding United States.

Locally, Lloyd worked on a rail line from Paducah to Memphis and another from Paducah to the Gulf of Mexico at Mobile, Alabama. Later he was chief engineer of the railroad from New Orleans to Jackson, Mississippi (1855–1856). He became chief engineer and general agent hired to build a railroad from Ferguson Point, on the Mississippi River, directly west to Dooley's Ferry on the Red River. The coming railroad was talked of throughout south Arkansas, except like many business risks, this one did not work out for investors.

"The site was secured and surveyed. It passed through Drew County about four miles south of Monticello on Rough and Ready Hill which, with its altitude of 155 feet above sea level, was the most elevated point of the railroad. The bed was completed, awaiting the rails, and about twenty miles of rails were laid beginning at the Mississippi River, but drought, excessive heat, mosquitoes, illness among the work crews, floodwaters damaging the roadbed, and an economic downturn kept the railroad from being completed. On the few miles of rails that were laid, the only machine to operate over the line was a handcar." The railroad took the name Mississippi, Quachita, and Red River. Investors in the stock, who paid $100 a share, soon discovered they had lost everything, resulting in a squabble — accusations of swindling, cheating and lying. About the only thing that survived this disaster was an old tale, repeated into the middle of the next century. "When the railroad was being built, a slave woman on the plantation of Thomas P. Dockery, in Quachita County, through which the railroad would pass, had quadruplets, three girls and a boy. She named the girls Mississippi, Quachita, and Red River; the boy she named Railroad."[4]

Throughout the 1840s the slavery issue continued to threaten the goodwill between the amalgamated states and the territories. Old Senator "States' Rights" John C. Calhoun's carefully prepared speech eloquently reiterated the southern position; if the South could not be made secure on the slavery issue, it would never remain in the Union.[5]

Politics, patronage, and pressure sprang into action with the passage of the Compromise of 1850, calling for California to be admitted as a free state; for new territories in the Southwest to be allowed to organize without restrictions on slavery; for protecting slavery in the District of Columbia; and a strict new fugitive slave law.

The last part, a new fugitive slave law, resurrected the old Federal fugitive slave law of 1793 as a means to protect Southern "property rights" in chattel; i.e., the slaves were an article of personal, movable property. Under the law, northern officials were responsible for returning a fugitive slave to his owner. Any person found guilty of assisting a fugitive slave was subject to six months' imprisonment, a $1,000 fine, and reimbursement to the owner for the market value of the slave. The law denied fugitive slaves a jury trial or protection under a writ of habeas corpus.[6]

For many years the abolitionists of the New England states, the Society of Friends, and other benevolent organizations established escape routes in the border states for transporting runaway slaves to freedom in free northern states and Canada. The statutes had little effect on the Underground Railroad run by dedicated abolitionists who felt that no man should be held in bondage, regardless that abolitionists' actions deprived the slave owner of his legally held property.[7]

A high percentage of slave owners controlled only ten or fewer slaves. Tilghman had five household servants. He certainly didn't want them stealing off in the night to go north. Nor did they. What really stirred up the South were a batch of northern states' laws. In an effort to overcome the Federal fugitive slave provisions of the Compromise of 1850, the legislatures of ten northern states passed their own personal liberty laws, which forbade state officers from aiding in the arrest of fugitive slaves, denied the use of their jails for holding runaways, and ordered jury trials for the fugitives. These personal liberty state laws openly defied the Federal laws and were an example of States' Rights being practiced by many northern states, categorically creating a situation where both sides would eventually have the devil to pay.

Associating with leading Southern businessmen and politicians, Lloyd was kept apprised of coming events. It was becoming more evident that the South and North were becoming uncivil on a great number of issues. The ugly situation of John Brown's terrorist attack at Harpers Ferry, Virginia, in 1859 sounded the alarm for the breakup of the Union in favor of Southern independence. An outgrowth of this event was unrest in the slave states, where young Southern sympathizers favored the Southern position of rebellion and secession.

The summer of 1860 found Southerners demanding protection of their supposedly peaceful expedient of withdrawing from the Union and resuming the sovereignty that they had partially surrendered to the Federal government in 1776. They proposed no war upon the government in Washington or upon any individual state. All they wanted, they said, was to be left alone. The *Charleston Mercury* argued that the North and

South were two nations, made by their institutions, customs, habits, and geography. Horace Greeley of the *New York Tribune* agreed to some extent when he remarked that "if the cotton states shall become satisfied that they can do better out of the Union than in it, let them go in peace."

It was known that if Abraham Lincoln were to triumph in the fall elections, he would take upfront action to keep the Union together. On November 5, 1860, he emerged victorious. This triggered the South Carolina legislature to vote unanimously for a sovereign convention to be elected for dissolving South Carolina's ties with the Union. At Charleston on December 20, 1860, all 169 convention delegates voted for independence from the Union. This act of secession was followed closely by the states of Mississippi, Florida, Alabama, Georgia, Louisiana, and Texas, which summoned conventions of their own and adopted ordinances of secession. While all of the Gulf States were prompt in following the lead of South Carolina and passed ordinances of secession, the action of the neighboring states was slow and vacillating. The early months of 1861 found Maryland, Virginia, North Carolina, Tennessee, Kentucky, Arkansas, and Missouri still in the Union.

As for West Pointer Lloyd Tilghman, which side would he choose? Much like his forefathers who participated in the American Revolution, Lloyd cherished self-government, and he was intensely Southern in spirit. There never was any question among his associates how he would stand when a decision became necessary. He would endorse secession, prompting him to begin recruiting secessionists for the Kentucky State Guard at Paducah.

3

A Godsend, and Kentucky Service

A written master plan or blueprint for the formation of the Confederate States of America has never been admitted, proven, or discovered. That a new nation within a nation could be concocted by a series of events over fifty years is a suspect notion. How could a civilized, wealthy country such as the United States of America be put asunder in that day and age? By the end of 1860 there was no turning back. After a half-century of filibustering, peace conferences, sermons, editorials, political action, and the novel *Uncle Tom's Cabin*, both sides had exhausted every possible reconciliation. All arguments had been silenced without any solution of the States' Rights issues that included slavery. The Mason-Dixon Line of 1767 held firm. The intangible words of the recent past were turning into a potential holocaust, which was almost sparked by fanatic abolitionist John Brown's terrorist raid at Harpers Ferry in 1859.

Following the November election of Abraham Lincoln, on December 20, 1860, South Carolina began the procession of secession of the southern states. Mississippi followed on January 9, 1861; Florida, January 10; Alabama, January 11; Georgia, January 19; Louisiana, January 26. These were overt actions sending a signal to the Federal government in Washington that the breach was serious.

An event occurred the first month of the New Year 1861, in Texas, with Tilghman's old commanding officer, General David E. Twiggs that set the stage for the full-blown conflict to follow.

Seventy-year-old General Twiggs had taken command of the Department of Texas based at San Antonio. Born in Georgia, the veteran general had strong Southern sympathies with Texas patriots such as Judge Simeon Hart, James Wiley Magoffin, and Sam Houston. At the time, General Twiggs was unsure what policy he should follow since the Texans were talking secession from the Union.

Seeking guidance, he wrote to General Winfield Scott, his former Mexican War commander and now his superior in Washington. Twiggs was puzzled by the ambiguity of General Scott's official reply: "The general does not see, at this moment, that he can tender you any special advice, but leaves the administration of your command in your hands, with the laws and regulations to guide, in the full confidence that your discretion, firmness, and patriotism will affect all of the good that the sad state of the times may permit."[1] With this reply, General Twiggs wrote back suggesting that he be relieved of command and a replacement be sent to Texas. Supposedly he did not want to be responsible for the first shot of the coming epic.

During the interlude of waiting for a replacement, the veteran General Twiggs gave evidence of being completely bewildered when he publicly remarked, "If an old woman with a broomstick should come with full authority from the state of Texas to demand the public property, I would give it to her."[2] Subsequently his old Mexican War colleague, Colonel Ben McCulloch, now a Texas Federal Marshal and Texas Ranger, accepted General Twiggs's surrender.

Gone in a penstroke, without a shot being fired, General Twiggs's 2,500 Federal troops laid down arms and departed Texas. Abandoned were cannon, howitzers, muskets, rifles, carbines, pistols, ammunition, commissary stores, wagons, and horses. Instantly the Texans heeded the southern call to arms and were equipped in style.

The new government being formed at Montgomery, Alabama, on February 4 could hardly contain itself that the back door to the new Confederacy was established by Twiggs's Texas land-grant; passage to the western states and Pacific coast; a doorway to the seaports of Mexico, such as Matamoros; Texas beef by overland cattle drives to Louisiana; the Red River egress for moving commerce to the Mississippi River; plus rail line connections to all of Dixieland. These things were secure. It was quite a legacy that General Twiggs bestowed on the nation still on the drawing board.

The separation of Texas from the Union in such a manner was heralded all over the world by the newspapers of the day. The articles appearing in the Paducah newspaper certainly caused citizen Tilghman to ponder his old commander's decision as well as make up his own mind. General Twiggs's 15 minutes of fame went down in ashes as he was immediately branded a traitor throughout the North and quickly dismissed from Federal service by order of President James Buchanan on March 1, 1861.

In May, Confederate President Jefferson Davis appointed Twiggs a major general in the Confederate States of America. The president, realizing the strategic importance of Ship Island to the Mississippi ports and the city of New Orleans, assigned Twiggs to the District of Louisiana, where he faithfully served the cause until his death in July, 1862.

General Twiggs's action certainly supported the earlier supposition that the U.S. Army had been unnecessarily scattered by Secretary of War John B. Floyd, a Virginian by birth. He was accused of stocking Federal arsenals in the south with rifles, pistols, and munitions in anticipation of their benefiting the Secessionists. Furthermore it appeared he stacked the western U.S. Army commands with officers of Southern leanings, such as General Twiggs in Texas; Bvt. Brigadier General Albert Sidney Johnston in California; Colonel W. W. Loring in New Mexico; Major General Edmund Kirby Smith, Mexican boundary commission; Major Henry Hopkins Sibley in Arizona and New Mexico; Major General Simon B. Buckner in Kentucky, and others.

Eventually, over 250 West Pointers, including 19 of Northern birth, chose to serve with the Confederacy. "General Twiggs was the only Regular Army officer who was charged with treason. Others of Southern sympathies had first turned over their Federal forces and U.S. property to proper Federal authorities before submitting their resignations."[3] These wholesale resignations weakened Federal forces badly, while at the same time providing experienced officers for the Confederacy.

Regardless, Secretary of War John B. Floyd was forced to resign in December, 1860. By May, 1861, he was appointed Brigadier General, C.S.A., and formed a brigade of Virginians, first serving in West Virginia in the fall of 1861. His 15 minutes of fame were scheduled to come, and like General Twiggs, General Floyd would die down like a spent rocket.

In the interim, the seceded states elected delegates to a convention that met at Montgomery, Alabama, on February 4, 1861. They organized the new republic, the Confederate States of America. Its provisional government immediately set out to enact measures for the common good of the Confederacy. U.S. forts, arsenals, post offices, railroads, and other public property were seized by the militia of the seceding states. The position of the Federal government in Washington became very difficult. It could either recognize the lawfulness of the acts of the seceded states, or maintain the authority of the present government and compel the submission of these rebel states to the Constitution of the United States. Conservative elements of both North and South made great efforts to bring about reconciliation. Various plans of settlement were proposed and resolutions adopted, but with nothing that would please either side, resulting in both sides rejecting the proposal of peace.

Abraham Lincoln, inaugurated on March 4, 1861, was determined to maintain the authority of the Federal government over the seceded states, as he promised to continue collecting public revenues at the ports as well as to reoccupy the forts, arsenals and other public property seized by the rebel states. Expeditions were sent to Forts Moultrie and Sumter at Charleston Harbor and to Fort Pickens at Pensacola Harbor, Florida. Before the Federal convoy arrived at Charleston Harbor, General P.G. T. Beauregard ordered Confederate batteries to open fire on Fort Sumter on April 12. The bombardment lasted 32 hours, forcing the Union to surrender on April 13, 1861. The telegraph immediately began clicking the news across the country that South Carolina forces had fired upon Fort Sumter, putting an end to the last hope of a peaceful settlement for both sides. The secession was now fully committed. Individuals now had to decide: Were they with the North or were they with the South?

Learning of the surrender, the fence-sitting border states rapidly called their own conventions of secession. Virginia seceded on April 17; Arkansas, May 6; North Carolina, May 20; Tennessee, June 6; conflicting sentiment on secession still lingered in Missouri and Kentucky.

All over the nation, newspapers were having colossal news days as one after another, southern states left the Union. The luck of the new Confederacy heightened when news leaked out that Federal troops had abandoned Gosport Navy Yard in Norfolk, Virginia, three days after the secession of Virginia on April 17. For 30 years the Gosport Navy Yard had been one of the largest and most important naval facilities in the country. There were of course, a token number of Federal troops guarding the facility. But the commandant incorrectly determined that the naval base was in danger of attack from the Virginia militia, so he put the torch to the base. Ten vessels were burned or scuttled, and waterfront buildings and barges were destroyed.

More important to the new government that moved in May from Birmingham, Alabama, to Richmond, Virginia, was the fact that the storage center at Gosport was still intact, stocked with 2,800 barrels of gunpowder, over 300 Dahlgren shell guns, and 1,200 heavy seacoast cannon.

With the cannon from Gosport, the Confederate military officers began strengthening their existing forts, such as Fort Sumter, Charleston, South Carolina; Fort Pulaski, Savannah, Georgia; Fort Saint Philip and Fort Jackson, New Orleans, Louisiana; Fort Morgan and Fort Gaines, Mobile Bay, Alabama; Fort Fisher, Wilmington, North Carolina; and river forts on the Mississippi such as Port Hudson, Louisiana; Vicksburg, Mississippi; and Arkansas Post, Arkansas.

In addition, hostile border states expanded the war zone, so construction of additional fortifications was necessary. A massive buildup of cannon was assembled at Columbus, Kentucky, and Island Ten on the Mississippi River, as well as the beginning of forts on the Tennessee and Cumberland Rivers to defend middle Tennessee.

For the time being, before the Confederate government could begin to purchase or produce weapons, it had to be content to utilize what the states' militia and arsenals held in their possession, plus the captured booty from the Gosport Navy Yard. It soon developed into a trying situation and unpleasant state of affairs, as the Confederate military began to divide into an eastern and western command system supplied by an errant Commissary Department.

Early in 1860, Governor B. Magoffin of Kentucky, in order to put his state in readiness for whatever might occur, had acquired the services of Simon Bolivar Buckner, appointing him inspector general.

The newly appointed inspector general was a native of Illinois who had graduated from the United States Military Academy in 1844, eight years after Tilghman. Buckner taught philosophy at West Point for a period, and then served in the Mexican War in 1846. He was wounded at the Battle of Churubusco. Buckner returned to West Point as a tactical officer and later saw frontier service before resigning in 1855. His civilian occupation was construction superintendent and he later became active in a Chicago real estate business. Concurrent with his civilian occupation, he became Adjutant General of the Illinois Militia, directing reorganization of the state's militia.[4]

Similar to Lloyd Tilghman, Simon Buckner had a mark of distinction, and in true spirit accepted the call of Governor Magoffin, accordingly switching his allegiance from Illinois to Kentucky in 1860. Buckner's first act was to draw up a bill that dealt with Kentucky's recruiting of local militia in order to strengthen the State Guard. Lloyd Tilghman was already doing that in Paducah. When newly elected President Lincoln of the Union requested four regiments of soldiers from neutral Kentucky as part of his first call for 75,000 volunteers to defend the Union, Governor Magoffin refused: "I say, emphatically, Kentucky will furnish no troops for the wicked purpose of subduing her sister Southern States."[5]

Although the Kentucky legislature approved and endorsed the governor's refusal to send troops to President Lincoln, Magoffin's control over the state's military affairs began eroding as the citizens of the state vacillated in their decision to become involved with either side. In a show of strength, Buckner ordered Captain Tilghman, with other State Guard companies, to Columbus, Kentucky (which overlooked the Mississippi River), to guard the western water approaches of the state. This training camp was short-lived and accomplished little.

Action in the legislature continued; appropriations for the Kentucky State Guard became minuscule, while the pro–Union lawmakers voted money for a second militia to be called the Home Guard. The Union newspapers in the state began to call for the disbanding of the pro–Southern Kentucky State Guard and the seizing of their arms from the arsenals. These events, and others, were enough to tell Tilghman and Buckner that their cause in Kentucky was rapidly sinking; swift decisions were needed in these tempestuous times. When Tennessee seceded in June, hundreds of young, restless Kentucky secessionists went singly or in small groups over the state line into Tennessee to enlist at Camp Daniel Boone, near Clarksville, Tennessee.

By 1861 the population of Paducah exceeded 6,000. The community enjoyed the benefits of a new railroad and had excellent river facilities, creating an alliance and relationship in an area that included

Kentucky, northern Tennessee, southeastern Missouri, and southern Illinois, across the river.[6]

Lloyd and Augusta faced an emotional drama as it became necessary for them to weigh their options: would they continue their comfortable lifestyle in Paducah or pursue their philosophy of States' Rights and cast their lot with the new Confederacy? Would they move north to where they had strong family ties and finances, or would they take flight of Paducah for the cause? It was a momentous decision, as the family would need to leave their home and friends of eight years. Their convictions were apparently deep-rooted. They both were intensely Southern in spirit, and there was never any question among their friends as to how they would stand when a decision became necessary. Unshaken, Augusta, with the eight children and five house servants, packed up and abandoned her home in Paducah, sailing on the steamboat *Dunbar* up the Tennessee River to the village of Danville. Here they boarded a train that ran from Bowling Green to Memphis. They alighted at Clarksville, Tennessee, their new Confederate haven.

Lloyd remained at Paducah, continuing to recruit local citizens who wished to join the Confederate cause and follow along with him to enlist in the Confederate army. As an incentive, Lloyd paid from his own pocket the cost of transporting the new recruits to Camp Daniel Boone in Tennessee.[7] Located a few miles south of the Kentucky line, seven miles east of Clarksville, it had been in existence for only a few weeks as Tilghman and his Kentucky recruits arrived the first week in July. The location had the necessary requisites for a training camp: wide, flat fields, an abundant water supply, ample forest for firewood, and it was within two miles of the Louisville & Nashville Railroad to receive its personnel and supplies.[8] At its earliest, Camp Boone was established for organizing the recruits into soldiers and companies. Where possible, the Kentucky enlistees were organized on a county basis, and Company D, of the 3rd Kentucky Infantry, was made up entirely of men from Paducah.

The most serious weakness of the new companies was the lack of suitable arms. The state of Tennessee had been pretty well swept of its arms early in the year; consequently, many of the newly formed units had few firearms to train with. Luckily, weapons such as squirrel guns and double-barreled shotguns had been carried along by the new recruits from their homes. The shortage of firearms plagued the Confederates for the next six months. The untrained recruits winced at Tilghman's discipline, but they soon realized under him that war was not a frolic.

Naturally, general officers were in demand to organize and train these raw recruits. Lloyd Tilghman, with his West Point training and service in the Mexican War, was appointed Colonel of the 3rd Regiment of Kentucky Volunteers, 3rd Brigade, 2nd Division of Forrest's Cavalry Corps, Army of Mississippi. It was organized July 5, 1861, and mustered into Confederate service the same date for three-year enlistment periods. Colonel Tilghman's appointment was confirmed July 19, and he accepted it September 1.[9]

The August elections in Kentucky played out the scenario in the state. The secessionist party barely obtained a third of the members of the Kentucky House, swinging the neutral state over to the Union. Up to this date, Simon Buckner had remained neutral, since both governments offered him a generalship if he went with their side.

His decision, like Tilghman's, was to join the Confederacy. He brought with him the highest concentration of secessionists in the state, estimated to be 5,000 men, most of the Kentucky State Guard. The loyalty of these men to the Confederacy and its cause seems to have outweighed their loyalty to their own state, which had now arrayed itself on the side of Union.[10] Buckner was appointed Brigadier General, C.S.A., on September 14. He remained at Bowling Green with a Confederate force, awaiting the arrival of Albert Sidney Johnston.

Having lost at the ballot box, the Richmond government decided to seize Kentucky by whatever means. With Kentucky remaining loyal to the Union, this meant there were many fence sitters to be plucked by either side. It was only natural to order Colonel Tilghman back to his old hometown of Paducah to pick up these late patriots. Returning in August with a recruiting major and some staff, Lloyd went to work recruiting and proclaiming that the Confederates would seize Paducah. To some degree this was truthful and came to pass on September 4, when General Leonidas Polk, C.S.A., moved into western Kentucky with Confederate troops and seized the towns of Hickman and Columbus on the Mississippi River.

Leonidas Polk was the Episcopal bishop of Louisiana. Related to President James Polk, he had attended West Point in 1827, converted while a senior, and was ordained a deacon in 1830. A classmate, Jefferson

Davis, prevailed upon him to accept a commission. Leonidas Polk was appointed Major General on June 25, 1861. The bishop-general was given the mission of fortifying and defending the Mississippi River, which he did by occupying the high bluff overlooking the river at Columbus, Kentucky. He placed 140 cannon to command the river and stretched a huge chain across the river to halt Union gunboats. Given the timeliness of his invasion, he steadied the early Confederate western theater of operations.[11] The "Stars and Bars" flew over the area, with great anticipation by the secessionists that Kentucky was about to be taken by Confederate forces.

While the Confederates were recruiting, building training camps, and establishing supply depots, the Federals were doing the same along the Ohio River. The Illinois Central Railroad collected recruits and supplies in the North and brought them south to Cairo, Illinois, across the river. Cairo became a staging area of the new Federal army, becoming headquarters for Brigadier General Ulysses S. Grant when he took command in early September. This frontier boomtown was at the strategic confluence of the Mississippi and Ohio Rivers.

Grant's response to General Polk seizing Columbus and Hickman in early September was a move to check the Confederate advance by attacking Paducah on the other side of the river. Traveling from Cairo by riverboats, his army of 5,000 bluecoats debarked on the Illinois side opposite Paducah on September 5. Grant had a wooden pontoon bridge placed across the Ohio River; this was undoubtedly one of the great engineering feats of the war. Constructed on 123 barges tied together, the span over the river was 3,000 feet long, or the length of ten football fields. When completed, Grant and his army crossed over the Ohio River unopposed and entered defenseless Paducah on September 6.

Grant's entry was accompanied by the posting of a "proclamation" asserting his friendly intentions. Such proclamations were common on both sides. The Paducah proclamation read:

Proclamation,
To the Citizens of Paducah!

> I have come among you, not as an enemy, but as your friend and fellow-citizen, not to injure or annoy you, but to respect the rights, and to defend and enforce the rights of all loyal citizens. An enemy, in rebellion against our common Government, has taken possession of, and planted its guns

upon the soil of Kentucky and fired upon our flag. Hickman and Columbus are in his hands. He is moving upon your city. I am here to defend you against this enemy and to assert and maintain the authority and sovereignty of your Government and mine. I have nothing to do with opinions. I shall deal only with armed rebellion and its aiders and abettors.

You can pursue your usual avocations without fear or hindrance. The strong arm of the Government is here to protect its friends, and to punish only its enemies. Whenever it is manifest that you are able to defend yourselves, to maintain the authority of your Government and protect the rights of all its loyal citizens, I shall withdraw the forces under my command from your city.

U.S. GRANT,
Brig. Gen. U.S.A., Commanding.
Paducah, Sept 6th, 1861

When Grant's troops arrived, men, women, and children came out of their doors looking pale and frightened at the presence of his Union troops. They had been expecting rebel troops all day. "The citizens were in awe," Grant said. "I never saw such consternation depicted on the faces of the people."[12]

In his report General Grant added: "As we neared the city, Colonel Tilghman and a recruiting major with a company of recruits raised in Paducah, left the city by railroad, taking with them all of the rolling stock."[13] A parade of mounted bluecoats along with four military bands marched through downtown Paducah, where Grant then issued a proclamation to the citizens that they were now under Northern control. The pontoon bridge remained across the Ohio River until October 8, when it was withdrawn. U. S. Grant fortified this city at the mouth of the Tennessee, where he built Fort Anderson.[14]

The question of Union military strategy in the fall of 1861 was as muddled as it was for the Confederate commanders. Generals Grant and Sherman received their orders from "Old Brains," H. W. Halleck, who took his orders from President Lincoln. Interestingly enough, it is documented that a Miss Anna E. Carroll was instrumental in what would be the Union strategy in the western theater.

Born into a famous Maryland family, Miss Carroll lived on her father's plantation for most of her life. With the outbreak of hostilities, she freed her slaves and began writing newspaper articles defending President Lincoln's actions. This early Civil Rights activist in the summer of 1861 also wrote a series of pamphlets, among which one advocated the

Union western forces to advance up the Tennessee and Cumberland Rivers rather than the Mississippi River, as was being planned by the Union gunboat fleet.

Miss Carroll had gone to St. Louis, and after a careful examination of the plan proposed, she wrote to Union Attorney General Edward Bates, the author of the expedition, that from her knowledge of the country and position of the Confederates, the mission would fail. She recommended that the fleet instead should be sent up the Tennessee River. Miss Carroll sent letters and maps to the Federal War Department. She also sent a mass of information concerning the roads, bridges, towns and railway connections, which was very valuable to the Federals.

The papers were carefully examined, and the Federal authorities saw the importance of Miss Carroll's plans. The original plan of the Federals was abandoned, and the land and naval forces massed on the Tennessee and Cumberland Rivers as she suggested. Ample proof exists of Miss Carroll's claim to the plan. She received letters from many well-known public figures of the day and reported conversations with President Lincoln and Secretary Stanton. All verified the existence of her plan. Her postwar petitions for compensation from Congress for her work were never acted upon, as Lincoln himself declared her request for $50,000 in compensation outrageous.[15] In part because she was wrapped up in the women's movement of that day, she was considered a controversial female figure of the war.

Whether the unimpressionable General Grant knew of such plans advanced by Miss Carroll is suspect, because lacking strategic avenues of advancing by rail or over land, he chose to move south in September by crossing the Ohio River and occupying Paducah, Kentucky, thus becoming an obstacle between General Polk at Columbus and the balance of the Confederate forces east of him at Bowling Green and Nashville.

4

Confederate Western War Department

Confederate strategy changed daily in the early months of the war. On September 14, 58-year-old General Albert Sidney Johnston, second ranking general in the new Confederacy, arrived in Nashville, Tennessee, to take command of the vast frontier department. Johnston, born in Kentucky, graduated in 1826 from the United States Military Academy. His military record was impressive, first in the Black Hawk War, then in the Mexican War in 1849, when he was a colonel in the U.S. Cavalry.

While commanding the Department of Texas in 1856, he was ordered to Utah Territory to quell Brigham Young's Mormon rebellion against the United States.[1] President James Buchanan sent a clear message to Brigham Young: "Don't consider dissolving the Union." It took Johnston two months to travel 1,200 miles to Utah with 2,500 soldiers. The Mormons, anticipating the military movement, burned Fort Bridger, Colonel Johnston's destination; in addition, they ambushed and destroyed the army's supply trains. A resolute Johnston constructed a temporary fort and requested 4,000 reinforcements, toughing it out over a cold winter with few supplies. Eventually negotiations between Brigham Young and the new governor of the territory settled their differences. Notwithstanding, Johnston, in a show of force with flags flying and bands playing loudly, marched his small army defiantly down the main street in Salt Lake City, demonstrating the power of the U.S. Army in the West.[2]

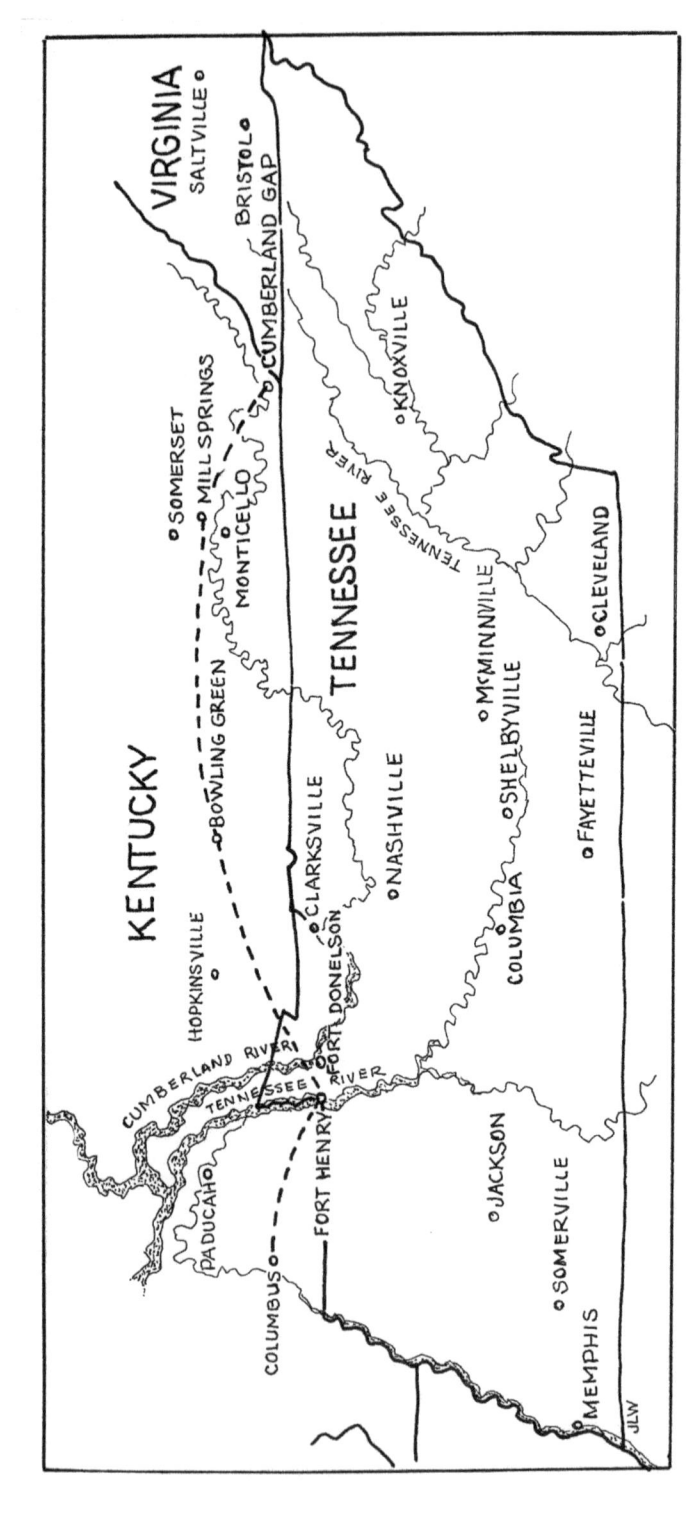

4. Confederate Western War Department

The press heralded the capitulation, making Colonel Johnston a man of note. Thereafter he was assigned to the Department of the Pacific, from which he resigned in 1861 to join the Confederacy. It took him four months to travel east to meet with his old friend Jefferson Davis, who immediately assigned Johnston to his home state of Kentucky as General, C.S.A.

The Frontier or Western Department was spread over 430 miles across Kentucky, from the gaps of the Cumberland Mountains to the banks of the Mississippi River at Columbus, Kentucky. The center of this massive defensive line would be Bowling Green, Kentucky, 70 miles north of Nashville, still occupied by General Buckner's Kentucky State Guard. General Johnston's military merit was being called upon to organize, equip, and train the volunteers as quickly as possible. Faced with 15,000 untrained newcomers and few experienced cadre, General Johnston appealed to Richmond for additional general officers.

Secretary of War Judah Benjamin replied, "There is an officer under your command whom you must have overlooked, whose claims in point of rank and experience greatly outweigh those of others. I refer to Colonel Lloyd Tilghman, whose record shows longer and better service and who is besides a Kentuckian, especially appropriate to the command at Columbus," under General Polk. "He therefore has been appointed Brigadier General; you will exercise your own discretion whether to place him in command at Columbus or not." Dated October 18, 1861.[3]

Upon arrival, General Johnston ordered Tilghman to relieve General J. L. Acorn of the Mississippi State Militia at Hopkinsville, Kentucky.[4] A principal defensive outpost, Hopkinsville was located 30 miles north of Clarksville and 11 miles east of Fairview, the birthplace of Jefferson Davis. These forces were to contain and discourage the Union troops stationed at Calhoun, Kentucky, under General T. C. Crittenden, who continued to send raiding and plundering parties across the Green River. The forces at Hopkinsville consisted of Mississippi Volunteers who were a long way from home with little knowledge of army life in the field. Tilghman found them in a terrible state of health and personal cleanliness. Through ignorance and neglect, the whole encampment was suffering from a raging epidemic of diarrhea and over 750 cases of measles. When Tilghman visited the hospital established at Hopkinsville,

Opposite: **The Western Theater of the Civil War, 1861–1862.**

vermin could be seen, and so offensive were the conditions that they prevented the soldier orderlies and nurses from attending to many of the sick soldiers.[5]

Tilghman inherited an infantry that was so unfit for duty because of sickness that the surgeon in charge stated to Tilghman that humanity demanded the men should not be drilled or trained. Tilghman wired General Johnston: "The raw troops are very raw, and it will take good handling to make them at all steady under the first fire in action. They are the poorest clad, shod, and armed body I have ever seen, but full of enthusiasm."[6]

The compassionate general, faced with a shortage of food, medical supplies, clothing, blankets and arms, immediately traveled to Nashville seeking help in supplying his withering troops. He soon discovered the task would not be simple.

During the first nine months of 1861, the state of Tennessee borrowed over six million dollars from the state's banks to recruit, clothe and arm the Tennessee Provisional Army. Consequently, Nashville became a giant Confederate arsenal and depot with warehouses bursting with food, clothing, medicine, muskets, saddles, knapsacks and blankets. Unknown to Tilghman, the Tennessee lawmakers authorized Governor Harris to make a military alliance with the new Confederacy, as between two independent nations; Tennessee agreed to turn over her military resources and all public property seized from the United States, and the Confederacy would reimburse the state for all military expenditures it had made before the state joined the Confederacy on June 24, 1861.[7]

To Tilghman's dismay, his plea for supplies was received with a deaf ear in Nashville, as the officers in charge explained that these supplies were solely for the Tennessee state forces and nothing could or would be given to him from this stockpile. Now desperate, Tilghman attempted to purchase supplies on the open market at Bowling Green and elsewhere in Kentucky but discovered the farmers and merchants, being badgered by both the Confederate and Union supply agents, refused the Confederate or Tennessee paper money, instead demanding gold or Kentucky paper money, which the general did not hold.

Returning to Clarksville headquarters he attempted to purchase supplies on Confederate credit. But the Confederate credit line had been closed in Tennessee because it was apparent the banks were not receiving reimbursements for their supplies as outlined in the agreement.

Tilghman had deep sympathy for the suffering of the men under his command. Still undaunted, he approached the Benevolent Society of Clarksville to tender their services for his men's personal needs. The Society agreed to make clothing and blankets at no cost, provided the general would secure all material for them. The Confederate Congress had not yet passed an Impressment Act that would have given him the power to impress property for subsistence and maintenance of the army. Not to be thwarted, Tilghman learned of a clothier in town who had five bales of cloth that totaled 1,722 yards. It had been purchased and paid for earlier for the Kentuckians' quartermaster stores and was to be made into clothing for the 5th Regiment of Kentucky Volunteers. The cloth was a combination of wool and cotton, a woven, light gray fabric called "jean cloth." Depending on the dirt roads and paths the wearer was using, the fabric turned into a whitish brown or deep coffee-brown; consequently, the troopers were called "Butternuts."

The cloth was in storage since August, the clothier said, and he knew of no one at Camp Boone to refer Tilghman to for further information about the disposition of the material. Quick-thinking Tilghman said that most likely the material had been forgotten about. Presenting no written authority except that of a general, the persuasive Tilghman told them he needed the material and must have it. The clothier accordingly delivered it over to him since it had already been paid for by the Kentuckians.

Two hundred women of the Benevolent Society went to work sewing clothing and blankets for the soldiers at Hopkinsville. As fast as possible the finished clothing and blankets were forwarded to the camp, and the improvement in morale and physical condition of the whole command was noted. Tilghman's short stay at Hopkinsville may have been beneficial to his men, but his boldness would be challenged by a higher authority at a later date.[8]

Elsewhere, voters of the new Confederacy went to the polls in early November. Running without opposition, Jefferson Davis was elected permanent president on November 6 for a six-year term. There was at this time only one political party — the Democratic Party. The new president issued a thanksgiving proclamation to the new nation:

Whereas, it hath pleased Almighty God, the Sovereign Disposer of events, to protect and defend us hitherto in our conflicts with our enemies as to be unto them a shield.

And whereas, with grateful thanks we recognize His hand and acknowledge that not unto us, but unto Him, belongeth the victory, and in humble dependence upon His almighty strength, and trusting in the justness of our purpose, we appeal to Him that He may set at naught the efforts of our enemies, and humble them to confusion and shame.

Now therefore, I, Jefferson Davis, President of the Confederate States, in view of impending conflict, do hereby set apart Friday, the 15th day of November, as a day of national humiliation and prayer, and do hereby invite the reverend clergy and the people of these Confederate States to repair on that day to their homes and usual places of public worship, and to implore blessing of Almighty God upon our people, that He may give us victory over our enemies, preserve our homes and altars from pollution, and secure to us the restoration of peace and prosperity.

Meanwhile in Kentucky, Grant's forces, after capturing Paducah, made further advances on November 6 as 3,000 bluejackets led by Grant sailed down the Mississippi River on steamer transports, landing on the shore at Belmont, across the river from Polk's armed Rock of Gibraltar at Columbus. In a daylong engagement, Polk's infantry and artillery bested the invaders, claiming a decided victory over Grant.

Although this was good news to General Johnston, it became obvious that the Federals were getting ready to invade Tennessee and that Polk's victory would be short-lived and merely a delaying action for things to come. Having been in command for less than two months, Sidney Johnston began to realize the ludicrous situation he had been assigned to by his friend Jefferson Davis.

Johnston soon consolidated his Kentucky line of defense by establishing a new line in Tennessee. The new line flowed west from Nashville to two forts under construction on the Tennessee and Cumberland Rivers.

While commanding at Hopkinsville, Tilghman, concerned with the weakness of the river line, wrote letters to General Johnston, warning of its condition. On his own time, Tilghman made a trip to the two forts under construction in early November, wishing to see what needed to be done, and discussing the defense situation with Major J. F. Gilmer.[9]

General Polk, commanding at Columbus, had his hands full defending the Mississippi stronghold from the troublesome U.S. Grant. Originally the construction of Forts Henry and Donelson was on his watch, but the general did very little to forward the work. On October 31, he sent a recommendation to Colonel W. W. Mackall at Bowling Green: "I beg leave to call the attention of the general commanding to the importance of the Tennessee and Cumberland Rivers. Of the very great importance of these channels of communication I need not speak. If they should be occupied and held by the enemy, they must necessarily prove of the most serious inconvenience to our army in Kentucky. Without disparagement to the parties in command, I beg to say that Colonel Tilghman, who I presume to be with you, is better informed as to the military aspect and capabilities of the country through which they run than any other person of whom I know, and I would suggest the propriety of having Colonel Tilghman put in charge of those defenses, if the exigencies of the service he is now upon would at all allow of such an arrangement. He might be with great advantage advanced to a higher military grade, and if in that command would form a very much needed link of connections between my command and that of General Buckner. The information I am daily receiving from that quarter makes this increasingly necessary. The space between General Buckner and myself is now very feebly occupied."[10]

In response to General Polk's suggestion, Special Order No. 89, dated November 14, Headquarters Western Department, was issued: "Brig. General Lloyd Tilghman will repair to Columbus, Kentucky, and report to Major-General Polk, by whom, in obedience to instructions from the Secretary of War, he will be assigned to the command of the fortifications at that point."[11]

W. W. Mackall, at Bowling Green on November 17, under Special Order No. 98, sent to Tilghman: "In turning over your command at Hopkinsville you will repair to the Cumberland and assume command of Forts Donelson and Henry and their defenses and the defenses of the intermediate country. You will push forward the completion of the works and their armament with the utmost activity, and to this end will apply to the citizens of the surrounding country for assistance in labor, for which you will give them certificates for amounts due for such labor. (Confederate paper). You will make your requisitions for quartermaster, subsistence, and ordnance stores upon the chiefs of the several departments at these headquarters. The utmost vigilance is enjoined."[12]

Mackall made a special effort to inform his friend Tilghman of the danger lurking at his new assignment. "The general regrets to hear that there has been heretofore gross negligence in this respect — the commander at Fort Donelson away from his post nightly and the officer in charge of the field batteries frequently absent. This cannot be tolerated. Your command is embraced in the division of Major-General Polk, to whom you will report monthly."[13]

An examination of these facts had to be frustrating to an officer like Tilghman. Others have written: "Polk's disinterest in the affairs of the eastern edge of his district and Major (J. F.) Gilmer's inexcusable neglect of his duties at Henry and Donelson both indicated a command failure at a departmental level." Throughout the fall and winter of 1861–1862, General Johnston was totally unaware of the debacle that existed at the inland forts. There is no evidence that he even knew that the forts were still in a defenseless condition. Instead, his absolute trust in his engineer, Gilmer, and his preoccupation with menial tasks at Bowling Green led him to believe that the forts were strong.[14]

With his new assignment in hand, General Tilghman boarded a steamboat at Clarksville for a trip west to Dover on the Cumberland River, where he would get a chance for another appraisal of the forts he would be responsible for under General Polk. His inspection and frank report back to Mackall sums up his frustration with the situation assigned to him: "November 29, 1861 — I have completed a thorough examination of Henry and Donelson and do not admire the aspect of things. I must have more heavy guns for both places at once, not less than four for each; one also of long range for each, say sixty-fours. Say to the general I have 1,000 unarmed men; no hope for any arms but from him. A message from Paducah and Columbus yesterday indicates a possible movement this way. Will he not let [me] have 1,000 arms from Nashville? I feel for the first time discouraged but will not give up. Answer me at Clarksville."[15]

An intermediary officer to Tilghman at Fort Donelson was Colonel James E. Bailey, also a resident of Clarksville. The 39-year-old colonel had been educated at Clarksville Academy, the University of Nashville, and eventually admitted to the practice of law in Clarksville in 1842. When Tennessee left the Union in June, he went with her. After a few months' duty in the military bureau organizing state troops, he was elected Colonel of the 47th Tennessee Infantry, which recently had been sent to Fort Donelson.[16]

With no possibility of Christmas at home in Clarksville, Colonel Bailey wrote his wife a letter on December 22: "The weather out of doors is gloomy and disagreeable; in my tent is tolerably comfortable. The boys have just finished their cabins sufficiently to enable them to cook in fireplaces. By Christmas I hope they will be all snugly housed. My own house will not be finished before the 1st of January. But if this weather gets to be extremely cold, I will move into one of the cabins of the men. We are getting along harmoniously — no trouble of any kind."[17]

Colonel Bailey then penned the current international news to his wife: "The U.S. and G. Britain gives me to believe that the war may be a very short one, God grant that it may be so that we may speedily return to the pursuit of civil life. Yesterday may be the happiest day in anticipation of so powerful an ally. I have said for months that if G. B. should take up arms with us, we will settle all our troubles in a short time."[18]

What Colonel Bailey, General Tilghman, and the entire civilized world were following at this time became known at the Trent Affair, involving James M. Mason of Virginia and John Slidell of Louisiana, named commissioners to Great Britain and France by the Confederacy as a separate nation. The two diplomats, having sailed through the Union blockade of Charleston Harbor, traveled to Havana, Cuba, to take passage on the British mail trawler, *HMS Kent*. En route out of Havana Harbor, the *Trent* encountered a Union warship, *San Jacinto*, that promptly fired two shots across the *Trent's* bow. The U.S. captain sent a boarding party demanding that Mason and Slidell be surrendered. The British captain acquiesced, and Messrs. Mason and Slidell were transferred to the *San Jacinto*, which transported the two men to Fort Monroe, Virginia. From here they traveled to old Fort Warren at Boston Harbor, Massachusetts, where they were imprisoned.

The Trent Affair — A Diplomatic Crisis

Immediately, England took a decided stand against the depredation the Federals committed against the British flag. England demanded a speedy and unconditional surrender of the ministers; if not complied with unhesitatingly, war would be instantly declared against the Union. To keep the two men imprisoned at Fort Warren risked conflict with England; to release them could be politically disastrous for the Lincoln administration. Southern newspapers spread the word, enthusiastically commenting on possibilities of war between the Union and Britain. This was the present situation on December 22, when Bailey wrote his wife.

Lord Lyons, the British minister to the United States, conferred with Secretary of State William H. Seward, acquainted him with the demands of his government, and requested immediate release of Mason and Slidell. On Christmas Day at the White House, President Lincoln and his cabinet met for discussion about the British demands. On December 26, as sober minds reconsidered the situation, it was agreed that the seizure of Mason and Slidell was illegal and that the two diplomats would be released, thus ending the crisis with Britain. It also ended the hope of the Confederacy that their new nation would be recognized early on by major foreign powers. Mason and Slidell were released on January 1, 1862, and sailed immediately for Southampton, England.[19]

As 1861 came to a close, the Confederate line of defense in Kentucky stretched across the southern part of the state from Columbus in the west to Cumberland Gap in the east, with the key point of defense at Bowling Green. Polk, with some 19,000 troops, occupied Columbus. The center of the long, thinly manned line was on the L&N Railroad at Bowling Green. There, Buckner's defenses were protecting Nashville with troops numbering approximately 23,000, under the command of General Johnston. The defense of the mountain passes between Bowling Green and far-off Cumberland Gap, a stretch of territory with dirt roads, ferries and poor communications, was the responsibility of General Zollicoffer, with an aggregate present of 9,417. In addition, the two forts coming under the command of Tilghman at this time had about 5,000 troops.[20]

5

A Trinity of Forts

From the first days of the conflict, Governor Isham G. Harris of Tennessee was concerned about the defense of the Mississippi Valley with its river tributaries. The Mississippi, Tennessee, and Cumberland Rivers, valuable travel arteries, could easily become proper avenues of advance for the Federals' land and naval forces. A flotilla of gunboats, teamed with steamboats acting as troop transports, could become a Union striking force capable of cracking open the South's heartland, jeopardizing towns such as Clarksville, Nashville, and Florence, plus hundreds of river farms and plantations along the way. At the same time, it could disrupt southerly rail connections, particularly the long routes running parallel to the front between Memphis on the Mississippi and Bowling Green, Kentucky. Governor Harris wasted no time; in April, 1861, he appointed a prominent civilian engineer, Adna Anderson, in Nashville, to locate and construct defensive works on the two rivers. At this date, any Confederate defensive forts would have to be built as far north in Tennessee as possible without violating Kentucky's neutrality. Aged General Daniel W. Donelson, a West Point graduate and engineer, was detailed as Anderson's military adviser, while Colonel Bushrod Johnson, a West Pointer himself, head of Tennessee's Provisional Army Corps of Engineers, sat in final judgment on their decisions.[1]

Anderson had the services of Major Wilbur F. Foster, another civilian engineer. They organized a surveying party to pick sites on the rivers for earthworks strong enough to mount guns to resist Federal gunboats and large enough to house infantry to repel ground assaults. They began

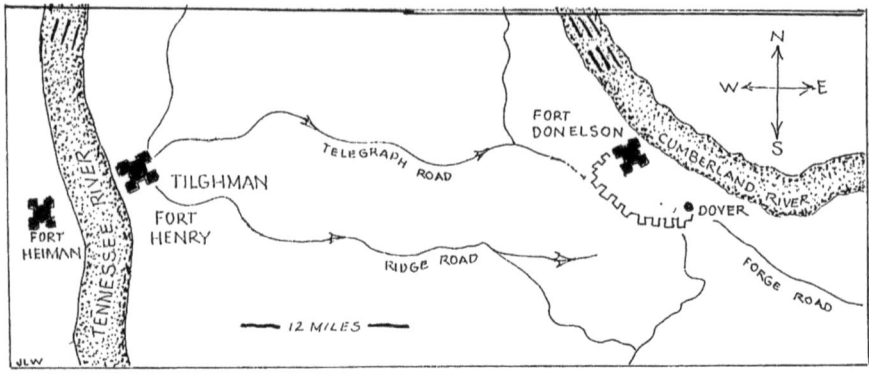

Forts Heiman, Henry and Donelson.

reconnoitering on May 10. On the basis of their studies, Anderson located the site of Fort Donelson, named for his colleague, on the Cumberland River a mile west of the village of Dover, and less than a dozen miles south of the Kentucky state line. Foster's surveyors laid out the works and a force began felling trees.[2] Fort Donelson's purpose would be to secure southern Kentucky — Hopkinsville, Russellville, and Bowling Green, and to protect Clarksville and the state capital at Nashville, located on the Cumberland River.

A dozen miles west of Fort Donelson on the Tennessee River, Donelson, with some misgivings, chose a site south of Kirkman's old landing on the east bank of the Tennessee. This site was named Fort Henry in honor of Gustavus A. Henry, a senator from Tennessee. Engineers Anderson and Foster objected because the place was on lowland dominated militarily by the heights on the opposite bank, which was Kentucky soil. Colonel Bushrod Johnson, Superintendent of the Tennessee Engineers, visited the disputed area and rationalized that a fort on bottom land had a better command of the river, on a bend of the Tennessee and at the head of a straight stretch of two miles — an excellent "field of fire" for defensive guns. He rejected Foster and Anderson's arguments.[3] Apparently no one noticed high-water marks on trees above, below and in the rear of the proposed fort, left over from normal winter floods.

This error in judgment at Fort Henry became an Achilles heel to A. S. Johnston's defense. What muddled the waters for the next few months was disagreement between the military engineers and the civil engineers. The West Point graduates recognized Dennis Hart Mahan at the academy as the undisputed authority on fortifications. The professor's treatise on field fortifications became the bible of the army operational engineer and thus was the last word to military engineers Donelson, Gilmer, and Johnson. The civil engineers — although many were West Point graduates — developed through surveying, bridge and railroad construction, and supervising the work of unskilled laborers, and they brought different, up-to-date skills. They had an inventiveness and aptitude for field expedients when textbook solutions authored by Eastern engineers were impractical or materials unavailable.[4] These men were Anderson, Foster and Tilghman. Ill judgment sometimes prevailed, yet never enough to hinder the completion of the forts.

The first of the twin forts to be constructed was Fort Henry on the Tennessee. As noted earlier, the fort was located on lowlands on a bend in the river. It enclosed an area of ten acres, with an 18-foot dry moat surrounding earthen parapets. In mid–June, the 10th Irish Tennessee began building the works and positions for seventeen guns. The colonel of the 10th was Adolphus Heiman, a Prussian-born Nashville architect and slave owner who had built the University of Nashville's Lindsley Hall and was a veteran of the Mexican War. Heiman pushed the digging and building so that the first gun was emplaced and test-fired with a blank shell on July 12. Initially, six smooth-bore 32-pounders and one six-pounder were set up. Ammunition was so poor it was necessary to add special quick-burning powder to each charge, creating the hazard of a premature blast and endangering the gun crews.[5]

Unfortunately, the fort was far from being completed. Local manpower was scarce because of the neutrality issue, plus many of the young Tennessee men had already enlisted in the Tennessee Army and were on their way out of the state. The construction slowed in the hot summer months with the inexperienced army volunteers who completed some breastworks but little else.

Before the Tennessee troops were incorporated into the Provisional Army of the Confederate States, the state of Tennessee commissioned officers with any military background and those with political influence. State commissions of major generals in June 1861 subsequently went to Gideon J. Pillow, ex–Congressman Felix Kirk Zollicoffer, Daniel S.

Donelson (60 years old, West Point 1825, and Speaker of the Tennessee House of Representatives), and Bushrod R. Johnson.[6]

At the forts the parade of experts continued to pass judgment. In September, Governor Harris sent Captain Jesse Taylor, a trained naval artillerist, to take command and instruct the gun crews at Fort Henry. Taylor reported back that the fort was not in the right place, would be a trap because its highest point was far below the high-water mark of the Tennessee River, and would flood by an ordinary spring rise of the river.[7] Governor Harris passed the communication on to General Polk, who washed his hands of it by forwarding it to the commanding general, Sidney Johnston.

Johnston, aware of the situation, sent 1st Lieutenant J. Dixon, another engineering officer, to examine the two river positions. He reported that Fort Donelson might have been better located, but Fort Henry was not situated very favorably although he acknowledged that it was a strong works. Instead of abandoning it, he suggested that the fort be completed, but an additional fortification to be built across the Tennessee River on the western bank atop Stewart's Hill.[8] Major J. F. Gilmer, on October 26, inspected both fort locations, concurring with all the others on their findings, and put into motion plans for the construction of a third fort to be located across the river from Fort Henry and named after the commander of Fort Henry, Colonel Adolphus Heiman.[9]

Time and events demanded that someone capable and qualified take charge of these forts immediately; therefore, General Tilghman was assigned in hopes that he could provide some direction. West Point's Dennis H. Mahan's principles in constructing field fortifications and regulating the defense of permanent works would be reviewed by the general. Even though he was weary from the incessant work in organizing and perfecting the Kentucky brigades at Hopkinsville, Tilghman hastened to his new assignment of bringing into perfect shape, if possible, the fortifications partially finished on the two rivers. After conferring with Major Gilmer, he reported back to General Johnston that light batteries should be added to each fort and the absolute necessity of occupying the opposite bank of the Tennessee River, now designated as Fort Heiman.[10]

At the outset, General Tilghman found Fort Donelson in good condition. Lieutenant Dixon informed Tilghman that he had completed the new battery on the Cumberland River and was preparing to mount the artillery pieces on it. He laid out a small works on the ridge, mounting two nine-pounders there. Trees were felled around the encampment to form a very good abatis for Fort Donelson.[11]

At Fort Henry, Major Gilmer requested four eight-inch Columbiads, four heavy guns of long range and four 32-pounders. These were to be delivered with platforms, chassis, and carriages, complete with 50 rounds of ammunition for each gun.[12] But some of the cannon at the two forts misfired and proved calamitous when they malfunctioned, causing loss of life among the men.

Prior to the arrival of Tilghman as commander of the twin forts, as a demonstration of things to come, the Federals in mid-October sent the gunboat *Conestoga* down the Tennessee on a reconnaissance, shooting several shells at the unfinished fortification in order to establish the proper range to the Confederate bastion.[13] This shelling could be heard at Fort Donelson as well, spurring a remarkable amount of energy and activity at both forts to hasten their completion.

As these defensive strongholds took shape, the citizenry in north Alabama became concerned about the effectiveness of the forts, especially Fort Henry, since its construction seemed to drag on with little progress in the summer and fall of 1861. Naturally they took their concern to their representative or local military commander. In this instance, General Tilghman received valuable help from Brigadier General Gideon J. Pillow, newly appointed general from Tennessee. Pillow told them straight out he did not consider the defense of the Tennessee River very adequate. The citizens inquired of Pillow what they could do to help the cause. Pillow's reply to them was in the form of a request for several thousand volunteers from Alabama to be stationed on the Tennessee River; 5,000 if possible, to help with the construction of the forts.[14] General Johnston, upon hearing of this, wired Governor A. B. Moore of Alabama that "as fast as they can be organized, equipped, and mustered they will be transported down the Tennessee River to Fort Henry, recommending that slave laborers shall be sent forward from the same point."[15]

At Florence, Alabama, S. D. Weakley, aide-de-camp to General Pillow, was placed in charge of mustering in such volunteers, announcing that he proposed to raise a regiment of men past middle life to serve during this emergency and the whole force would be armed with shotguns and rifles.[16] This would be a tall order on short notice to be filled at Christmastime.

Tilghman connected Forts Henry and Donelson by telegraph to Cumberland City, a distance of 35 miles, placing them in communication with Bowling Green and Columbus.[17] Stealthily the general began to assemble his staff. Captain Powhatan Ellis Jr. became his adjutant general[18]; Lieutenant Colonel M. A. Haynes, chief of artillery[19]; Lieutenant Foot, acting aide-de-camp[20]; and all supplies from the Quartermaster Department would be drawn by requisition under approval of H. L. Jones, assistant quartermaster.[21] Undoubtedly there were several Negro servants and cooks on staff.

Events in Kentucky continued to unfold as delegates from 64 counties had time to meet in eastern Kentucky at Russellville to form a Confederate provisional government for Kentucky, with George W. Johnston elected governor and Bowling Green selected as the capital of the new Confederate state government. The Confederate Congress at Richmond on December 10 admitted Kentucky as their twelfth state. This paper government did not last very long, collapsing in early 1862.

The question facing General Johnston, head of the command, and General Tilghman, in charge of the forts, was how and when the Federals would attack the forts. During the American Revolution, the patriots had Paul Revere and his famous midnight ride, dashing across the countryside warning that the British were coming. The prearranged signal would be flashed from the steeple of the Old North Church: Two lanterns would mean the British were coming by water, and one, by land. But now, with divided loyalties in Kentucky and Tennessee, would any Confederate patriot appear for the cause, warning, the Yankees are coming, the Yankees are coming?

Ironically, Tilghman's progress report on January 2, 1862, was sent to Major George Williamson, Assistant Adjutant General to General Polk at Columbus, and not to General Johnston. It read:

> HEADQUARTERS,
> Fort Donelson, January 2, 1862.
>
> Maj. George Williamson,
> *Assistant Adjutant-General, Columbus*:
>
> SIR: In transmitting weekly report (ending 31st) of the troops under my command I am happy to be able to report a favorable progress in all matters connected with the command. The large difference in the weekly report between "Present for duty" and "Total present and absent" will, I hope, be cured in a few days.

The regiments of Colonels Bailey and Stacker have only just organized, and freed now somewhat from feeling themselves bound to court the good-will of their men in order to secure their election, aided by a positive order against granting any furloughs, I hope to be able to restore matters to a more wholesome status.

I have still near 2,000 unarmed men in my command. I have not men enough armed at this post to man one-half the lines within the fortification, much less to effect anything at points which command my whole work. I beg you to call the attention of the general commanding division to this unvarnished state of things.

A most satisfactory progress has been made in the main fortification, an inclosed work. A very few more days will close up the gap and give us a very good work.

The heavy batteries are progressing rapidly and will be very efficient. I shall be ready to place all the guns in position as fast as they arrive. I am straining a point to make the armament sufficient to answer the aim we have in view. I look for some of the heavy guns tomorrow. My entire command is now comfortably housed for the winter. The houses are admirably built, well situated, and present an appearance of real comfort that will compare favorably with any command in the field.

On yesterday I reviewed and inspected the entire command at Fort Henry, and am gratified at being able to report the entire command in a most admirable state of efficiency. Everything will be ready to receive the additional armament now on its way. A heavy rifled gun (82-pounder) arrived at the fort on yesterday and will be in place to-day.

As shown by weekly report, I have had an addition to the force at Fort Henry in the Alabama troops; seven companies are now on the ground; the remaining three will be in place on Saturday. The companies are tolerably armed. Five of them only were inspected, the others arriving this morning. These troops are, as I understand it, for the work south of the Tennessee River.

The negro force (500) will be here in a few days. I have had no instructions on this point, and desire to know fully the views of the general commanding. I have conversed with Major Gilmer once on the subject, but deem it prudent to ask for further instructions.

I will present to the general commanding division a statement of advantages to arise to the Government from the covering of the immense rolling-mills owned by Hillman & Bro., below this place. These mills have become an absolute necessity to the whole country. I hope he may find it practicable to protect it, and shall examine the river just below the mills with a view to this object and report.

Respectfully, your obedient servant,
LLOYD TILGHMAN,
Brigadier-General, C. S. Army, Commanding.

In the early days of the New Year with its uncertainty and instability, the Confederate officials at Bowling Green, mimicking their Federal contemporaries, decided they had time for a court of inquiry for Tilghman's actions at Hopkinsville. A court of inquiry is limited to finding an answer to a question without determining guilt or innocence. A ruckus over relatively nothing developed at a time when General Tilghman expected complete cooperation from all commanders. Was this all about Tilghman's sudden rise in rank and standing, or was there sound reason for the good of the service?

General Tilghman's partner in the forming of the Kentucky State Guard, General Simon Buckner at Bowling Green, upon learning that Tilghman had requisitioned the fabric at Hopkinsville that belonged to Buckner's Kentucky Commissary Department, became vindictive and brought charges against Tilghman on January 3, 1862, to wit: "Conduct to the prejudice of good order and military discipline."[22] Before any military court would convene, Tilghman sent a blistering handwritten letter to General Buckner and in no uncertain words outlined and defended his actions. "My position was a critical one at Hopkinsville, and nothing but good resulted from my actions. As to any inconvenience your 2nd Brigade, Kentucky Volunteers may have sustained, the beneficial effects at Hopkinsville balance out to the bad against the other troops." As the two men had to work together, they did achieve some sort of reconciliation. Concluding, Tilghman told Buckner, "This trivial matter should have been resolved in Nashville with a personal meeting." No court of inquiry was held.[23]

It also came to Tilghman's attention that Buckner made this off-the-cuff remark: "I decided that this is probably the only course left to prevent the improper interference of General Tilghman with the command and administrative duties of other officers." This ruffled Tilghman even more than the charges of the inquiry. There was some substance to this remark because by Tilghman's abrupt manner in having to hurry to assemble his staff, he provoked some officers. He also irritated some who dealt with him because of his perfectionist, aristocratic mannerisms. General Buckner's remarks were in reference to an incident with Major J. F. Gilmer, Chief Engineer of the Western Department, stationed at Nashville. Gilmer had sent Mr. T. J. Glenn, a civil engineer, to place obstructions in the Cumberland River at a distance of about 1,000 to

1,200 yards from the guns at Fort Donelson. Late in November, Mr. Glenn wired Gilmer: "General Tilghman has ordered me to suspend work. Instruct me immediately." Gilmer replied: "You will continue the work for obstructing the Cumberland River. It will be impossible for me to reply upon any work being done properly if each subordinate brigadier general be allowed to suspend operations ordered by me. I must therefore earnestly request that the general commanding the Western Department hold Brigadier General Tilghman responsible for the act now reported, and forbid the repetition of like interference for the future."[24]

Tilghman, who was under the command of General Polk at Columbus, could not complain to Bowling Green; thus, he fared poorly in this dispute with Gilmer because General Johnston had complete confidence in his chief engineer. The truth of the matter: Tilghman, when he took command in November, said that manpower was being wasted on various projects that Gilmer had instigated. He realized that the slave power Gilmer was expending below the fort was needed for the construction of breastworks at Forts Donelson and Heiman. He ordered Mr. Glenn to cease work immediately; consequently the complaint by Glenn. Tilghman tried to explain that the obstruction project was badly planned and represented a waste of effort. Tilghman was curtly informed by Johnston's headquarters that in the future he was not to interfere with Gilmer's activities.[25]

Later Tilghman claimed he never received adequate support, that he was cast on his own resources, compelling him to assume responsibilities that may have worked a partial evil in order for him to accomplish an end.[26]

There were others who thought Lloyd Tilghman was not a particularly popular man with the soldiers and officers of his command. "Colonel George W. Stacker, the original commander of the 50th Tennessee, resigned to avoid serving under him. The new commander, Colonel Cyrus A. Sugg, apparently didn't like him either. Colonel John W. Head of the 30th Tennessee also intended to resign and said just that in front of his troops during a dress parade."[27] He did not follow through with this threat; later he cooperated with Tilghman.

Colonel Bailey, in a letter to his wife on February 2, made a reference to the Stacker matter: "We have for some days been very quiet here. Stacker's regiment has returned and in addition we have some cavalry.

More than half the force report sick with measles, with eight or nine deaths. You no doubt heard of Stackers's resignation, caused by some differences with Genrl. Tilghman. Colonel Head also intended to resign, had gone so far as to announce the fact on dress parade, but fortunately for his reputation he did not do so. He has since reconsidered the matter and expresses his great satisfaction at not taking a false step. With Tilghman his relations are now reestablished and I hope that hereafter we will have harmony and that they will pull together. My own regiment not in as good condition as I would like. It requires great exertion to get the different company officers to do their duty, and sometimes I have almost despaired of getting them to do so. This day is wet and disagreeable. The morning very cold; the boys out in the ditches and in the wood throwing up defenses. We hope to finish all this within a week or two. The men and officers are so crazy to get to their houses, that I am compelled to doing myself that pleasure."[28]

Tilghman denied that on occasion he interfered with other officers' duties. He maintained that the charges were totally without foundation and grew out of the capricious spirit of subalterns who acted in a way contrary to the military order. He was a no-nonsense general, the first choice of the volunteers.

In a show of support, Lieutenant Colonel Mackall, an old classmate of Tilghman's from the academy and serving as Sidney Johnston's adjutant, wired Lloyd: "And for the sake of old times—you did right, I know you will succeed. The General desires me to say that we now require vigilance and energy and he is satisfied that in these you will not fail. He hopes to stop the movement for some time on this line and that Generals Polk and Tilghman will delay them."[29]

Patriotic ideas of how to defend the rivers were prevalent among the citizens of Tennessee. James M. Hamilton of Nashville, on January 13, outlined in a letter to General Tilghman how the rivers could be made impregnable, "blowing every gunboat out of the river that passed over it." He had submarine batteries that could be constructed for less than one hundred dollars. "The machine is cheap, simple, easily constructed and will do its work of destruction. Ten machines will be quite sufficient for the Cumberland, what number for the Tennessee I could not say. I will have correct drawings made of my machine and will submit them to you, claiming nothing for my services in getting them up and submerged."[30] This was not a new idea, having been first used in 1776 in the harbors on the East Coast. It had been disapproved on moral grounds because targets were struck without warning. But this was a new war. On January 18, General Polk at Columbus informed Tilghman, "Lieutenant Pharr on board the *Chance* will be bringing submarine batteries to Fort Henry. On his arrival, Dr. H. L. Saunders will lay the charged submarine batteries."[31] Tilghman wired back to Lieutenant Pharr: "You are hereby directed to assume the entire control of the system of submarine batteries to be placed in the Tennessee River near this post. The steamer *Dunbar* is placed at your disposal, and the requisite number of men will be detached. Col. Heiman will explain to you my views on this subject as to placement of batteries. You will report instantly to these headquarters."[32] "Torpedo" is the generic term for a variety of naval mines employed by the Confederates during the war. Some torpedoes were set adrift in a river current, or on weights to float just beneath the surface, to strike a ship's hull in random collision.

Fort Henry finally took shape. "It became a five-sided, open-bastioned work, rising out of the marshes. Its walls rose some twenty feet from the water's edge, were about twenty feet thick at the base and sloped upward to about ten feet thick at the parapet. Seventeen guns were mounted on solid platforms. Eleven covered the river, and the other six were positioned to repel a landward attack. Two heavy guns, a 10-inch Columbiad and a 24-pounder rifled cannon, were the most effective weapons of the water battery. The rest consisted of seven 32-pounder smoothbores. An access road was built by piling stones, logs, and dirt through the marsh. To the east was a long ridge that rose above the fort. There the Confederates constructed rifle pits of about four feet high and four to six feet thick to protect the garrison from the landward approaches. By the end of January, they constructed yet another ring of rifle pits to keep any attacker even farther from the fort."[33]

Every preparation to meet the enemy's attack was progressing forward, although there continued to be a shortage of artillery for Forts Donelson and Heiman. Efforts throughout the fall to procure cannon seemed to have been ignored by Confederate authorities. But what was not needed by Polk at Columbus, or Bowling Green and Nashville, found its way slowly to the twin forts. "Many of the guns were defective and even dangerous," declared one ordnance officer. "One battery from the

Memphis foundry lost three guns in a month by bursting, one of them in the battle at Belmont on November 7."[34] When Tilghman inspected a battery of two iron six-pounders and two bronze nine-pounders made at a Clarksville, Tennessee, foundry, "he declared them to be worthless." The nine-pounders were of very little account as all guns were mounted in a wretched manner. "He fumed about a total ignorance of all mechanical principles evidenced in the construction of the carriages."[35] Such outbreaks by the general lent support to the later charges, as discussed, that he was overwhelmed by his new responsibilities, was fatigued, becoming difficult with his subordinates regardless of rank. He had become irksome.

On January 15, Lieutenant Colonel Haynes, Chief of Corps of Tennessee Artillery, arrived from Columbus to take charge of the artillery forces at all points. Tilghman directed him to Fort Donelson to take charge, while he would remain in charge of Fort Henry. Unexpectedly, Tilghman's 21-one-year-old cousin, Lieutenant Oswald Tilghman of Easton, Maryland, who was Adjutant with the Tennessee Light Artillery, is recorded as "transferred to the staff of his kinsman, General Lloyd Tilghman, in command of the defenses of the Tennessee and Cumberland Rivers."[36] It would be a short assignment.

January 15, Fort Donelson to General Tilghman: "In regard to ammunition, all things are ready. I have thrown out pickets below base. The whole command turned out and put to cutting trenches. The men are cool and determined. Colonel J. W. Head."[37]

January 17, Danville to General Tilghman or Col. Heiman: "The ammunition here is for 24-pound and 10-inch Columbiad. W. O. Watts."[38]

From Powhatan Ellis to General Tilghman: "Col. Head expects a good part of the ammunition opened yesterday to be worthless." Tilghman to Col. Mackall at Bowling Green: "I must have some artillery officers at once."[39]

Throughout the month, rain had been falling at a steady pace in Kentucky and Tennessee, further hampering Tilghman in his quest to complete and arm three forts. The rainfall was good news to the Union navy, as it meant the rivers would be rising, which would permit them to strike the Confederates at their fortifications on the Mississippi, Tennessee, and Cumberland Rivers.

5. A Trinity of Forts 59

Guarding the Mississippi River, General Polk was first to sound the alarm on January 17 when he wired Tilghman: "What is the state of affairs with you now,"[40] as General Grant commenced to make another move on Columbus. "I require strong reinforcements," Polk wired Judah Benjamin at Richmond.[41] On this same date at 4:00 A.M., an excited Tilghman wired Colonel Mackall at Bowling Green: "We have four gunboats, one transport, and I think one mortar boat just below us. I am prepared for this much."[42] By daylight three gunboats, accompanied by transports, appeared off Panther Island, three miles downriver from Fort Henry. After they chased a small makeshift rebel boat armed with two rifled guns, using the island as cover, the monsters fired 22 shots that fell short of their position, Fort Henry.[43] Their object was to draw out Confederate fire, thus obtaining the position of the fort's artillery. The next day a lone gunboat returned to reconnoiter, again firing at the fort. Thereafter the gunboat returned to its base at Cairo, Illinois.[44] With all of the firing for two days, Colonel Haynes at Fort Donelson, twelve miles east of Fort Henry, replied: "The cannonade against your fort was distinctly heard and helped our men to work."[45]

The buildup of Confederate forces on the Tennessee River over the past five months had been done in bits and pieces. By this time, General Tilghman had an aggregate of 2,600 soldiers located at Fort Henry, Fort Heiman across the river, Paris Landing five miles south of the fort, and a light battery and rocket guard at Bailey's Landing three miles north of the fort.[46] Most of the men were new to military life, having volunteered for service in the infantry. They were new to camp life, its marching and drilling, and were poorly equipped with double-barreled shotguns, old Tennessee muskets, or rifles. Few of the cavalry had either sabers or pistols and were only armed with whatever weapons they had brought with them. The appearance of the gunboats was something they had never seen before; when the shells came at them whistling "Yankee Doodle," they quickly discovered they were not Fourth of July fireworks.

These Union ironclad monsters were menacing and frightening to the citizenry. With a 175-foot superstructure, they were about the largest thing afloat these men had ever seen. The bows and bulwarks consisted of three feet of oak timber bolted together and covered with wrought iron plates two and a half inches thick. They were 50 feet in breadth, drew only five feet of water when loaded, and their width in proportion to their length gave them the steadiness in action of a stationary land battery. They were pierced for nine to 13 Columbiads and the bow gun was an 84-inch rifled cannon. These gunboats packed a wallop of firepower never tested before by the Union navy, as the coming engagements would be a month before the battle of the Monitor-Merrimac at Hampton Roads, Virginia.

At 10:00 P.M. on January 17, Tilghman informed Bowling Green: "Two gunboats, with transports between and two barges with wagons, returned near position of this morning, reporting to have landed on south side — my pickets all out on both sides. I must prevent lodgment opposite me — have only two thousand men of all arms — must be reinforced by two regiments and battalion of cavalry. Quartermaster at Nashville shamefully negligent of my known wants."[47]

There were always vigilant citizens who supplied military information to the commanders via government operators located at telegraphic centers. From Danville, the general received:

D.S. Chilton
Govt. Operator

Paris, Jany 18
at 7 o'clock.

Two reliable gentlemen Mr. D. Matthews and C.A. Duncan from Murray, Kentucky, bring information of a force of Federals of about six thousand strong composed of infantry, cavalry, and artillery — eight miles west of Murray marching in direction of Fort Henry. There is also a force of about two thousand landed below by the boats yesterday marching in direction of Murray from north east.

S.D. WARD
Government Operator
at Paris.[48]

At 8:00 A.M. the next morning the government operator at Paris wired: "A certainty that there are 12,000 Federals — 30 cannon — 400 wagons, and 1800 cavalry this side of Farmington, Kentucky."[49]

January 19, a wire from Tilghman to Mackall at Bowling Green discussed the situation at Fort Henry and Fort Heiman. "Smith is at Murray [this was General C. F. Smith, 2nd Division, U.S. Army of the Tennessee] with seven thousand five hundred men — including one thousand cavalry, and twelve field pieces. I have possession of the hill [the location where Fort Heiman was to have been built] and fortifying hard.

Can make it strong if time is allowed. One Alabama company of cavalry came tonight. Sent back boat for the others — have moved six hundred men and three pieces field artillery from Donelson here. Await anxiously to learn about re-enforcements. I must and will hold the hill if I can make men behave well."[50]

Now in his fourth week in command of the three forts, Tilghman would try desperately to finish the uncompleted Fort Heiman. Since October the construction on this fort had gone forward by fits and starts and now was still waiting for cannon for the fort's defense. The five hundred Negroes that the governor of Alabama promised never materialized. Fifteen Negroes were sent from Henry County, but they never arrived until the 22nd of January. Ten companies of Alabama volunteers, as promised by the governor, did show up and report to Tilghman at Fort Heiman.[51] This was the regiment of men "past middle life" who were serving in this emergency, a force armed with shotguns and old muskets. Their good intentions were to help construct Fort Heiman. Colonel Foster was in charge of the Alabamians on their arrival and was the one responsible for recruiting and forming the companies. The colonel was carrying a note from the governor, "by whose order an election of officers must be held, his or General Tilghman?"[52] To resolve the muddled election problem, Tilghman issued a Special Order: "Foster in charge of Alabama Regiment at Fort Heiman is assigned to duty with that Regiment as Lt. Colonel, under a new acting Colonel Captain Clare." This placed Captain Clare in temporary command until the regiment could have elections.[53] This deliberate move by Tilghman, although for the good of the service, did not sit well with the volunteers from Alabama, and especially T. J. Foster. In an eight-page, legal-sized paper, he chastised General Tilghman about the state of affairs.[54] Tilghman's defense was that he was placing an experienced officer in charge until the elections could be held. There would be no elections, as the Federal forces were marching down the west bank of the river with 2,000 infantry and 200 cavalry. Tilghman's cavalry scouts said the enemy made camp on the Murray Road, which led to Fort Heiman. The bluecoats were equally untried in warfare, as were the graycoats. The rain and muddy roads beyond description slowed Smith's forces. It became necessary for them to establish an encampment for the men and animals, which resulted in a two-week delay in advancing on the fort.

When word of the shelling of Fort Henry was received by the fighting Bishop Polk, he telegraphed Tilghman: "Am informed column four thousand infantry, six hundred cavalry, and two batteries artillery are moving from Farmington towards Murray. I have sent one thousand cavalry to attack their column in rear and to harass them. Will send along two regiment of infantry from the rear as soon as they can be put in motion."[55] On January 22, General Polk wired Tilghman: "I have ordered six companies of Colonel Gee's Regiment to Danville — the other three will follow as soon as they reach Memphis. He is instructed to report to you."[56] The help en route for Tilghman was 70 miles away. The rivers were still rising.

6

Eve of Disaster

There were some who thought the Federals would not attack the forts until April or May. General Johnston himself did not hold this view and on one occasion said that "anyone who did not expect a winter advance by the Federals was deluded."[1] The veteran general pointed out the offensive campaign the Union armies were operating on three fronts in Kentucky: the first against Polk at Columbus and Hickman, utilizing the Mississippi River to aid in their movement and the capture of Paducah; another against Fort Heiman and Fort Henry, located on the Tennessee River, now at hand; a third on the L&N Railroad, confronting General Buckner at Bowling Green.[2]

In addition, a fourth front had been developing rapidly as both sides maneuvered for position of advantage in recruiting men from Kentucky and Tennessee into their respective armies. What began as a recruiting contest in early summer of 1861 had grown into a conflict in the fall and winter of 1861. In July when General Polk was in command of the Western Department, he became concerned about the hostility of the citizens of eastern Tennessee whose pro–Union spirit was being agitated by many prominent politicians and citizens.[3]

The principal railroad connecting Polk's Western Department with Virginia passed through this disaffected region. The bishop desired that the security of the supply line should be established by moral influence rather than by military force, and the administration of the district would be committed to the hands of a good politician. President Davis on July 26 appointed General Felix K. Zollicoffer to proceed to east Tennessee where, under difficult circumstances, he was expected to preserve peace, protect the railroad, and repel invasion.[4]

Felix K. Zollicoffer, born in 1812, worked as a youth on the family plantation in Tennessee and attended Jackson College in Columbia. At age 16 he entered the newspaper trade in Paris, Tennessee, later becoming editor of the *Columbia Observer*. He volunteered for military service during the Second Seminole War, returning from the Florida campaign a year later as a first lieutenant. This was the extent of his military service. By 1842, he was associate editor of the *Nashville Republican Banner*, served as State Adjutant General and Comptroller, was elected a state senator, and in 1852 was elected to the U.S. House of Representatives. A champion of States' Rights, he remained in Congress until 1859. In 1861 he attended the Washington Peace Conference, which failed in its mission. He had significant political power in the state. When Tennessee seceded, Governor Isham G. Harris appointed Zollicoffer a brigadier general of Tennessee State Troops, assigned to command Camp Trousdale, north of Nashville. On July 9 he accepted a brigadier general's commission in the new Provisional Confederate Army.[5] Possessed of a magnetic personality, six feet tall and erect in form, with rugged features, he commanded respect wherever he went.[6] Zollicoffer was not a military genius; in fact, he was a far better politician than he was a general.[7]

At this time, Kentucky was attempting to maintain a position of neutrality with respect to active participation in the war on either side. Early in July, Lieutenant William Nelson, U.S. Navy, was ordered by the War Department to raise an army in southeastern Kentucky. Nelson carried on his recruiting and training activities at Camp Dick Robinson in Garrard County. He was authorized to issue commissions from the Federal government to those who would raise commands; and he distributed these commissions so generously that he gave rise to the expression "as numerous as Kentucky colonels."[8]

While Nelson was distributing "Lincoln guns" shipped from Washington and rounding up mules and wagons for an expedition into east Tennessee, Zollicoffer was proposing to arrest the advance by forming a chain of infantry posts at Cumberland Gap and other paths leading across the mountains.[9] At the western anchor of this 300-mile defense line, Polk landed Confederate forces at Hickman and Columbus, and on September 6, General Grant seized the city of Paducah. "The neutrality of Kentucky has been broken by the occupation of Paducah, and Richmond ordered Zollicoffer to take arms." On September 9, Zollicoffer replied, simply stating: "I ordered three regiments into Kentucky today."[10] Before he left Knoxville to join his troops at Cumberland Ford (the present city of Pineville, Kentucky), he wrote his wife, Virginia, a letter. "In this great conflict which will tax our people to the utmost, I will endeavor to do my duty. The responsibility is great. I feel my want of experience and knowledge of war for so large a command — now about 10,000 men."[11]

Later Polk was superceded by General Albert Sidney Johnston, who became Zollicoffer's commander in chief. Zollicoffer lost no time in obtaining permission from General Johnston to exercise his discretion in attacking the enemy. General George H. Thomas, who took over the Union command, started advancing to recover eastern Kentucky. At Rockcastle Hills on October 21, Zollicoffer was driven back into Cumberland Gap. In November, Zollicoffer moved from Cumberland Gap, advanced 70 miles northwest to Mill Springs on the Cumberland River, and crossed the rain-swollen river to Beech Grove, Kentucky. Here Zollicoffer's luck began to diminish as he was joined by Major General George B. Crittenden, who had been in command at Knoxville, and was ordered to Kentucky to assume command of all of Zollicoffer's forces. Crittenden was surprised to find Zollicoffer still on the right bank of the Cumberland River, for he had previously been ordered to re-cross the river.[12] The Confederates were stuck there because the river was greatly swollen, with high, muddy banks. Meantime, Union General Thomas left Lebanon, Kentucky, on December 31 and marched in heavy rain over muddy roads, reaching Logan Cross Roads on January 17, ten miles from the Confederate beachhead. Rather than have his back to the river, the experienced Crittenden decided to take the initiative, moving out at midnight in a driving rainstorm to attack Thomas early on the morning of the 19th, near Mill Springs, Kentucky, thus bringing about an impetuous adventure that ultimately ended in failure.

The morning was dark and a drizzling rain was falling as General Zollicoffer realized there was a lull in the fighting at this point. Because of the smoke from the battle, mixed with the mist in the air, confusion arose on both sides as to the location of their enemy. Colonel Speed S. Fry of the Federal forces had made a similar observation, riding a short distance to ascertain the true state of affairs. As he was returning, "he met a mounted officer wearing a waterproof coat without insignia. This was Gen. Felix Kirk Zollicoffer who, in the confusion of the battle, had lost his sense of direction and had calmly approached the ranks of the 4th Kentucky under the impression that it was a regiment of his own brigade. Zollicoffer commanded Fry to order his men to cease firing; and Fry, believing the stranger to be a Union officer, obeyed. Zollicoffer was about to ride away when his youthful aide dashed out of the woods and, firing at Fry, exclaimed, 'It is the enemy, General!' Fry then drew his revolver and fired at Zollicoffer, while at the same time giving the command to his troops to fire. Zollicoffer fell from his horse, pierced by several balls. He was dead."[13]

News of Zollicoffer's death quickly spread through the ranks of both armies, where it was received by the Confederates with grief and disheartenment. Crittenden went forward as planned, leading the small army into a bloody battle, but Zollicoffer's tragedy, together with the disparity in arms and terrible rains, soon caused the Confederate regiments to retreat in confusion and disorder until the retreat became a virtual rout. Realizing his perilous situation with a disorganized army, Crittenden moved quickly back to the Cumberland River, which he crossed over to the south side. There was great panic by the Rebels to board the little ferry that crossed and re-crossed the raging river. Like a long funeral procession, the Confederates left Kentucky and returned to Tennessee.[14]

General Zollicoffer's body was removed to Nashville, where it lay in state in the Hall of Representatives at the capital. Interment was at the old City Cemetery at Nashville.[15]

Johnston's defense line, which Zollicoffer helped build across southern Kentucky from western Virginia to the Mississippi, had collapsed on the eastern end. All of Kentucky and middle Tennessee was in danger of falling to the Union armies.[16]

Back at Fort Donelson, General Tilghman was running out of time to complete his montage of forts and defense lines. The remoteness of the area, time lapses in securing supplies, ammunition, trained soldiers, and officers would not be overcome, as everything seemed to be en route. Tilghman's uneasiness with the forts was apparently reflected in the tone of one of his dispatches to Governor Harris. Harris wired: "Your dispatch of last night just received. Colonel Gaultz cavalry sent today. You may avoid the defeat — the responsibility of which you seem to seek to fix in advance, signed Harris, Governor of Tennessee."[17]

General Johnston and Governor Harris, deeply concerned about their defense with the collapse of the eastern anchor of the line, on January 21 ordered Colonel Bushrod R. Johnson, Superintendent of the Tennessee Engineers, to report to Fort Donelson. Tilghman received the wire: "B. R. Johnson will take command of Fort Donelson Brigade with pleasure if you can place him in that position. He has not a

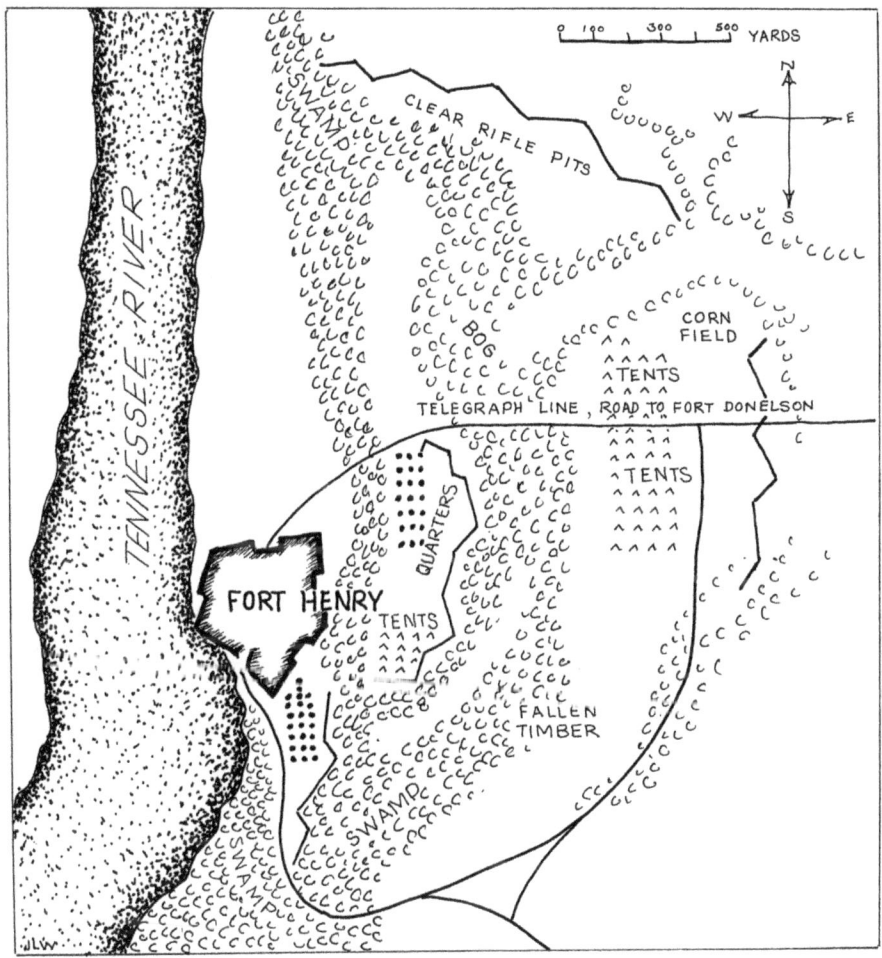

Fort Henry on the Tennessee River.

Confederate commission. He will leave for Fort Donelson as soon as assigned."[18]

Bushrod R. Johnson, born in Ohio to a Quaker family, graduated from West Point in 1840, spending seven years in the old army on the frontier, a veteran of the Seminole Indian Wars in Florida, and then saw service in the Mexican War, where he was attached to the Quartermaster Department. It was at this time that he was forced to resign from the army because of a vague and guileless bribe proposal by him to a superior officer that backfired. Thereafter he operated a military school in Kentucky and, later, the Western Military Institute at Nashville. He was a politician and a friend of Governor Harris. He was swiftly commissioned a brigadier general in the Confederate army on January 24; earlier, on January 21, he took command of Fort Donelson for a week while Tilghman was absent to work on Fort Heiman.

The Yankee Quaker's gloomy appraisal of what he found at Fort Donelson prompted a wire to Governor Harris. "Forces weakened here by detachments withdrawn, cavalry and infantry ought to be sought. Can arm 500 more infantry; need field artillery; need 536 sporting rifles. One more regiment of new troops will be as many of that description as will be desirable here. Should be pleased to get one good regiment of old troops. Fort Donelson is now our weakest point. I trust it will be duly strengthened."[19]

General Bushrod Johnson wired Tilghman at Fort Henry: "I have sent a telegram to Gov. Harris requesting every man you can arm, and 700 to be armed at Fort Donelson. Colonel Bailey received word that his guns are still at Richmond and will remain there for fifteen days. You promised to send me three officers who were sent to you by General Johnston. They have not arrived. I manned parapet guns today with all forces, not one thousand strong, and explained the kind of defense necessary as far as I could."[20]

Colonel Haynes, who was in daily contact with Tilghman, confided, "I am informed that there is much dissatisfaction in regards to the appointment of General Bushrod Johnson to command here, and that several officers will send in their resignations; I have advised against such a course. Now is not the time to do anything to weaken ourselves. I am in command of guns without trained and qualified men."[21] The old U.S. Army was small in number; undoubtedly some of the officers remembered the rumor and resignation of Johnson.

Tilghman's adjutant informed the general: "The line from here to Cumberland City is not working now on account of lightning. I start the telegraph expeditions as soon as Major Jones can get wagons. Twenty-seven of Forrest's cavalry arrived this morning destined for Fort Henry. Four guns were sent from Nashville with no ammunition with them."[22] On January 22, Ellis further advised: "Telegrams being sent now for 1,000 shoes. Box guns received this morning on the *General Anderson*. Bailey's regiment falling sick rapidly and becoming demoralized."[23] Sick call was not any better at Fort Henry. Surgeon A. H. Voorhies reported 40 men in the hospital, 183 sick in quarters, and 187 sent to general hospital.[24] The rain and cold, damp weather was taking its toll on the volunteers.

On January 24, Ellis reported: "Lieutenants Martin and McDaniel of the Tennessee Artillery have arrived here from Columbus, assigned as instructors of heavy artillery by Colonel Haynes. The artillery has been formed into a battalion, so leave the two companies from Nashville with Major Baker; its head guns have been placed in their position by General Johnson. Whenever you can get over, General Johnson is anxious to discuss with you some points about the defense of this place."[25]

Tilghman never did accept Johnson's request to meet, as he was too busy at Fort Henry. He knew Fort Henry was well built, as it was completed before he took command, and he had strengthened it greatly by building embrasures and epaulments of sandbags, making it a formidable resistance against any fair odds. In case of an attack by land he had given instructions as to the exact ground each one was to occupy.[26] Lieutenant of artillery W. Watts, in his report of ordnance on January 21, added, "I deem it my duty to state that the water line is in the main ditch, 5 feet scant below the mouth of the ditch draining the magazine and lower terreplein of the fort. The mouth of this 18 inches below the bottom of the magazine which is 3 feet, 10 inches below the powder terreplein— making six and a half feet necessary for the water to enter the magazine." He continued his report with a very important observation: "River rising not so fast, but if the rise should be met by a rise in the Ohio, makes it probable that it will come up to this mark in a few days."[27]

Everyone who lived in proximity to the Tennessee and Cumberland Rivers was a weatherman. The citizens depended on the rivers for their personal transportation and commerce from one state to another. They well knew the flood stages of these mighty rivers, so naturally, without a shadow of a doubt, they knew that Forts Heiman and Henry would be goners if the floodwaters developed into something tangible at that moment. The Tennessee River begins at Knoxville, Tennessee, where the Holston and French Broad Rivers meet, flowing southwest through Tennessee and Alabama. Then the river curves northward and flows back into Tennessee and then northwest across Kentucky, emptying into the Ohio River at Paducah. This navigable river is 650 miles long. The Tennessee at Fort Henry and Fort Heiman flowed northward by the forts, Fort Henry on the eastern bank, with the fort facing the northwest, and Fort Heiman on a bluff on the western bank of the river. The mass of water that had cut off Zollicoffer and his men in the middle of January would take maybe a week to reach the vicinity of Fort Henry. The exact date this would occur was a guess. The Cumberland River rises in the rugged Cumberland Mountains in eastern Kentucky, is 720 miles long, and empties into the Ohio River at Smithfield. It too flows northwesterly, and would pass Fort Donelson, which was located on the west bank of the river at Dover.

Tilghman in the last week of the month concentrated on completing Fort Heiman on the west bank. On the last day of the month, Major Gilmer reached Fort Henry for an inspection. "General Tilghman and his engineers pressed these defenses forward so rapidly, night and day, that they only require a few days' additional labor to put them into a state of defense. BUT NO GUNS have been received at Fort Heiman except for a few field pieces ... the lines of infantry cover, however, which have been thrown up are capable of making a strong resistance, even without the desired artillery."[28] The heights of Fort Heiman were occupied by the 27th Alabama Regiment, two companies of Alabama Cavalry, the 15th Arkansas, and an unorganized section of a light battery, amounting to all of 1,100 volunteers. What Gilmer didn't know was that most of these troops had just entered the service. But Tilghman knew.

Diary entries of J. P. Cannon, M.D., 27th Regiment, Alabama Infantry, revealed the truth of the situation. "The war was coming to our very doors; the time had come for every man to shoulder his gun. President Davis issued an urgent call for volunteers; there were no examinations by surgeons as to physical condition, nor were youth or old age a bar to eligibility: every man or boy capable of handling a gun was gladly received, no questions asked. On December 24 (Christmas eve), 1861, ten companies of about 100 each had been enrolled and assembled at Florence, mustered into the service of the Confederate States by General S. D. Weakly. In the afternoon of the same day, with 1,000 double-barreled shotguns and 1,000 long Bowie knives in place of bayonets, they proudly marched to the river where a boat was waiting to bear the men to war. On the morning of December 26, we arrived at Fort Henry, a small fort on the east bank of the Tennessee: it looked formidable to us, who had never seen anything like it before. We were not allowed to land, but proceeded to the opposite side of the river in Calloway County, Kentucky. Here it was intended for us to build a fort, Heiman, which, with the assistance of Fort Henry, was to create an impassable barrier to all craft and sink the Lincoln gunboats to the bottom of the river. It required several days to complete our arrangements, such as laying off camps, stretching tents, building bunks, etc. Our rations consisted of a fair article of beef and cornmeal, which was supplemented by luxuries we got from home on the steamboats which made regular trips. Little work was done in the building of the fort and we spent the month of January in regular routine duties: we scarcely broke dirt and not a cannon was on our side of the river."[29] The reason for this idleness was that there were no pickaxes, shovels, et cetera, available to build the fort. The inclement weather soon found a lot of volunteers on sick call, the plague of newcomers to the service.

The well planned Federal advance would be a joint attack by the U.S. Army and the U.S. Navy on Fort Henry and Fort Heiman. Flag Officer A. M. Foote's flotilla of gunboats, teamed with steamboats converted to troop transports, left the Cairo, Illinois, assembling base for the Union expedition on February 2 with four armored vessels, the *Essex, Cincinnati, Carondelet,* and *St. Louis*; three wooden gunboats, the *Tyler, Conestoga,* and *Lexington*[30], reaching the Tennessee by evening. On the fourth, the ships anchored six miles downstream (north) of Fort Henry. Rear Admiral Henry Walker, U.S.N., described the weather: "Heavy rains had been falling, and the river had risen rapidly to an unusual height. The swift currents brought down an immense quantity of heavy driftwood, lumber, fences, large trees, and it required all the steam power of the *Carondelet* with both anchors down, and the most strenuous exertions of the officers and crew working day and night, to prevent the boat from being dragged downstream." Walker continued: "The next morning we saw a large number of white objects, which through the fog looked like polar bears coming down the stream, and ascertained that they were the Confederate torpedoes forced from their moorings by the powerful current. The overflowing river, which opposed our progress, swept away in broad daylight this hidden peril; for if the torpedoes had not been disturbed, or had broken loose at night while we were shoving the driftwood from our bows, some of them would surely have exploded near or under our vessels."[31] Twelve torpedoes were sunk in the chute of the river at the foot of the island. For want of powder and time, none were sunk in the main channel. As pointed out, those sunk were rendered utterly useless by the heavy rise in the river.[32]

On February 4 at 4:30 A.M., the Confederate sentinel at Bailey's Landing downriver sent up a rocket signal announcing the approach of the Union gunboats and transports loaded with Yankee soldiers.

Shortly after daylight the pickets on both sides of the river reported a large fleet coming up, and the smoke from several gunboats became visible over Panther Island.

During this time, the rising Tennessee River had reached flood stage, and Colonel Heiman had a force of men at work on the abutments at Fort Henry trying to keep the water out of the fort. The lower magazine already had two feet of water in it, and the ammunition had been removed to a temporary magazine above ground.

With the approach of the flotilla, the eleven guns in the fort bearing on the river were immediately manned and everything held in readiness for the attack. By 9:00 A.M. the gunboats commenced throwing their shells at the quarters of the pickets and other buildings at Bailey's Landing and at the same time began landing cavalry.

By noon, five gunboats came into sight in the main channel. All Confederate troops except the artillery force were marched out of range of the Federal guns. The gunboats formed in line of battle across the channel about two miles downstream of the fort.

About one o'clock they opened fire with shell and shot, which was immediately returned by Heiman's rifled gun and the 10-inch Columbiad. The rifled gun was fired in quick succession and with good effect while the Columbiad on the fourth shot broke a clamp and could not be fired again.

5. A Trinity of Forts 73

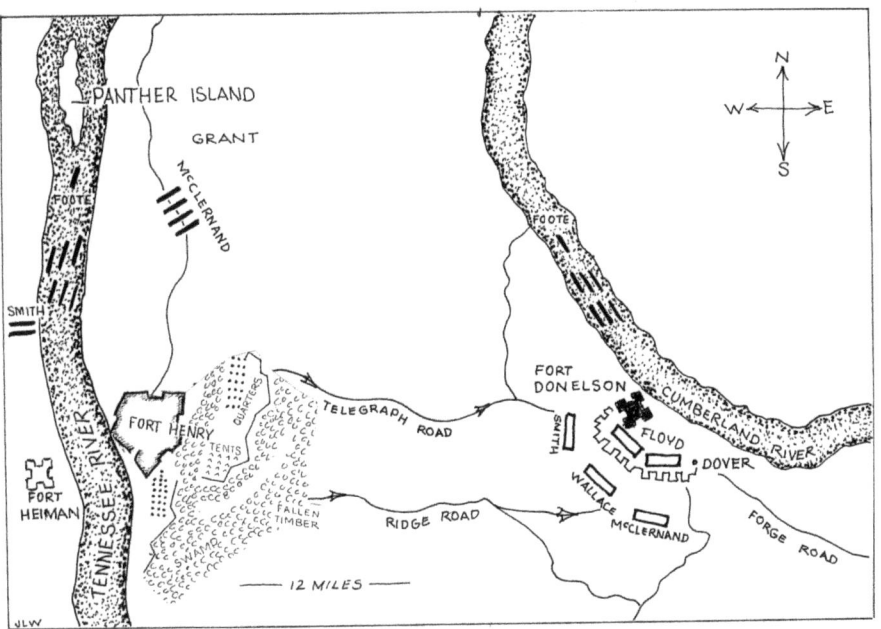

Scope of the Confederate calamity as Fort Henry is attacked.

As the gunboats advanced closer to the fort, Heiman's men opened with the eleven guns that were bearing on the river. The engagement lasted for half an hour. Some of the Union shots fell in and around the fort and others fell a quarter of a mile beyond the fort. After this heated exchange, the gunboats withdrew for the day.

Colonel Heiman wired Tilghman at Fort Donelson that the Federals were landing large forces three miles north of the fort. He added that he was convinced he could not hold Fort Heiman on the opposite heights; therefore it would be prudent to move these men back to Fort Henry. On Heiman's request, Tilghman came in person to Fort Henry, crossing the peninsula from his headquarters at Fort Donelson, arriving at midnight with Major Gilmer's Corps of Engineers and three companies of cavalry. Lieutenant Colonel Haynes, Chief of the Artillery, would join later.

On February 6, Colonel Bailey seemed very comfortable at Fort Donelson as he wrote his wife a long letter: "The Lincolnites have landed from 4,000 to 6,000 men three or four miles below Ft. Henry. The day before yesterday began with 7 gunboats and heavy fire on that fort but without any injury. Yesterday the cavalry from that place were drawn into combat and fired on by infantry, with a loss of one man killed, the wounded enemy said to be two. We have heard nothing from them today, but I suppose the heavy rain which fell last night will curtail their operations." Colonel Bailey continues the war news to his wife: "Our men are all hard at work on the fortification and will finish them in a day or two. We are expecting large reinforcements, and will be able to thump them soundly. It is all a mistake about the Yankees having so large a force. It cannot possibly exceed 7,000 men. Our nominal force at Henry and Donelson is larger, but having so many being sick, the effective strength is not so great. We will catch the last man of theirs if reinforcements come in time." Bailey reiterates: "I work hard constantly to have everything to required standard and feel good in restoring harmony in other regiments." Like everyone else, he missed his home, finishing his letter with: "I will always love and cherish you and the children. That after a little while we will be together again, never to part. I know that until now I never could appreciate my sweet wife."[33]

On the fifth, Tilghman directed the evacuation of all forces from Fort Heiman except three companies of cavalry who would stay as scouts. Tilghman reasoned that with muddy roads, Smith's infantry could do little to harm Fort Henry if they ever did arrive at Fort Heiman.

Dr. Cannon's diary entry: "About midnight we had a night alarm. Boys, get up quick, leave everything except guns and cartridge boxes, fall in without a bit of noise. Boarding the boat which was waiting for us, with lights all covered and with renewed caution to keep perfect silence, we steered direct to Fort Henry. The gunboats could not be seen on account of the darkness."[34] General Tilghman shepherded the Alabama companies across the raging Tennessee to Fort Henry, where they were ordered to take position with the main body of troops camped outside the fort. They were detailed to throw up earthen banks to keep the rising river out of the gunpowder magazine and construct a temporary earthen bridge across the flooding backwater for an avenue of escape. Without adequate cannon, Fort Heiman became an ineffective, time-costly defense that ended up being abandoned by Tilghman.

That night Tilghman stayed aboard the steamer *Dunbar*, which lay about a mile and a half south of the two forts.[35] Early morning on the sixth revealed heavy black smoke rising over Panther Island, manifesting the fact that the Federal flotilla, in cooperation with Federal land forces, were beginning the advance on the two forts. Although General Tilghman had his headquarters and brigade at Fort Donelson, he spent much of January servicing the other two forts, which was quite fatiguing and consumed a great deal of travel time. With the appearance of Foote's gunboats, Tilghman returned to Fort Henry to make a quick assessment of the situation facing him.

On the eastern bank of the river he had Grant's 12,000 bluecoats and cavalry between Bailey's Landing and the fort; on the western bank of the Tennessee he had Smith making his way south towards the uncompleted Fort Heiman, with 7,000 infantry and cavalry. At Panther Island, Foote's gunboats had 54 high-power cannon. To face the enemy, Tilghman had 2,600 unseasoned, poorly armed infantry and an assortment of 12 cannon, which was a no-win situation. As field officer in charge he had several options. He could abandon Fort Henry and Fort Heiman because of the overwhelming odds that faced him; or he himself could retire to Fort Donelson, leaving Colonel Heiman behind to defend and ultimately surrender the works. But there was a third option: Tilghman decided to stay at Fort Henry and make a successful defense in order to buy time for reinforcements to arrive at Fort Donelson from Bowling Green, Clarksville, Columbus, and elsewhere. This stratagem by General Tilghman was crowned with success, as the Confederate military rushed additional forces to Fort Donelson.

Realizing the precarious position of the soldiers in and around the fort area, he ordered the men to get out of the fort and away from the range of the Union navy's powerful guns. The troops moved out of harm's way, positioning themselves to make a quick retreat if necessary. Tilghman retained a small company of 65 trained artillerists for the fight. With the rashness of hope and courage, they would fight until compelled to surrender — self-sacrifice and gallantry for the cause.

Because of the rise in the river, Fort Henry lay almost before the Union gunboats at eye level. "This was fortunate, for the naval cannon had elevation limitations and would mean that Foote could employ point-blank fire against the fort. Still, the fort's eight-foot parapets were formidable, and the fourteen feet of earth could absorb much beating from enemy guns."[36] Also, "twelve of Tilghman's heaviest guns would bear upon the flotilla, including the 10-inch Columbiad hurling a 128-pound shot, a re-bored 24-pounder firing a 62-pound ball, and two 42-and eight 32-pounders, also capable of doing great damage to the boats. As the naval gunners came closer they could see the black muzzles of the Confederate cannons peeking through embrasures formed from the sand-filled cotton sacks."[37]

7

The Surrender of Fort Henry

Rear Admiral Walker described his view of the day's action: "The 6th dawned mild and cheering, with a light breeze, sufficient to clear away the smoke. At 10:20 the flag officer made the signal to prepare for battle, and at 10:50 came the order to get under way and steam up to Panther Island, about two miles below Fort Henry. At 11:35, having passed the foot of the island, we formed in line and approached the fort four abreast — the *Essex* on the right, then the *Cincinnati*, *Carondelet*, and *St. Louis*."[1] The *Tyler* and *Conestoga* had succeeded in removing six torpedoes, as the others had been torn loose and carried downriver. The *Cincinnati* was the flagship. They each were carrying thirteen guns, and the *Essex* carried nine guns.[2]

"As we slowly passed up this narrow stream, not a sound could be heard, nor a moving object seen in the dense woods which overhung the dark and swollen river. About noon the fort and the Confederate flag came suddenly into view, the barracks, the new earth-works, and the great guns well manned. The flag-steamer, the *Cincinnati*, fired the first shot as the signal for others to begin. At once the fort was ablaze with the flame of her eleven heavy guns. The wild whistle of their rifle-shells was heard on every side of us."[3]

Inside the fort, Tilghman and Heiman took position at the center battery to observe the movements of the gunboats as they approached. Captain Jesse Taylor's artillery company of Tennesseans manned the heavy guns and had 50 men present for duty. The captain, a native of Lexington, Tennessee, was an officer of skill and courage, and the imminent battle with the Federal fleet showed how well his guns were served. As the Union navy opened with shot and shell, their fire was returned by the fort's heavy seacoast cannon brought from Mobile. When the gunboats came into range of the lighter guns, then the whole eleven guns erupted and continued firing without a moment's intermission.[4]

Shot after shot was exchanged with admirable rapidity by the rookie artillerists. It was good while it lasted; unfortunately, calamitous happenings began to take the fort down. The 24-pound rifled gun exploded with a terrific bang, disabling every man at the piece; a shell from the fleet, exploding at the mouth of one of the 32-pounders, ruined the gun and wounded all the men serving it. Then a premature explosion of a 42-pounder killed three men and wounded others. A priming wire accidentally spiked the 10-inch Columbiad. Their reliance on the 32- and 42-pounders was diminished when they found that they had not the proper ammunition for them. Within an hour, Tilghman had five men killed, 11 wounded, and five missing, with four guns disabled. Tilghman ordered the gun captains to concentrate their fire on one particular vessel and to pay it a special compliment. The *Cincinnati*, flying the flag officer's pennant, was made the chief mark.

Foote was in the pilothouse of the *Cincinnati*, which received 32 shots. The Confederate heavy shots that struck her had the effect of a thunderbolt, ripping the side timbers and scattering the splinters over the vessel. The chimneys, aft cabin, and boats were completely riddled, and two of the guns disabled. One sailor was killed and several wounded. At the same time the firing from the armored vessels was rapid and well sustained, and seemingly accurate, and they could occasionally see the earth thrown in great heaps over the rebel guns. The Confederates' heavy shot broke and scattered iron plating as if it had been putty and often passed completely through the casemates.[5]

The *Essex* fired 70 shots from her two nine-inch guns, but the feeling of joy on board the ship was suddenly changed to calamity when a shot from the fort pierced the casemate just above the porthole on the port side, then traveled through the middle boiler, opening a chasm for the escape of scalding steam and water.

Captain Porter, his paymaster, Lewis, and acting master's mate S. B. Brittan, Jr., were standing in a direct line of the passing ball. Young

Brittan, being in the center of the group, was struck on the top of the head by the ball and his brains scattered in every direction — earning him a place among Union heroes as the "Boy Brittan" of Forceythe Wilson's poem.[6] The exploding boiler killed the *Essex's* two pilots, several men were badly scalded, and some jumped overboard and drowned in the swirling, ice-cold Tennessee River. The disabled gunboat drifted back downriver carrying with it 10 dead, 23 wounded, and five missing from this single Columbiad shot from the fort.

The *Carondelet* fired 107 shells and solid shot at the fort and was struck in about 30 places by the Confederates' heavy shot and shell, with none of her officers or crew killed. The *St. Louis* fired 107 shots during the action and was struck seven times. No one on board the vessel was killed or wounded.[7] The *Tyler*, *Conestoga*, and *Lexington*, with 15 guns in all, formed the second or rear line. These wooden gunboats engaged the fort at long range in the rear of the ironclads.[8]

By this time the gunboats, by a steady advance, had reached positions not over 600 or 700 yards from the fort. Tilghman's artillerists became very much discouraged when they saw their two heavy guns disabled and the Federal boats apparently unaffected, still drawing nearer and nearer. Then two of the 32-pounders were struck almost at the same instant, and the flying fragments of the shattered guns and burst shells disabled every man at the two guns. The rifle shot and shell penetrated the earthworks as readily as a ball from a Navy Colt would pierce a pine board and soon so disabled other guns as to leave Tilghman with but four capable of being fired.[9]

Seeing this, General Tilghman did everything possible to encourage and urge his exhausted men to further efforts. He assisted to serve one of the pieces himself for at least fifteen minutes, but his men had lost all hope, and there were no others to replace them at the remaining guns. The Federal gunboats improved very much their close-in gunfire as they closed in on the fort; at 200 feet, knowing full well the fort was finished, they began target practicing, i.e., sweeping the entire fort and surroundings with their guns ripping the fort's parapets to pieces.

Tilghman would not entertain the idea of surrender, inquiring why some of the guns had ceased firing. He was told of the men being killed and wounded and that there were no men to relieve them. At this,

Tilghman threw off his coat, sprang on the chassis of the nearest gun, stating he would work it himself: "I shall not give up the work."[10]

He ordered Colonel Heiman to get 50 men of his regiment to come and assist the remaining gunners in the fort. Colonel Heiman himself started out of the fort, but before he could reach his command, the rising Tennessee River was quickly turning the fort's levees of dirt into a ten-foot-high mud bank, and he realized that further resistance was foolish. Tilghman now consulted with Major Gilmer and Captain Taylor as to the situation, and the decision was that further resistance would only entail useless loss of life.

Tilghman's mind turned to saving his infantry and cavalry encamped at the outworks of the fort. He sent Colonel Heiman with instructions to his commanders to withdraw as quickly as possible and move to Fort Donelson on the other side of the peninsula. By now the farmers and backwoods volunteers were frightened beyond belief with visions of being crushed and taken prisoner by the overwhelming, well-equipped Union army marching their way — look what those black monsters had done to their fort! Lacking wagons, they abandoned all supplies, skedaddling along the telegraph lane to Fort Donelson, cousin Oswald with them.

"The end came about 1:50 P.M. Hoping to allow his main force to escape to Fort Donelson, Tilghman sought to parley with the Federals. Unsure of the position of Grant's land force, he reluctantly affixed a small white cloth to a stick and mounted the parapet. The dense battle smoke hid his flag, however, and the conflict continued for another five minutes. Tilghman then ordered Captain Taylor to strike the Confederate colors from the main flagstaff. Orderly Sergeant John Jones braved the Federals' fire, ran to the flagstaff, clambered up to the yardarm, and lowered the Stars and Bars.

When reports of this reached Colonel Haynes, he sought to raise the flag again and yelled at Tilghman, "I will not surrender, and you have no right to include me in the capitulation as an officer of this garrison, I being here only for consultation with you." He then rushed off to join Heiman and Gilmer in the escape column headed for Fort Donelson.[11]

Commodore Foote ordered his vessels to cease firing and remain where they were, while a small yawl was put out from the fort carrying Tilghman's adjutant and an engineer. Approaching the flagship, the Confederate officers relayed the message that General Tilghman wished to communicate with Foote and requested permission to come aboard. The naval officer agreed, dispatching two officers to take possession of the fort while at the same time assuring Tilghman that his men would be permitted to retain their sidearms and be treated with the highest consideration due prisoners of war. The formal surrender was made to the naval forces, Lieutenant Commander Phelps acting for Foote and Captain Jessie Taylor representing General Tilghman.[12] On February 6, 1862, General Tilghman unconditionally surrendered himself and Captain Taylor's company of Tennesseans, 12 officers, 66 men in Fort Henry, and 16 men in the hospital boat.

Captain Jesse Taylor, C.S.A., had his own sardonic observations of the battle: "On the morning of the attack, we were sure that the February rise of the Tennessee had come; when the action began, the lower part of the fort was already flooded, and when the colors were hauled down, the water was waist deep there; and when the cutter came with the officers to receive the formal surrender, she pulled into the sally port; between the fort and the position which had been occupied by the infantry support was a sheet of water a quarter of a mile or more wide, and running like a millrace. If the attack had been delayed forty-eight hours, there would hardly have been a hostile shot fired; the Tennessee would have accomplished the work by drowning the magazine. The fight was over; the little garrison were prisoners; but our army had been saved. We had been required to hold out an hour; we had held out for over two."[13]

As the Union flag was raised over the fort, General Tilghman was escorted to the flagship *Cincinnati*, where he joined Commodore Foote. In surrendering, the Rebel general remarked, "I am glad to surrender to so gallant an officer." Foote replied, "You do perfectly right, sir, in surrendering, but you should have blown my boats out of the water before I would have surrendered to you."[14]

"As for the Confederate commander, Lloyd Tilghman never planned on surrendering himself at Fort Henry. It was purely an emotional decision made in the heat of battle. Tilghman's original plan was to fight briefly with the batteries, rejoin his column marching towards Fort Donelson, and renew the fight there. He was in command of both forts and thus responsible for each one equally. By surrendering himself at Fort Henry, he was derelict in his duty to defend Fort Donelson."[15]

Present were extraneous circumstances, i.e., combat fatigue brought on by exhaustion and stress of the battle.

Foote told one friend that Tilghman had appeared aboard his flagship shell-shocked, wringing his hands and exclaiming, "I am in despair, my reputation is gone forever." Foote then reassured the man of his gallantry: "More than two-thirds of your battery is disabled, while I have lost less than one-third of mine." Foote promised to forever attest to Tilghman's valor, and the naval officer not only wrote to his own superiors to that effect, but encouraged his prisoner to do likewise to Richmond authorities. Foote then turned to Tilghman, saying, "Come, General, you have lost your dinner, and the steward has just told me that mine is ready." Arm in arm, the victor and vanquished disappeared into Foote's cabin. Whatever the truth of this story, Tilghman certainly escaped the indignity imposed upon his subordinates as they were rounded up by the sailors.[16]

The strain of the bombardment and surrender was telling on the general. He had no choice but to await Grant's move, leading to a passive and reactionary defense of the fort. Even an interview with a newspaper reporter attested to Tilghman's state of mind. "General, will you be kind enough to give me the correct spelling of your name?" Tilghman replied haughtily, "Sir, I do not desire that my name should be made use of at all, in connection with this affair, except as it may appear in the reports of General Grant." When told his name was needed only for the list of prisoners, Tilghman shot back, "You will oblige me, sir, by not giving my name in any newspaper connection whatever."[17]

At least one reporter failed to oblige Tilghman in this manner. An *Easton Gazette* article dated February 15, 1862, put Tilghman in the headline:

The Stars and Stripes Again Waving in Tennessee.
Fort Henry Captured.

A LARGE NUMBER OF CANNON AND MORTARS TAKEN.

THE SURRENDER OF THE FORT—FIVE THOUSAND REBEL INFANTRY CUT AND RUN, LEAVING EVERYTHING BEHIND THEM IN THEIR FLIGHT.

GENERAL LLOYD TILGHMAN, THE COMMANDER OF THE FORT, WITH ONE HUNDRED OTHERS TAKEN PRISONERS.

WASHINGTON, Feb. 7—The Navy Department, at two P.M. to-day, received the following highly important dispatch:

U.S. Flag Steamer Cincinnati, *Off Fort Henry, Tennessee River*, Feb. 6, 1862. HON. GIDEN WELLS, Sectary Navy:

7. The Surrender of Fort Henry

The gunboats under my command — Essex, Commander Porter; Carondelet, Commander Waiter; Cincinnau, Commander Stenabel; St. Louis, Lt. Commanding Paulding; Conestoga, Lt. Commander Phelps; Taylor, Lieut. Commanding Gwinn, and Lexington, Lieut. Commanding Shirk — after a severe and rapid fire of one hour and a quarter, have captured Fort Henry, and have taken General Lloyd Tilghman and his staff and 60 men as prisoners.

The surrender to the gunboats was unconditional, as we kept an open fire upon them until their flag was struck. In half an hour of after the surrender I handed the fort and prisoners over to General Grant, commanding the army, on his arrival at the fort in force.

The Essex had a shot in her boilers, and after fighting most effectually for two-thirds of the action, was obliged to drop down the river, as I hear that several of her crew were scaled to death, including the two pilots. She, with other gunboats, officers and men, fought with the greatest galantry.

The Cincinnati received 31 shots, and had one man killed and eight wounded — two seriously.

The fort, with twenty guns and seventeen mortars, was defended by Gen. Tilghman with the most determined gallantry.

I will write as soon as possible.

I have sent Lieut. Commanding Philips and three gunboats after the Rebel gunboats.

A. M. FOOTE, Flag Officer

The artillerists from the surrendered fort were detained separately from the general. Because they were confined to a small area of the gunboat, it became necessary for U.S. Navy personnel and prisoners to mess together. Everyone was treated with every courtesy; even in war, the breaking of bread with the enemy was a symbol of peace, but only at the dining table.

While some dined, Foote dispatched three timber-clad gunboats to continue the Federal initiative by moving upstream for a distance of one hundred and fifty miles, capturing along the way the important railroad bridge at Danville, Tennessee. Continuing their penetration, the gunboats spread havoc with small farms and plantations along the way, taking potshots at the farm buildings, wharfs, unarmed wooden boats, putting ashore raiding parties, destroying any rebel war materials or goods that were found on the bank of the river, plus offering freedom to any slave who wanted to come aboard. Upon reaching Muscle Shoals in Florence, Alabama, the raiders turned their gunboats about and returned downriver to join the flotilla in time to proceed down the Cumberland River for the attack on Fort Donelson. The loss of control of the river destroyed communication and transportation between the parts of Tennessee on either side of the river.

On the west bank of the river, poor roads and mud continued to hinder General Smith's Union men. Finally reaching the bluff at Fort Heiman, without any opposition from the Confederate cavalry, General Lew Wallace, with 2,500 bluecoats, was left to guard the site of Fort Heiman and the lately surrendered Fort Henry across the river. General Smith, with the balance of his force, retraced his steps northward, was ferried across the Tennessee, and marched to reinforce General McClernand's brigade now bivouacked around Fort Henry.[18]

Meantime, Grant's fledging brigades continued likewise to be hindered by mud and poor roads and did not arrive in the vicinity of Fort Henry until after the naval bombardment. The troops did hear the shells of both combatants, cheering at the whistling of the shot and balls as they slammed into the fort or the boats. While there was some daylight left, Grant ordered his cavalry to chase after Heiman's van of retreating Confederates and harass them if possible.

Dr. Cannon's spirited 27th Alabama Infantry diary recounts: "The cannonading continued at the fort incessantly for about an hour and a half when it ceased as suddenly as it began. We were immediately ordered to 'right face, forward march' up the river; it soon dawned on us that the fort had surrendered and we were retreating from the Yankees.... The impulse to go faster seemed to strike all of us at the same time, while the dashing past of small squads of frightened cavalrymen and an occasional shot in the rear served to accelerate our speed. We followed a dirt road leading up the river and had not covered more than a mile when we were confronted by a perfect torrent of a creek which, swollen by recent rains, was rushing down from the hills towards the river like a millrace and was fully fifty feet wide. The stream was so deep and the current so strong that small men could not swim it alone, so locking together, tall and short, by fours we plunged in and all made a successful landing on the opposite shore.

"We turned across the country towards Fort Donelson, the Federals' cavalry charging upon our rear occasionally. Night ended the pursuit, but not our troubles, for it set in cloudy and so dark we could not see our file leaders. All night long we groped our way over hills and hollows, wading numberless creeks and branches and finally reaching Fort Donelson at daylight, exhausted and almost starved: 36 hours without food, a 15-mile run through mud and water without a minute's rest was pretty rough on a lot of raw soldiers who had never seen any active service."[19]

Any heightened anticipation of General Johnston's at Bowling Green of Tilghman stopping the invading navy and ground forces at Fort Henry had now been squelched. As the clicking of the wireless began to announce the fall of Fort Henry, everyone wondered how a fort, a culmination of seven months' construction, could topple in less than two hours. The fort was devastated and in shambles. The answer was that Tilghman had been outgunned by the naval force and surrounded on the ground by Grant's army.

General Tilghman reported as follows to Colonel Mackall at Bowling Green:

Fort Henry, Tenn., *February 7, 1862,*

Through the courtesy of Brig. Gen. U. S. Grant, commanding Federal forces, I am permitted to communicate with you in relation to the result of the action between the fort under my command at this place and the Federal gunboats on yesterday.

At 11.40 o'clock on yesterday morning the enemy engaged the fort with seven gunboats, mounting fifty-four guns. I promptly returned their fire with eleven guns bearing on the river. The action was maintained with great bravery by the force under my command until 1.50 P.M., at which time I had but four guns fit for service. At 1.55 P.M., finding it impossible to maintain the fort and wishing to spare the lives of the gallant men under my command, on consultation with my officers I surrendered the fort. Our casualties are small. The effect of our shot was severely felt by the enemy, whose superior and overwhelming force alone gave them the advantage.

The surrender of Fort Henry involved that of Captain Taylor and Lieutenants Watts and Weller, and one other officer of artillery; Captains Hayden and Miller, of the Engineers; Capts. H. L. Jones and McLaughlin, quartermaster's department, and Acting Assistant Adjumen under my command. They sustained their position with consummate bravery as long as there was any hope of success. I also take great pleasure in acknowledging the courtesy and consideration shown by Brig. Gen. U. S. Grant and Commander Foote and the officers under their command.

I have the honor to remain, very respectfully, your obedient servant,

LLOYD TILGHMAN,
Brigadier-General, C. S. Army.

Tilghman makes no reference to the menacing Tennessee River or flooded fort.

There was praise for Tilghman from Colonel Heiman: "I may be permitted to state that the self-sacrificing heroism displayed by Tilghman in this terrible and most unequal struggle challenges the admiration of all gallant men and entitles him to the gratitude of the whole people of the Confederate States. His tact and skill while in command of the defense of the Tennessee and Cumberland Rivers proved him a most skillful and gallant leader."[22]

The effect of the Union victory was far-reaching, and there was much carping about Tilghman throughout Dixie. The general was vilified for the surrender of the fort and men; words such as "treason," "treachery" and "avoidance of duty" sprung up and were uttered by uninformed Confederates. Regardless, Tilghman was aboard the flagship *Cincinnati* as a prisoner of war. The ironclad returned downstream and put him ashore at Paducah, his old hometown. But there was no cheering for the Confederate, as he was on his arrival placed in the custody of Brigadier General Sherman. General Sherman told Tilghman that he and the other prisoners, who were on their way, would be sent to either St. Louis or Cincinnati for parole.[23]

General Grant, savoring the capture of his first general in the war and in the absence of any firm Federal POW policy, suggested to Sherman that Tilghman and the other captured men from Fort Henry be held incommunicado in confiscated secessionist homes, where they might have the freedom of the town while awaiting their paroles. "When everybody realized that Paducah was Lloyd Tilghman's home and might pose problems to Sherman's control of the city, Grant suggested that the Fort Henry prisoners be sent to Cairo, Illinois, and then be transferred to the Alton, Illinois, prison. Even then the officers could stroll about town."[24]

All of this civil liberty ceased when Secretary of War Stanton and General McClellan learned of it. They telegraphed their opposition to paroles and exchange. At one stroke, Washington hardliners swept away all local attempts to shape POW policy. "The rebels would be incarcerated as prisoners of war."[25]

Learning of this, Tilghman dispatched a personal letter to Brigadier General Crittenden, U.S.V., son of Senator Crittenden of Kentucky, a prominent Southern political leader, objecting to his uncivil removal instead of being paroled as promised by General Sherman. At this early stage of the war the political pipeline between the sides had ruptured; the appeal went unanswered, so there would be no parole for the general. On February 17, Tilghman was on his way up the Mississippi River to be incarcerated as a prisoner of war at the Alton, Illinois, prison north of St. Louis.

Below is a copy of Lloyd Tilghman's official report on the bombardment of Fort Henry. An accompanying note indicates that he first attempted to file the report from the prison in Alton:

Richmond, VA., *August* 9, 1862.
General: Inclosed you will please find a copy of my official report of the bombardment of Fort Henry, on February 6, 1862, by the Federal fleet, together with accompanying papers. The original of this report was forwarded from Alton, Ill., but, not having reached your office, I have prepared a copy of the same at the earliest moment practicable since my release from Fort Warren, Mass.
I remain, respectfully, your obedient servant,
LLOYD TILGHMAN,
Brigadier-General, C. S. Army, Commanding.
S. Cooper,
Adjutant and Inspector General C. S. Army.

The forces under Tilghman at Fort Henry were organized as follows:

TILGHMAN (approximately 2,700–3,300, Feb. 6, Fort Henry)
    6 infantry regiments + 1 battalion
    3 batteries of light and heavy artillery
    2 battalions + 1 company + miscellaneous cavalry
1st Brigade (Heiman)
    10th, 48th Tennessee Infantry
    27th Alabama Infantry
    Culbertson's Light Artillery Battery
    Gantt's Battalion, Tennessee Cavalry
2d Brigade (Drake)
    4th Mississippi Infantry
    15th Arkansas Infantry
    51st Tennessee Infantry
    26th Alabama (Garvin) Infantry (2 companies)
    Crain's Light Artillery Battery
    Alabama Cavalry Battalion (Hubbard, Houston)

Milner's Cavalry Company
Padgett's Spy Company
Milton's Ranger Detachment
Taylor's Company, Tennessee Artillery Corps[28]

Here is Lloyd Tilghman's report on the battle of Fort Henry to Colonel W. W. Mackall:

Feb. 12th, 1862.

Col. W. W. MACKALL, A. A.-Genl. C. S. A., Bowling Green:

Sir,—My communication of the 7th instant, sent from Fort Henry, having announced the fact of the surrender of that fort to Commodore Foote, of the Federal navy, on the 6th inst., I have now the honor to submit the following report of the details of the action, together with the accompanying papers, marked A, B, containing list of officers and men surrendered, together with casualties, etc.

* * * * * * *

The wretched military position of Fort Henry, and the small force at my disposal, did not permit me to avail myself of the advantages to be derived from the system of outworks, built with the hope of being reinforced in time, and compelled me to determine to concentrate my efforts, by land, within the rifle-pits surrounding the 10th Tennessee and 4th Mississippi regiments, in case I deemed it possible to do more than to operate solely against the attack by the river. Accordingly, my entire command was paraded and placed in the rifle-pits around the above camps, and minute instructions given, not only to brigades, but to regiments and companies, as to the exact ground each was to occupy. Seconded by the able assistance of Major Gilmer, of the Engineers, of whose valuable services I thus early take pleasure in speaking, and by Colonels Heiman and Drake, everything was arranged to make a formidable resistance against anything like fair odds. It was known to me, on the day before, that the enemy had reconnoitred the roads leading to Fort Donelson, from Bailey's Ferry, by way of Iron Mountain Furnace; and at 10 o'clock A. M., on the 5th, I sent forward, from Fort Henry, a strong reconnoitring party of cavalry. They had not advanced more than one and a half miles in the direction of the enemy, when they encountered their reconnoitring party. Our cavalry charged them in gallant style, upon which the enemy's cavalry fell back, with a loss of only one man on each side.

Very soon the main body of the Federal advance guard, composed of a regiment of infantry and a large force of cavalry, was met, upon which our cavalry retreated. On receipt of this news I moved out in person, with five companies of the 10th Tennessee, five companies of the 4th Mississippi, and fifty cavalry, ordering, at the same time, two additional companies of infantry to support Captain Red at the outworks. Upon advancing well to the front I found that the enemy had retired. I returned to camp at 5 P. M., leaving Captain Red reinforced at the outworks. The enemy were again reinforced by the arrival of a large number of transports. At night the pickets from the west bank reported the landing of troops on that side, opposite Bailey's Ferry, their advance pickets having been met one and a half miles from the river.

* * * * * * *

To understand properly the difficulties of my position, it is right that I should explain fully the unfortunate location of Fort Henry, in reference to resistance by a small force against an attack by land co-operating with the gunboats, as well as its disadvantages in even an engagement with boats alone. The entire fort, together with the intrenched camp spoken of, is enfiladed from three or four points on the opposite shore, while three points on the eastern bank completely command them both—all at easy cannon range. At the same time the intrenched camp, arranged as it was in the best possible manner to meet the case, was two thirds of it completely under the control of the fire of the gunboats. The history of military engineering records has no parallel to this case. Points within a few miles of it, possessing great advantages and few disadvantages, were totally neglected; and a location fixed upon, without one redeeming feature, or filling one of the many requirements of a site for a work such as Fort Henry. The work itself was well built; it was completed long before I took command, but strengthened greatly by myself in building embrasures and epaulments of sand-bags. An enemy had but to use their most common sense in obtaining the advantage of high water, as was the case, to have complete and entire control of the position. I am guilty of no act of injustice in this frank avowal of the opinions entertained by myself, as well as by all other officers who have become familiar with the location of Fort Henry. Nor do I desire the defects of location to have an undue influence in directing public opinion in relation to the battle of the 6th instant. The fort was built when I took charge, and I had no time to build anew.

* * * * * *

The case stood thus: I had, at my command, a grand total of two thousand six hundred and ten men, only one third of whom had been at all disciplined or well armed. The high water in the river, filling the sloughs, gave me but one route on which to retire, if necessary; and that route, for some distance, in direction at right angles to the line of approach of the enemy, and over roads well-nigh impassable for artillery, cavalry, or infantry. The enemy had seven gunboats, with an armament of fifty-four guns, to engage the eleven guns at Fort Henry.

* * * * * *

I argued thus: Fort Donelson might possibly be held, if properly reinforced, even though Fort Henry should fall; but the reverse of this proposition was not true. The force at Fort Henry was necessary to aid Fort Donelson, either in making a successful defence, or in holding it long enough to answer the purposes of a new disposition of the entire army from Bowling Green to Columbus, which would necessarily follow the breaking of our centre, resting on Forts Donelson and Henry. The latter alternative was all that I deemed possible. I knew that reinforcements were difficult to be had; and that, unless sent in such force as to make the defence certain, which I did not believe practicable, the fate of our right wing at Bowling Green depended upon a concentration of my entire division on Fort Donelson, and the holding of that place as long as possible; trusting that the delay, by an action at Fort Henry, would give time for such reinforcement as might reasonably be expected to reach a point sufficiently near Donelson to co-operate with my division by getting to the rear and right flank of the enemy, and in such a position as to control the roads over which a safe retreat might be effected. I hesitated not a moment. My infantry, artillery, and cavalry, removed, of necessity, to avoid the fire of the gunboats, to the outworks, could not meet the enemy there. My only chance was to delay the enemy every moment possible, and retire the command, now outside the main work, towards Fort Donelson, resolving to suffer as little loss as possible. I retained only the heavy artillery company to fight the guns, and gave the order to commence the movement at once. At 10¼ o'clock Lieutenant McGavock sent a messenger to me, stating that our pickets reported General Grant approaching rapidly, and within half a mile of the advance work; and movements on the west bank indicated that General Smith was fast approaching also.

*   *   *   *   *   *   *

At 11.45 A. M. the enemy opened from their gunboats on the fort. I waited a few moments, until the effects of the first shots of the enemy were fully appreciated. I then gave the order to return the fire, which was gallantly responded to by the brave little band under my command. The enemy, with great deliberation, steadily closed upon the fort, firing very wild until within twelve hundred yards. The cool deliberation of our men told from the first shot, fired with tremendous effect. At twenty-five minutes of 1 o'clock P. M. the bursting of our 24-pounder rifled gun disabled every man at the piece.

This great loss was, to us, in a degree, made up by our disabling entirely the *Essex* gunboat, which immediately floated down stream. Immediately after the loss of this valuable gun we sustained another loss still greater, in the closing up of the vent of 10-inch Columbiad, rendering that gun perfectly useless, and defying all efforts to reopen it.

*   *   *   *   *   *   *

It was now plain to be seen that the enemy were breaching the fort directly in front of our guns, and that I could not much longer sustain their fire without an unjustifiable exposure of the valuable lives of the men who had so nobly seconded me in the unequal struggle. Several of my officers, Major Gilmer among the number, now suggested to me the propriety of taking the subject of a surrender into consideration.

Every moment, I knew, was of vast importance to those retreating on Fort Donelson, and I declined, hoping to find men enough at hand to continue awhile longer the fire now so destructive to the enemy. In this I was disappointed. My next effort was to try the experiment of a flag of truce, which I waved from the parapets myself. This was precisely at ten minutes before 2 o'clock P. M. The flag was not noticed, I presume from the dense smoke that enveloped it, and, leaping again into the fort, I continued the fire for five minutes, when, with the advice of my brother officers, I ordered the flag to be lowered, after an engagement of two hours and ten minutes with such an unequal force.

The surrender was made to Flag-Officer Foote, represented by Captain Stemble, commanding gunboat *Cincinnati*, and was qualified by the single condition that all officers should retain their side arms, that both officers and men should be treated with the highest consideration due prisoners of war, which was promptly and gracefully acceded to by Commodore Foote.

*   *   *   *   *   *   *

Confident of having performed my whole duty to my government in the defence of Fort Henry, with the totally inadequate means at my disposal, I have but little to add in support of the views before expressed. The reasons for the line of policy pursued by me are, to my mind, convincing.

Against such overwhelming odds as sixteen thousand well-armed men (exclusive of the force on the gunboats) to two thousand six hundred and ten badly armed, in the field, and fifty-four heavy guns against eleven medium ones, in the fort, no tactics or bravery could avail. The rapid movements of the enemy, with every facility at their command, rendered the defence, from the beginning, a hopeless one. I succeeded in doing even more than was to be hoped for at first. I not only saved my entire command outside the fort, but damaged, materially, the flotilla of the enemy, demonstrating thoroughly a problem of infinite value to us in the future. Had I been reinforced so as to have justified my meeting the enemy at the advanced works, I might have made good the land defence on the east bank. I make no inquiry as to why I was not, for I have entire confidence in the judgment of my commanding general.

  * * * * * * *

Respectfully, your obedient servant,
LLOYD TILGHMAN, Brig.-Genl. Comdg.

Official.
ED. A. PALFREY, A. A. Genl.
A. and I. G. Office, *Aug.* 29*th*, 1862.

8

Armageddon on the Cumberland, and the Surrender of Fort Donelson

The eastern end of the Confederate defense had been scattered in mid-January by Union General George Thomas, who soundly defeated the rebel forces of Generals Zollicoffer and Crittenden at the Battle of Mill Springs, Kentucky. This defeat left Bowling Green, the present Confederate capital of Kentucky, as the new eastern terminus of Johnston's shrinking defensive positions. Johnston had established his headquarters here for directing military operations. The position of the city had little defensive value. Nevertheless, the Central Army of Kentucky parked here to discourage the enemy from making further intrusions into Kentucky. Recruiting slowed down after the first rush of volunteers for Confederate service in 1861. As a matter of fact, when the Confederate government removed from Montgomery, Alabama, in May, 1861, and moved to Richmond, Virginia, the cause, for Kentucky and Tennessee, was removed 700 miles away. No longer was it a local affair; the remoteness of the capital contributed to a lack of manpower or weapons for Johnston's Western Department.

Assembled at Bowling Green were about 14,000 Confederates under Generals Buckner and Hardee. At nearby camps such as Clarksville and Hopkinsville, Generals Floyd, who had just arrived from Virginia, and

8. The Cumberland and Fort Donelson

Pillow had another 11,000 men. The forts on the Tennessee and Cumberland Rivers had garrisons totaling about 5,500. At Columbus, a hundred miles away, Bishop Polk had 12,000 effectives. The total varied from day to day because of sickness among the men. All told, Johnston was lucky to field 40,000 soldiers, and they were scattered in all directions. Union forces, by contrast, were poised, ready, and equipped. At Paducah, Grant had some 20,000 men plus the support of Commodore Foote's flotilla of gunboats. General Don Carlos Buell, based at Louisville, had possibly 60,000 bluecoats along the railroad north of Bowling Green and the Green River.[1]

To meet this crisis and strengthen Johnston's staff, President Davis ordered General P.G. T. Beauregard, hero of Sumter and Manassas, to Bowling Green. He arrived on February 4. Generals Johnston, Beauregard, Hardee, and Buckner then conferred as to the next course of action. The news of the collapse of Fort Henry and Tilghman's surrender came like a thunderbolt, although Johnston admitted that he never intended to give Tilghman any additional troops. With the deed done, the officers concluded and unanimously resolved that preparations should at once be made for the removal of forces at Bowling Green to Nashville. Johnston wired orders for his commanders to evacuate all positions in Kentucky; furthermore, "He ordered the combined Confederate forces to hold Fort Donelson until he could move his army at Bowling Green across the Cumberland River at Nashville. *The Donelson troops were then to abandon the fort and move south as well.*"[2] Plain matter of fact, General Johnston had no intention of saving Fort Donelson.

Johnston, shaken by Grant's success at Fort Henry, ordered Confederate forces to Clarksville where they could take a defensive stand if necessary. General Gideon J. Pillow, without a command, was ordered to Clarksville to coordinate the Confederate forces arriving for the defense of Fort Donelson.

"Pillow arrived on the night of February 5, and, according to his welcome by the *Clarksville Weekly Chronicle*, his presence was a source of gratification to everyone. After making a hurried inspection of the defensive works, he wired Johnston: 'None of the defensive works completed, none of the four heavy guns were ready for use, and there were no artillerists ... if Fort Donelson should be overcome, we can make no successful stand without a larger force.' Johnston quickly responded by dispatching the divisions of Brigadier General John B. Floyd and Brigadier General Simon B. Buckner from Russellville. Sidney Johnston sent Floyd on his way with authority to make the dispositions for the defense of Clarksville, Fort Donelson, and the Cumberland River at his own discretion.

"Pillow displayed great industry at Clarksville and had transformed that post into a well-functioning distribution point for forwarding men and supplies downriver to Fort Donelson. He also advocated marching north, and with the assistance of Floyd's and Buckner's divisions, falling upon Grant's exposed forces. This plan had merit, but the usual quarreling among celebrated brass about WHO was in charge, nixed the offensive plan. The opportunity was foolishly lost."[3]

Johnston ordered Generals Buckner, Floyd, and Pillow to Fort Donelson to reinforce Bushrod Johnson and Colonel Heiman's cadre of 5,500 men. Bushrod had hurried back from Nashville to replace the captured Tilghman. By nightfall on February 12, Fort Donelson and its immediate vicinity was crowded with about 15,000 anxious rebels ready to avenge the loss of Fort Henry and to protect Nashville from Grant's invasion. General Pillow, who arrived at Fort Donelson from Clarksville with 2,800 men, pronounced that the watchword for Fort Donelson was LIBERTY OR DEATH.[4]

The fort was located north of the river town of Dover. Donelson, like the other forts, was built and pieced together over a period of seven months by companies of volunteers and some leased slaves from Alabama. Like all other earlier forts, it was a bastion of logs and earth located on fifteen acres on the west bank of the Cumberland River. The earthworks were ten feet high, elevated one hundred feet above the river's shoreline. The water batteries were not part of the fort and had been engineered by Major Gilmer, who placed the batteries on the Mississippi River at Columbus and Fort Henry. The batteries were on the river, while the fort was situated on a hill behind to protect them. The ammunition was stored in bombproof magazines.[5] Although Fort Donelson was Tilghman's headquarters, the general made few structural changes except to add armament when available. Fort Donelson, in the course of preparation, was better located and planned than its twin fort, Fort Henry, which "was nothing more than an area of about an acre, enclosed by levees of dirt some eight or ten feet high."[6]

8. The Cumberland and Fort Donelson

On February 6, 1862, the *Louisville Daily Democrat* proclaimed:

> Cotton is no longer king. Mud is monarch of all. It has issued its proclamation against the advance of armies and dug its trenches and pitfalls in all the camps.... Byron's dream of darkness could be paraphrased into a hymn descriptive of the empire of mud. Mud on all the roads — mud on door steps, gardens, and fields — and mud enough to bury streets ... man is not only made of clay he is clothed in it. He cannot "put off this muddy vesture of decay" in or out of life. The mud has been ground, worked, toughened, and prepared, as if for building purposes, and any mud just from anywhere out of doors, thrown into an oven, would come out a regular "brick." The world seems to he soaked, steeped, and melted; as if providence, disgusted with it, intended to run it over in a new mold. The ground hog came out on the first of February, and went back in out of the mud. It's just seven miles from Water Street to Broad Street — six miles deep and one mile long. The soldiers are not in entrenchments but endrenchments, drenched with mud. A half an hour's walk in the fields gives a man a free sample of a ten acre farm on his boots, back, head, legs, and body generally. If a soldier were to ground his arms, his musket would sink down until the fire in the center of the earth fired it off before it touched a solid part. Three fourths of the earth used to be water — now the remaining one fourth is mud.... [We] are blockaded and besieged by the imperial armies of mud.

On the seventh, Grant rode over from Fort Henry to make a personal reconnaissance of the fort, discovering it was next to impossible to move his infantry and cavalry because of high water and muddy bottomland. With a change in the weather on the 11th, Grant marched his forces from Fort Henry campgrounds with 15,000 men, including eight batteries and part of a regiment of cavalry, moving his army slowly across the 12-mile peninsula. By 11:00 A.M., the lead elements were within three miles of Fort Donelson's outer trenches when they encountered a strong detachment of Confederate horsemen intending to resist any further progress. "The gray troopers were under the command of Nathan Bedford Forrest, who ventured forward of the trenches to observe any enemy movements. Forrest promptly dismounted his men and formed a line of battle along the crest of a ridge, and for the next few hours, each side fired, charged, and withdrew without significant advantage gained. The Confederate cavalrymen kept up a constant fire, however, with the overall effect of delaying the Federals until about 3:00 P.M. At this time, orders were given for all Confederate forces to withdraw back into the outer works."[7]

That afternoon and the next day the Federals spent time in taking up ground to make their investments as complete as possible. Their line was generally along the crest of ridges, with artillery being protected by being sunk in the ground and spread in a semicircle upon the hills. Grant's plan was for "the troops to hold the Confederates within his lines, while the gunboats should attack the water-batteries at close quarters and silence the guns if possible. Some of the gunboats were to run the batteries, get above the fort and above the village of Dover."[8] Grant had his foe trapped in their own fort.

At this time the spring weather turned bitterly cold and blizzard-like, as the mild rain turned to fine sleet, and finally wet snow, with temperatures plunging to 10°. Within the fort's boundary were 15,000 camped Confederate forces with their animals, now all struggling to keep warm. Although one hundred log huts had been built for the fort's cadre, they provided little relief to such a large crowd, and when the temperature remained below freezing, many paced back and forth all night to prevent themselves from freezing to death; others who lay down were frostbitten. They were forbidden to light fires because of Union sharpshooters, and the only food was cold hardtack. Their clothing froze to their bodies and much of the drinking water froze.

The boys in blue, another 20,000 or more, fared no better. Aside from some seasoned troops from Missouri, Grant's regiments had come from the depots in Illinois, Indiana, and Ohio, so freshly formed that they had hardly changed their civil garb for soldiers' uniforms before they hurried here. On the long march, many had abandoned their coats and blankets. The shelter tents had not arrived.[9] Neither side had expected the return of winter weather. Even the mud froze.

It's a wonder, with guns, caissons, and wagons frozen to the earth, that Union Generals Smith and McClernand would attempt to nudge forward in probing attack on the 13th. Firing soon became general from the batteries on both sides and was kept up all day. The Illinois regiments made a charge upon the rebels and came up within a few feet of the entrenchments, but were repulsed with a heavy loss.

In the afternoon the gunboats, four in number, came up and tested the water batteries and, after a long and fierce battle, were driven back. Lost at this exchange was Captain Dixon, an engineer in the Confederate army. General Polk had previously cited him for his action at the

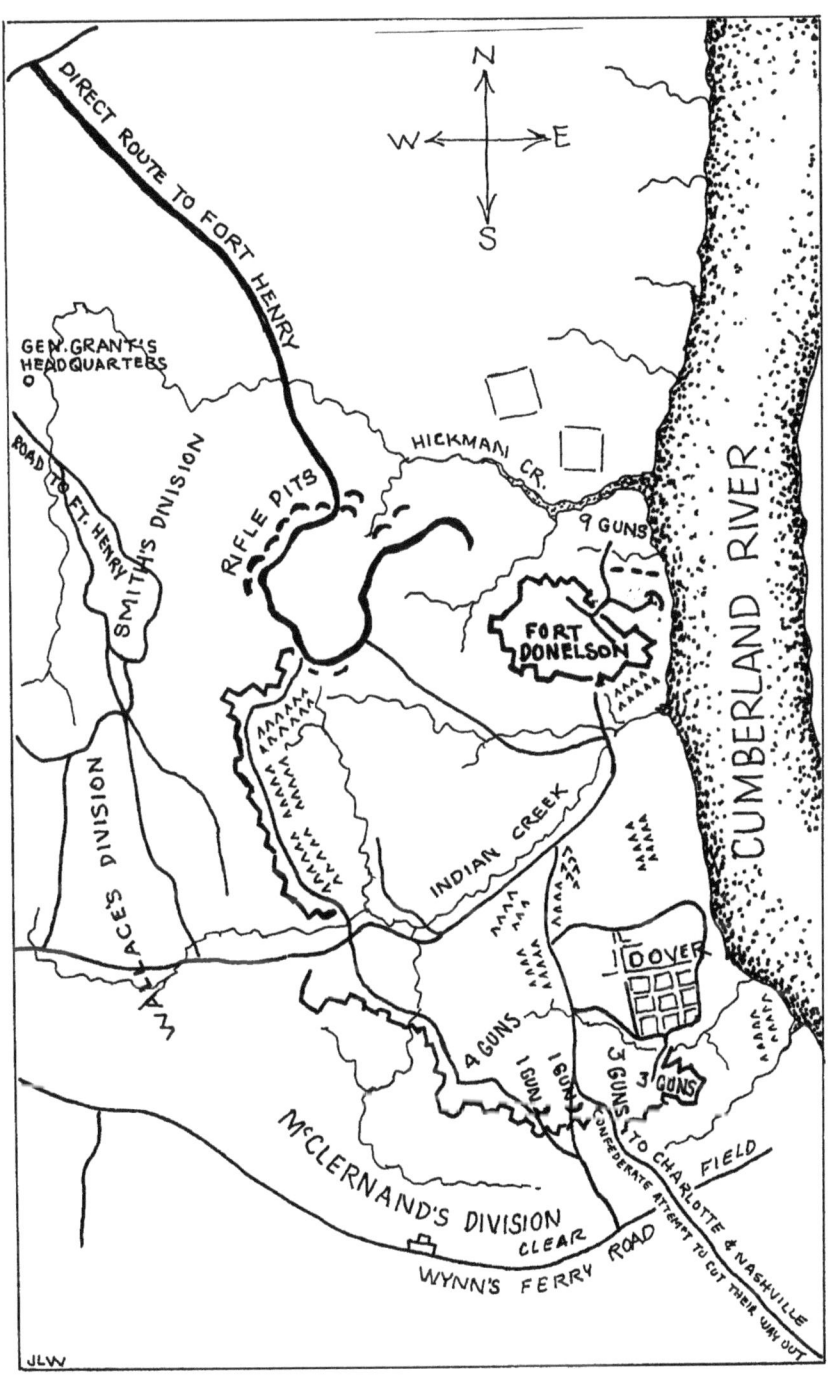

Fort Donelson on the Cumberland River.

Battle of Belmont. Of his work, General Tilghman wrote: "To Captain Dixon, of the Engineers, I owe my special acknowledgements of his ability and unceasing energies. Under his immediate eye were all the works proposed by myself at Forts Donelson and Heiman that he executed." Dixon, who commanded these batteries, was killed when a ball struck one of the Confederate cannons and knocked off a nut, which struck Dixon in the head, and killed him instantly."[10]

February 14 found the two shivering armies skirmishing. That afternoon the black-hulled iron monsters and their wooden ships reappeared, steaming up the Cumberland; as they approached Fort Donelson's two water batteries, they began to bombard the fort. Their fire was immediately returned by the more powerful Confederate cannon mounted on the shore, which, due to the position of these guns, enabled the Southern gunners to throw cannonballs into the holds of the ships, crippling their machinery. Foote's flagship was hit 59 times, wounding Foote and rendering his boat useless. Two other ironclads lost their steering from direct hits and drifted aimlessly downstream on the Cumberland. The more effective and powerful Confederate cannon had won the day. The Union fleet retreated downstream.

General Floyd, senior commander in the fort, tempered by the day's water victory, had the convoluted idea that the best thing the Confederates could do was to cut their way out of the fort, retire upon the Charlotte Road, and make their move back to Nashville to join General Johnston's forces. This would mean a stiff fight the next day; nevertheless, the other generals approved the plan, since these were their orders from General Johnston.

At 5:00 A.M. on the 15th, in freezing weather, Pillow moved forward, aided by Buckner's division, to assault the Federal line. After a morning's fighting, the Federal line on Grant's right was broken, and the road lay wide open as an avenue of escape. For whatever reason, the Confederates misread one another's concept of the mission and did not take advantage of the reprieve. Instead, Pillow, flushed with his success, attacked Wallace's Union position in hopes of rolling his troops back into Smith, turning the Federal position. In this effort he was aided by Buckner, but the combined advance made little headway as the weakened Confederates became worn out from the bitter weather and lack of food, retiring from the field in early afternoon.

Top: Cumberland River Defense at the Fort Donelson National Battlefield. Today, a quarter of Fort Donelson battlefield is protected by the National Park Service (National Park Service). *Bottom:* Original cannon on site at Fort Donelson.

Top: Another view of the Cumberland River Defense at Fort Donelson. *Bottom*: This log hut is representative of the 100 huts built within the walls of Fort Donelson by the Confederate garrison (James W. Raab).

8. The Cumberland and Fort Donelson

Some of the Confederates' success was due to the fact that some of the Union men had run out of ammunition. When restocked, the bluejackets re-closed the gap, seized the Charlotte Road back from the exhausted rebels, and went on to occupy every yard of ground back to the Cumberland River, making the Confederates' situation worse than it had been in the morning.

Lieutenant Richard L. McClung, whose 15th Arkansas Tilghman had ordered to Fort Donelson, kept a diary: "The men left behind all their blankets and clothes, as they expected on leaving camps, to return again to Fort Henry after a few hours. This lack of clothing was not a problem until Friday, February 14, when the men were exposed to rain and snow and hail by turns. Four to five inches of snow were on the ground by the next morning." His summary of the battle for Donelson was brief: "The snow covered the ground, the sun was shining, bayonets glittered, muskets fixed — artillery boomed — rank thinned — blood ran — men died, twelve hours bloody work on this day."[11]

Indeed, it was a bloody day for both sides. The Federal forces lost 500 men killed, 2,108 wounded, and 224 missing. The Confederates lost 2,000 men killed or wounded.[12]

Lieutenant McClung became ill and was placed in the post hospital. He penned in his diary that he watched details bury the slain who had frozen. Mass burial ditches were used for those killed in battle. The dead were carried by three men on a rail (being frozen) and thrown and 75 together.[13]

Later that evening the triumvirate of generals met in Dover to decide the fate of Fort Donelson. These West Pointers were an assortment of commanding officers whose division of counsel, antagonism, personality, and uncertainness of action would cancel out whatever dim hope there may have been that General Johnston could defend Nashville by stocking Fort Donelson with this appointed group.[14]

General Pillow observed that the Union occupation of the rifle pits was an open gateway for the bluecoats to the Confederate river battery. He believed the army ought to cut its way out of the fort, carrying with them as many as possible, leaving the killed and wounded on the field.[15] General Buckner disagreed, stating it would cost three-fourths of the army to get the other fourth out, and that he did not think any general had the right to make such a sacrifice of human life. General Floyd, who had never wanted to come to Fort Donelson since he considered it a trap, began fearing for his life. Having been Secretary of War under President James Buchanan, he believed he would be executed as a traitor if captured by Grant. He was running scared.

> General Pillow then rose up and said, "Gentlemen, as you refuse to make an attempt to cut our way out, and General Buckner says he will not be able to hold his position a half hour after being attacked, there is only one alternative left, that is capitulation," and then and there remarked that he would not surrender the command or himself; that he would die first.
> General Floyd then spoke out, and said that he would not surrender the command or himself.
> General Buckner remarked that, if placed in command, he would surrender the command and share its fate.
> General Floyd then said, "General Buckner, if I place you in command, will you allow me to get out as much of my brigade as I can?"
> General Buckner replied, "I will, provided you do so before the enemy receives my proposition for capitulation."
> General Floyd then turned to General Pillow and said, "I turn the command over, sir."
> General Pillow replied promptly, "I pass it."
> General Buckner said, "I assume it. Give me pen, ink, and paper, and send for a bugler."
> General Pillow then started out of the room to make arrangements for his escape, when Colonel Forrest said to him, "General Pillow, what shall I do?"
> General Pillow replied, "Cut your way out, sir."
> Forrest said, "I will do it," and left the room.[16]

Colonel Forrest, returning to his cavalry, said, "Boys, these people are talking about surrendering, and I am going out of this place before they do or bust hell wide open."[17] They hurried off, escaping across swollen Lick Creek, south of the fort. He would fight another day.

After the meeting, great activity prevailed at the Dover wharf. It did not take General Floyd long to rally his Virginians, find several steamboats, confiscate them, remove himself from Fort Donelson, and be on his way to Nashville. General Pillow followed suit: with his staff, he found a smaller boat, crossed over the Cumberland, and was freely on his way to Nashville. Floyd and Pillow took all the transports, and escape was hopeless for the others.

This left Generals Buckner and Johnson still in the fort complex with 14,000 demoralized Butternuts who had not bargained for this after the previous day's hard battle. General Buckner at dawn sent a messenger to Grant to learn what terms would be accepted by him if Buckner surrendered the garrison.

"No terms," answered Grant, "but unconditional and immediate surrender can be accepted. I propose to move immediately upon your works." Grant's demand for an unconditional surrender of the fort earned him his nickname, as the press corps earlier had associated his initials to such monikers as "*U*nited *S*tates" Grant, "*U*ncle *S*am" Grant, and now "*U*nconditional *S*urrender" Grant. Grant and Buckner had been classmates at West Point and friends before the war. When Grant was down on his luck in the 1850s, Buckner had lent him money. Later he met Grant and found him large-hearted, but for now Buckner had no choice but to accept the unchivalrous terms. At headquarters in the Dover Hotel he surrendered the Confederate forces.

Lieutenant McClung found out about the surrender at 8:00 A.M. that Monday morning when he walked past a Confederate battery. He saw a gunner standing by his gun and asked him, "What yon white rag there and another yonder mean?" The gunner replied, "We are all surrendered, goddamn you. That is what it means."[18]

The soldiers unceremoniously received the surrender by word of mouth, resulting in an exodus of hundreds from the fort. No one will ever know the true number surrendered; the estimate of 12,000 captured is suspect and the real number most likely lower, but who was counting after a six-day battle. Bushrod Johnson commented, "It is proper to state that many of the men and officers commenced to leave the fort as soon as they were aware of the proposed surrender, and hundreds of them made their way to their homes. I have not learned that a single one who attempted to escape met with any obstacle."[19]

In all likelihood, cousin Oswald Tilghman was one of the many rebel stragglers who took leave of Fort Donelson, traveling the road with others who went missing and making his way to Nashville. The capital was in turmoil, as disjointed Confederate companies and brigades from everywhere streamed southward through Nashville on their way to Murfreesboro, Tennessee. Oswald likely joined their ranks. Somewhere in Tennessee on April 30 he was taken prisoner by the Federals and imprisoned at Smyrna Camp Grounds, south of Nashville, and held prisoner until exchanged on October 31, 1862.[20]

The Federals were not prepared for such a quick capitulation of a large body of soldiers; provost guards and sergeants had to be detailed, which took time. The weather continued cold with snow on the ground, and without established guard posts the men could walk, if they knew where they were going. It didn't take long for General Bushrod Johnson to figure this out. On the 18th, towards sunset, he and Captain J. H. Anderson of the 10th Tennessee strolled out of the fort entrenchments walking towards the rifle pits on the hill. Finding no Yankee sentry to challenge them, they kept on walking beyond the fort's encampment and made their way to freedom.[21] It was a long, cold trek back to Nashville for Bushrod.

In the intervening time, 70 miles east of the fort at Bowling Green there was general mayhem. As agreed at their earlier meeting, Hardee, Johnston and Beauregard had decided a course of action, i.e., the army should be removed to Nashville, and if Fort Donelson fell, the two commands were to be operated independently. Hardee set to work to remove the Central Army of Kentucky and its supplies from Bowling Green. He had little time to plan the movement, because by the 14th, Buell's bluejackets brought up artillery and began to shell Bowling Green. Most of the shells exploded near the depot, where Hardee was feverishly loading one last train. "The Confederates should have retired to Nashville by rail, but the overloaded railroad system broke down, and most of the troops had to march."[22] Arkansas General Hindman was given the assignment to vacate Bowling Green.

Hindman met the crisis and began to set fire to public buildings in Bowling Green in order to deny their use to the Federals. However, things soon got out of hand as other kinds of buildings, including private homes and property in Bowling Green and its environs, were burned. Josephine Covington wrote to her father on March 2, 1862: "The greater part of the town has been destroyed. Part of the square was burned by the rebels, but a couple of days after the Yankees arrived, some drunken ones burned the other half."[23] Hindman applied the torch. A reporter with the *Indianapolis Daily State Sentinel* reported, "Fires were distinctly seen in the distance, which proved to be barns, outhouses, grain and haystacks, and straw piles set on fire."[24] A correspondent with the *Cincinnati Commercial* said, "The rebels left nothing at Bowling Green except a few old wagons."[25]

The weather did not assist the movement south by the Central Army of Kentucky. "It commenced to snow, a cold wet snow. The men traveled 13 miles the first day, 14 the second, and 17 on February 15, camping 10 miles north of Nashville."[26] "Finally the army reached the Cumberland River, crossed the river with difficulty, since the bridge had been destroyed, and moved through the city. Crowds pressed close to the soldiers, taunting them for their cowardice, and begging them to turn on the enemy. Hardee marched his men out the Murfreesboro Pike and encamped five miles east."[27]

Buell's Yankees cautiously pursued the Rebels retreating from Bowling Green. Hindman, who was covering the retreat, burned the bridge across Green River and obstructed the road by felling trees. He killed various kinds of animals and threw them in ponds along the route to decompose, rendering the water unfit for use. A captain in the 57th Indiana said of the Confederate retreat, "The destruction to the country is beyond anything you can conceive."[28]

General Albert S. Johnston (Martin Callahan Collection, U.S. Army Military History Institute).

This march was no different from others. Men were dying at places where no fighting occurred; these unmarked places, scattered without pattern, bear resemblance to Captain Junius N. Bragg's writings: "Their white bones are the links which bind them to liberty."[29] Confederate service records reveal, "Pvts. Thomas J. Erwin and John Hudson were left on the road sick between Bowling Green and Nashville. Pvts. Thomas

Creed and John H. Harris were absent sick while on the march from Bowling Green, Kentucky, not heard from thereafter."[30]

Both armies suffered with the same ailments, indispositions, malnutrition, and maladies such as measles, mumps, typhoid fever, pneumonia, and diseases of the bowels. After the bloody battles began, the complaints turned to gunshot wounds, amputations, and frostbite. If the soldier was lucky enough to survive the field hospital tent or house, the more serious cases found their way to community hospitals such as those found at Hopkinsville, Clarksville, Bowling Green, Nashville, and other towns. The Federals had similar arrangements in the towns they occupied.

Nashville, capital of the state of Tennessee, was a large town with over 17,000 inhabitants. "When the army began entering Nashville, on account of exposure to the snow, rains and bitterly cold weather on the 60-mile march, more than 5,400 soldiers required medical attention. An abundance of yellow ribbons were seen to identify homes, churches, schools, hotels, and other public buildings — as hospitals."[31] Added to Hardee's sick soldiers were the casualties, sick, and wounded from the Fort Donelson battle. Johnston now found his army encumbered by casualties and sickness.

General Johnston, traveling in advance of Hardee's division, had reached Nashville as news of Donelson's surrender circulated. The streets and roads leading southward to Franklin and many other towns were jammed with all sorts of wagons as families sought safety from the "damn Yankees." "General Johnston made no attempt to defend Nashville on the Cumberland, appointing General Floyd, recently of Fort Donelson disdain, the responsibility of restoring order in the capital. In the meantime, Johnston retired along with Hardee's division to Murfreesboro."[32] Johnston, as far as can be determined, remained outside the city. "He issued only a few orders and several of his subordinates did not know where to locate him."[33] Here Johnston attempted to consolidate and stabilize his command, now dwindled to about 17,000 men. Meanwhile, Don Carlos Buell's advance guard entered the sacrificed city.

The western bastion of Albert Sydney Johnston's line at Columbus was now under the command of Beauregard, who condemned the fortification without seeing it, much to Bishop Polk's disgust. Although the location had been approved by Major Gilmer, preparation for the evacuation of Columbus began immediately. Within five days the quartermaster, commissary, and ordnance stores, including 140 pieces of artillery, were moved to the fortifications now being completed downriver at Island Ten.[34]

In summary, Dr. Cannon penned: "Back home in Alabama, we were entertained with red hot speeches, picturing in glowing terms the glorious destiny of the 'young nation' which had just been born, and urged to hurry or the boys in Virginia would clean out the Yankees before we had a chance to show our mettle. We got a good deal of experience crowded into six weeks after we landed, but there was not much glory."[35]

As the fort was assailed by the Federal fleet and Grant's army, Colonel Bailey was in command of the fort's water batteries. The character of his service at Fort Donelson was described by Captain Ross of the artillery, who said, "It is due Col. J. E. Bailey to say he worked with the regiment night and day, remaining much of the time with us at night, encouraging us to persevere. In the land battle of the 15th, he led his regiment promptly into action on this cold day, and was distinguished in the fighting, repulsing a Federal movement that threatened the flank of General Buckner."[36]

Bailey was now a prisoner of war. He would be sent to prison at Fort Warren, Boston Bay, joining General Tilghman and other high-ranking officers.

As the case may be, the myth, the grand excuse of Fort Donelson was created. "Could the Confederates, full of fight, have successfully continued their defense or escaped? Were they surrendered because of delusion, cowardice, and betrayal? Did the Southern people or the Confederate government itself require a scapegoat? As it played out, General Buckner became the martyr, and Pillow, Johnston, and Floyd, the scapegoats,"[37] nullifying any claim to earlier fame.

Nevertheless, with the fall of Fort Donelson, the Confederacy was forced to give up southern Kentucky, much of middle and west Tennessee, the Tennessee and Cumberland Rivers, and the railroads.

All of this happened within two weeks after General Tilghman's imprisonment. Shortly thereafter, Clarksville fell into Union hands with virtually no Confederate resistance. In the absence of correspondence or records, it is presumed that General Tilghman's wife and children remained at Clarksville. All three forts were occupied by the Federal forces for the balance of the war as points of supply, recruitment, and haven for refugee slaves seeking freedom.

Today, Fort Donelson is a national battlefield, with Fort Donelson and Fort Heiman retaining most of their earthworks. Unlike Donelson and Heiman, Fort Henry is today primarily submerged under Kentucky Lake, scoring one for the civil engineers.

9

A Prisoner of War at Fort Warren, Massachusetts

The surrender of the twin forts so early in the war was a great coup for Grant, heralding his rise to power. He was promoted to major general on February 16, 1862. Equally impressive was the capture of 15,000 rebel volunteers, 20,000 stands of arms, 48 pieces of artillery and 17 heavy guns, 2,000 to 4,000 horses, plus large quantities of commissary stores. This was a huge deficit for the Confederate western armies to absorb.

"Grant's army now moved to secure the fruits of victory. Bands struck up 'Yankee Doodle' and even 'Dixie' as the Union brigades marched into Dover. C. F. Smith's men soon had the Stars and Stripes floating over the fort, and bohemians of the news corps soon disembarked from steamboats to fan out like locusts through both Union and Confederate armies to seek stories." "A motley, care-worn, haggard, anxious-looking crowd of rebels" was the way the *Boston Journal* described the human flotsam at Dover landing. The dejected Confederates stood around glumly in groups, drinking heavily from liberated whiskey and brandy stores. A brisk trade sprang up between the erstwhile antagonists — rebel tobacco, Bowie knives, and trinkets being exchanged for Yankee beef and biscuits. "Christian Commission officials, who arrived quickly from Cairo after the battle, estimated that injured Confederates alone filled the 23 log-house hospitals at Fort Donelson and Dover."[1] Buckner's surrendered forces were collected as rapidly as practicable near wharfs, under their respective regimental commanders. They were permitted to retain their personal possessions such as clothing and blankets, and the commissioned officers were permitted to keep side arms.

The cold weather continued, and men gathered in groups to keep warm aboard the boats while discussing their future as prisoners of war. There were in existence U.S. Army regulations for POWs. At the beginning of hostilities in 1861, both sides used the old parole of honor for their captives, i.e., the soldiers were paroled when captured, then sent to a neutral area. The parole served as a waiting period (usually ten days) that could be spent outside a prison. When an official exchange of soldiers was made, the paroled soldier was free to return to his unit.[2] As the war escalated and more men were captured, larger makeshift prisons became necessary. Tent compounds, surrounded by high wooden fences with guards, were easily constructed as makeshift stockades. In addition, existing prisons, forts, courthouses, government buildings, and warehouses were put to use. Fort Donelson's POWs, however, soon outstripped the capacity of local compounds.

Federal transports were brought upriver to the Dover wharf, where each was loaded with 600–800 Confederate prisoners who were guarded by two companies of Federals. They sailed down the Cumberland River on February 18, passing Smithland and Paducah on the way. Reaching Cairo, Illinois, early in the evening, they remained on board overnight. After taking on coal and commissary stores, they proceeded up the icy Mississippi River en route to St. Louis, Missouri, which they reached on the 20th. Here the citizens received them with great cordiality; those who came out to see the prison boats contributed to the comfort of the men by furnishing articles of necessity.[3]

On the 21st, they sailed for Alton, Illinois, and on the 22nd the soldiers and officers had the pleasure of meeting General Tilghman, who had been given free run of the town by his escort, Colonel Murphy.[4] This kindness and courtesy extended to Tilghman came to an end when General Halleck issued General Order No. 50, which decreed, "Where there are any considerable number of prisoners of war, their officers should be separated as soon as possible from the privates."[5] The soldiers were separated from the officers, marched off the transports, and then conveyed by railroad cars to Camp Douglas, Illinois. The remaining company and field officers were returned to St. Louis.

On February 27, the officers were loaded on boxcars that moved eastward, traveling via Terre Haute and Indianapolis, arriving at Columbus, Ohio, on March 1. The men were marched through the principal streets, and then four miles to Camp Chase.

On March 4, the senior officers were informed they were being sent to Fort Warren prison in Massachusetts. Leaving the capital city, the officers traveled by railroad through Cleveland, reaching Buffalo, New York, early on March 5. The snow was deep on the ground as they passed through Rochester, Utica, and Albany. At each point where they stopped, the officers were subjected to the idle gaze of the curious and inquisitive northerners. Arriving at the depot in Boston on the sixth, they were conveyed by a small boat to their destination, Fort Warren, situated on a small island in the protected waters of Boston Harbor.

Massachusetts Bay was an inlet of the Atlantic Ocean on the Massachusetts coast, extending about 65 miles from Cape Ann to Cape Cod. The prison, sitting on George's Island not far out in cold, windswept Boston Harbor, was a forbidding and depressing sight to the southerners. The old 19th-century seacoast fortress was constructed of thick granite walls and floors, pentagonal in shape. As they debarked, the Confederates realized for the first time that they were now being confined on an isolated island, unable to fight any longer for their cause. And it was cold; the frigid weather, a climate strange to their warm homeland, led them to believe that "it was a place to convert inmates to the theological belief of the Norwegians that hell has torments of cold instead of heat."[6]

Once landed, the settled prisoners had the pleasure of joining ranks with Generals Tilghman and Buckner, who had preceded them. One of these officers was Lieutenant Colonel Randal W. McGavock, C.S.A., former mayor of Nashville, who wrote: "Very soon we were surrounded by a number of political prisoners from Maryland who received us with a great deal of cordiality and immediately ordered breakfast for us, and I must say that it was the best meal I have set down to since entering the army. Our Generals and these gentlemen were so kind to us that I really forgot that I was a prisoner, but fancied that I was in the select society of congenial minds who had happened together by some freak of fortune in this inhospitable latitude."[7]

The fortress had been a training base for Massachusetts regiments, but was now designated a federal prison under the command of Colonel J. E. Dimick, a professional soldier who up to this time had been commanding officer at Fortress Monroe. Early in the war the prison was a stockade for smugglers, blockade runners, persons of suspect loyalty to the Union, military offenders, and spies; recently it had been stocked with political prisoners from the state of Maryland and diplomats Mason and Slidell of the Trent affair.

The senior POWs were processed according to the rules that had been established by Colonel Dimick. The well known and wealthier prisoners such as Tilghman and Buckner were formed into groups of eight for assignment to rooms in the officers' quarters of the fortress. The other officers, with limited or no funds, were assigned to rooms 17 by 50 feet in size, with double-deck bunks.[8] The officers' quarters had iron cots, mattresses, blankets, and heat from an anthracite coal fire that made the rooms comfortable. Initially, General Tilghman shared a room with Colonel Heiman, Colonel Gregg of Texas, Lieutenant Jackson of Alabama, and Lieutenant Colonel McGavock.[9]

Dining options varied. Officers with means feasted and fared excellently; those with limited money at their disposal ate reasonably well, and the less affluent had to be satisfied with regular U.S. Army rations.[10] Tilghman and other officers were invited to join the Baltimore dinner of the Maryland political prisoners, who had everything properly arranged, including French cooks, waiters, "as well served as can be found at any first class hotel in the country." This mess enjoyed fresh salmon, roast and boiled mutton, macaroni, fresh cheese, green peas, Irish potatoes, radishes, lettuce and dessert. Colonel Dimick could furnish the best rations, cigars, liquors, and such for the 72 inmates if they paid him $2.00 apiece per week.[11]

One of the discussions on the long train ride to Fort Warren was the existence of U.S. Army regulations, known to both sides, in regard to desertion. West Pointers Tilghman and Buckner, plainly aware of what they were forfeiting when they joined the Confederacy, expressed concern when captured that their action could be construed as desertion to take up arms with the enemy, a crime for which the usual penalty was execution. Even President Lincoln himself showed anger as he alluded to the large numbers of those in the army and navy who had been favored as officers [who] had resigned and proved false to the land which had pampered them.[12] In addition, "Reaction in northern Kentucky to Buckner and other Kentucky Rebels threatened to turn violent as they passed upriver towards captivity in Massachusetts. Civil authorities had issued a warrant for Buckner's arrest on the charge of treason against the state of Kentucky, and for several days following the surrender, the United States government was unsure of what to do with him."[13] Unfortunately, the trauma for the generals did not end, although it may have postponed any desertion charges. The local *Cape Ann Advertiser*, on March 7, voiced the abolitionist opinion "that the two Confederate leaders might be kept in close confinement so as to reflect upon their crimes against America." By a strange coincidence, the adjutant general informed Colonel Dimick on the following day that the secretary of war had ordered the two men restricted to special apartments and denied any contact except with his permission."[14] The generals were not even permitted to use the latrine at the same time as did others in the area. It was solitary confinement.

Within the confines of Fort Warren in a court in absentia, the Confederate officers, the imprisoned victims of the Donelson debacle, closed ranks agreeing upon a common verdict: Pillow deserted them, robbing them of a victory they had paid blood to win.[15] The other rascal they blamed was Floyd, former governor of Virginia, who returned to Virginia and was stripped of his command. Buckner was left to bear the blunders of his superiors.

In the same token, a cry of condemnation arose in the press against General Sidney Johnston, upon whom rested the responsibility of these disasters. Why hadn't he sent the troops at Bowling Green to attack Grant, instead of marching towards Nashville? There was adequate time. Why had the works at Columbus been made for a garrison of 13,000 men, and armed with 140 heavy guns, and the twin forts had only 30 cannon pieces? Had a reasonable portion of time and labor been misspent by Polk at Columbus?[16] In retrospect, Pillow and Floyd became the scapegoats for the affair, losing their fifteen minutes of fame, while Buckner emerged the martyr. The aristocrat, Tilghman, who commanded both forts, became insulated from damaging public accusations because of his confinement.

The *Richmond Enquirer* was critical of this treatment of the persecuted generals, calling it the one black spot on Fort Warren's record. The harsh treatment of solitary confinement provoked General Tilghman's influential mother to travel to Washington and gain a favor from United

States Secretary of War Stanton, who ordered "the restraining order to be modified sufficiently, to permit the men to walk on the ramparts for exercise and fresh air. They did so separately, under guard; furthermore, they were forbidden to speak to their fellow officer prisoners or to recognize them in any way."[17]

There was no overcrowding at Fort Warren in 1862; the apartments given the prisoners were warm and neat and had adequate sleeping arrangements. We must assume that Buckner and Tilghman were provided similar accommodations in their rooms, although separated from the rest of the apartments. Lieutenant Colonel Randal W. McGavock of the 10th Tennessee, who often commanded Fort Donelson on a temporary basis in Tilghman's absence, kept a detailed diary of his imprisonment, later published by the Tennessee Historical Commission. His entries mirror many of the routines, events, and privileges that Buckner and Tilghman enjoyed even though in solitary confinement. The basic rules of procedures were given to Colonel Dimick when he took command of Fort Warren. "The prisoners were to be securely held, treated with kindness. Prisoners would be allowed to provide themselves with such comforts as they required and could afford, including articles of food, clothing, and small sums of money. They might have newspapers, send and receive letters, and visitors might be permitted upon proper authorizations from Washington."[18]

There is no question that Fort Warren was the country club of Civil War prisons. A few of McGavock's entries:

> — I have occupied the day in reading, walking around the fort viewing the shipping, etc.
> — Received a box today, containing fine whiskey, brandy, cigars, cheese, sardines, etc.
> — My tailor sent me clothes today. [He was permitted a tailor outside the prison.]
> — This evening I enjoyed very much the music of the Union brass band.
> — The issue of *London Times* received by yesterday's steamer contains a very correct view of the battle and surrender at Fort Donelson.
> — This morning I walked for the first time entirely round the little island on which Ft. Warren is situated. It contains about twenty-five or thirty acres.
> — Eight of the political prisoners from Maryland were offered a release today.
> — Twenty-six prisoners reached here this evening, including Major W.

Lafayette McConnico of the 10th Tennessee Regiment who served as acting assistant adjutant-general under General Tilghman at Fort Henry.

— My father sent two hundred dollars in gold; it was converted into Federal Treasure Notes.

[May 16:] I have been a prisoner now just three months today. I think it high time that some steps were taken to release me.

[June 3:] Capt. Stoke says that we will all be exchanged very soon. Both governments have agreed upon the terms.

[June 6:] U.S. Secretary of War states that a general exchange has been agreed upon by the two governments.

— I walked down to the play-ground and witnessed a game of football by the younger men, and pitching quoits by the old gentlemen.

— McConnico gave us a treat for tea — nice strawberries and cream, and cake ... they were purchased at the sutler for eight cents, basket and all. By returning the basket you are allowed two cents.

— We have an English servant from the Revere House to attend our room.

— The money market in N.Y. yesterday shows that gold is sixteen per cent premium ... stocks will certainly commence tumbling down very soon.

[July 23:] The telegraph this evening brings intelligence of an agreement between Generals Dix and Hill on the subject of exchanges, which goes into operation immediately. It created quite a stir among the prisoners here. Some of them commenced packing their trunks.[19]

It was becoming impossible for both sides to continue to hold the growing number of POWs in the prison pens. Yet efforts at an effective exchange system had been held up for months because of rancorous disputes between both sides because the North did not wish to recognize the Confederate government.

Finally through the efforts of Major General John A. Dix, USV, and Major General D. H. Hill, C.S.A., the Dix-Hill Exchange Cartel was signed at Haxall's Landing on the James River in Virginia on July 22, 1862. Under the Cartel, an exchange system was worked out, officer for officer, private for private, or a certain number of privates for commissioned officers, depending on rank.

"This has been a busy, bustling day in the fort. Everyone is packing his trunk and procuring as far as their means will allow, all those little articles that they may require. The sutler has done a brisk business, also the express men that run to Boston. Lieutenant Pearson, the commissary of the post, and who keeps the money of the prisoners, told me today that over twelve thousand dollars had been checked from him in the last sixty days. I really think that the prisoners here in the last six months have expended over twenty-five thousand dollars in clothing and one thing or another.[20] I leave a small box with Lieutenant Pearson containing two quilts — one given to me by General Tilghman and one by Ann Waters. I leave them with him for safekeeping until sent for."[21]

The 28th of July was a glorious day for the prisoners in Fort Warren. Colonel Dimick received an order to have the prisoners ready to start for the main locality of exchange, which would be City Point, a giant staging area and supply depot on the James River below Petersburg.[22]

Generals Tilghman and Buckner were immediately turned out of close confinement. "The scene of meeting between them and their fellow prisoners was wonderful. Many of them shed tears of joy."[23] With the Cartel in place, there was no time lost in emptying the overcrowded prisons.

July 31 was the day of departure from Fort Warren, many men having been there for five months. "The prisoners were drawn up in line in the shade of the fort and the roll called. Amid the sweet strains of the fort's band the prisoners bid adieu to set sail on the *Ocean Queen*, one of the largest Union transports afloat."[24] Their restful existence ended.

On the third of August they cast anchor below Fortress Monroe, Virginia. In a short time a transport called *Knickerbocker* came alongside and took the men off and then moved to a point above the fort where several other transports were lying loaded with other Confederate prisoners. While here, some five or six transports came downriver loaded with Federal forces.[25]

The officers landed on August 5 at a point called Eakin's Landing, some fifteen miles below Richmond. The debarkation was as rapid as possible; "nearly every man as he stepped off the boat seemed to draw a long breath and looked like he felt better and happier."[26] General Tilghman was officially exchanged for Union General J. F. Reynolds, who had been captured at Gaines Mills, Virginia, during the Peninsula campaign.[27] General Buckner was exchanged for General C. A. McCall. The Richmond authorities were embarrassed, as there was no one present to receive the exchanged officers. There was no band and no transportation. The freed officers walked to Richmond.

The coming exchanges of Confederate forces would significantly aid the manpower-deficient Confederacy, which was having difficulty recruiting new volunteers to the ranks. General Grant strongly believed that the exchange of prisoners was of great disadvantage to the North. He wrote, "Every man we hold, when released on parole or otherwise, becomes an active soldier against us. If a system of exchange liberates all prisoners taken, we will have to fight on until the whole South is exterminated."[28] The great battles at Gettysburg, Vicksburg, and Chattanooga in 1863 settled the POW controversy, as the Federal authorities decided to cease further deliveries of POWs, sowing the seed for the horrible prisoner of war camps of both sides.

Colonel McGavock continued to capture the tone of the day, proving the incarcerated soldiers remained firmly committed to the Southern cause, as the officers chose to return to the war after five months of imprisonment. August 7: "This morning I called with General Tilghman and the officers of Brigade to see the Secretary of War, Mr. Randolph — who informed us that we must proceed to Vicksburg and reorganize our Regiments. He answered all questions asked with great promptness and clearness, stating the Confederacy had abundance of arms, having received three ship loads recently from Europe." On August 8: "General Tilghman and myself called today on the President — but he was engaged with the Secretary of State on important business and we did not see him. I met his aide-de-camp, Col. William Preston Johnston, son of General Sidney Johnston. Just as we went in General Buckner came out, in company with Cols. Hanson and Brown, whom he had recommended for brigadier generals. We dined at the Exchange and during the day I drew my back pay — procured my transportation ticket to Vicksburg and my passport."[29]

Colonel John C. Brown, 3rd Tennessee, was made brigadier general at the end of August, and Colonel Roger W. Hanson, 2nd Kentucky, was appointed brigadier general on December 13. On the final day of fighting at the Battle of Stone's River, Hanson was mortally wounded. He died near the battlefield on January 4, 1863, a brigadier general for only twenty-two days.

General Simon Bolivar Buckner was promoted to major general on August 16 and sent to Braxton Bragg at Chattanooga to command the Left Wing, Army of Mississippi. General Buckner, the last surviving

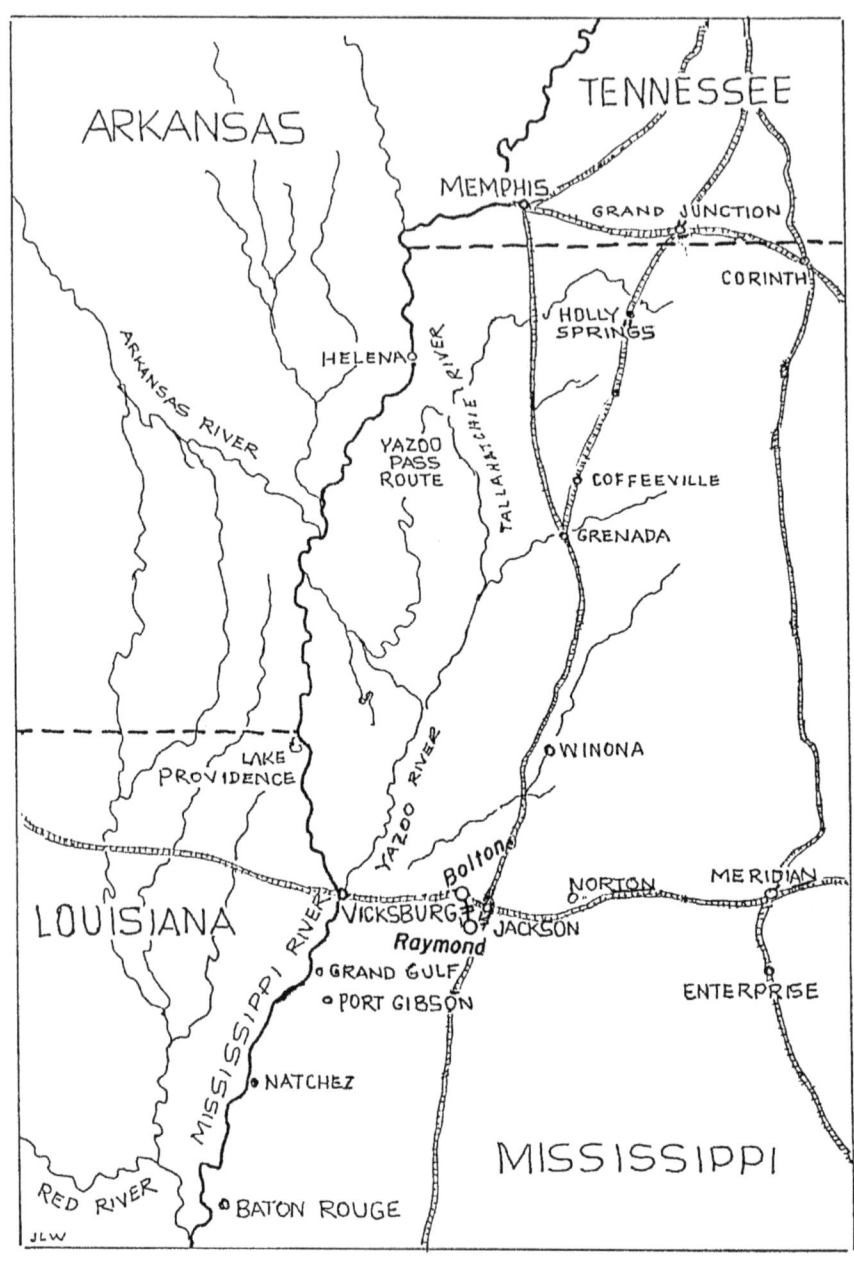

Mississippi railroads. Without the Confederate cavalry to control the railroads, Pemberton was doomed.

general of the Southern armies, would live until 1914. His son and namesake was killed as a general in World War II.[30] General Tilghman and Colonels Heiman, Bailey, and McGavock were afforded no reward, via promotion, for their dedicated service at the three forts or for their imprisonment. The Henry-Donelson prisoners were provided only brief furloughs, followed by reorganization of their regiments. Colonel James E. Bailey rejoined at Clinton, Mississippi. Colonel McGavock left Richmond on August 10 for Vicksburg. "The cars were so crowded that I found it very difficult to get on at all. Finally, I got into a boxcar filled with Negroes going to Jefferson County, Tennessee. They were mostly children purchased in Richmond at very high prices — for an investment. I suppose that the man considers it safer than holding Confederate paper."[31]

10

The Exchange Cartel, and the Attacks on Iuka and Corinth

In accordance with the Dix-Hill Exchange Cartel Agreement, Confederate agents for the parole and exchange of prisoners of war were to communicate with Union agents by correspondence or otherwise, prepare lists of the prisoners for parole and exchange, and attend to the delivery of the prisoners at the place agreed upon. Tilghman was ordered by the Richmond authorities to return immediately to Mississippi to begin receiving the paroled Confederate POWs as they arrived at Vicksburg from the northern prison pens.

Tilghman departed by train from Richmond. He passed through Knoxville, Tennessee; Dalton and Tunnel Hill, Georgia; and Mobile, Alabama, on his way to Jackson, Mississippi. He was assigned to the Army of the West. Tilghman's family was living in Clarksville behind enemy lines; no visit was possible. McGavock's diary reveals: "August 22nd, reached Mobile where I met General Tilghman, Maj. Barbour, Maj. Ellis, Col. Heiman, Maj. Grace, Col. Murphy and several other Fort Warren acquaintances. The general and staff left this evening for Jackson; the prisoners have not been delivered yet at Vicksburg." "August 31: I see a dispatch that some prisoners have left Camp Martin in Indiana on the 23rd."[1] Most of the POWs would be from the Fort Donelson debacle and battles at Shiloh.

McGavock continued, on "September 4: I reached Jackson, Mississippi, and stopped at the Bowman House — a large four-story house but a very bad table. General Tilghman and Staff are here. I am very disappointed at the appearance and size of Jackson. The houses indifferent, the State Capitol is a poor affair, the Governor's Mansion is large and occupies a whole square, but looks very dilapidated. Maj. McConnico went down to Vicksburg this morning with about two hundred Federal prisoners. One of them had no pants on — but his blanket wrapped around him. This was a shame. He should have been furnished with pants."2

Trains filled with returned Confederate prisoners began arriving in Vicksburg. On September 7, 3,000 butternuts were recorded; on the 10th an additional 4,000 rebels reached there. Tilghman issued an order for all officers to go there at once. Of course, Col. McGavock went along looking for his regiment. "On the way we met two long trains filled with returned prisoners from Camps Morton and Chase. The balance will be here in a few days. It is my first visit to Vicksburg and I hope my last, as it is an ugly, dirty, and disagreeable place."3 The returned POWs were divided among General Bragg, the Army of Northern Virginia, and a regiment to Port Hudson, Mississippi. Others were discharged on surgeons' certificates, and the balance was to be organized into companies, battalions, and regiments. The latter were to remain for the Army of the West and sent to Clinton, Mississippi, located a mile outside of Jackson, where General Tilghman would oversee the exchange under the Cartel Agreement.

On September 25, McGavock left Jackson in the morning for Clinton, to meet with his regiment. The Colonel said, "The men were all exceedingly glad to see me, which was very gratifying. The regiment numbers about 450 privates. Some 200 joined the Federal army at Camp Douglas — and I notice that they were mostly the young men of the regiment. I understand that they all deserted the Federal army as soon as they got a chance." On the evening of the 28th, he went to Jackson to carry the rolls of the companies to Adjutant General Sam Walker.4 At this time, discord arose between General Tilghman and Colonel McGavock.

September 30: "Left Jackson this morning in company with General Tilghman and others for Clinton. Went out to my camp about 10 o'clock. General Tilghman made speeches to three Regiments encamped here. The burden of his remarks to my Regiment was in regard to their reorganization [elections]. He said that we had some good officers, but many very bad ones — and recommended some half dozen of his Kentucky friends for Captains. He then told them that he had provided everything for them — from a ten-penny nail to a locomotive if they needed such a thing and if they did not get everything that they were entitled to — it would be the fault of the Regimental officers and not his fault. In his speech to Quarles's Regiment, he pitched into General Pillow pretty severely — and charged him with having caused all our misfortunes at Fort Donelson. He is quite a demagogue — and lets off a great deal of gas."[5]

Later, when Tilghman caught up with Pillow, he made him answer for accusations about his inept defense of Fort Henry. Pillow lamely responded that he had been misinformed.[6] Although disgraced, Pillow never gave up on the Southern cause: He led a brigade at Stones River; he was constantly assigned to various duties by President Davis, including conscript duty for two years; and finally he was placed in charge of Union prisoners in the last months of the war.

October 1: "Col. Heiman made speeches to all of the companies today and read a letter from General Tilghman recommending six gentlemen that he spoke of yesterday for Captains."

October 2: "Today the companies in the 10th Tennessee Regiment were reorganized — and I think the organization better than ever before. None of the gentlemen that General Tilghman recommended received a single vote."

October 3: "Today we held an election in our Regiment for field officers. Col. Heiman, Maj. Grace and myself were elected without opposition, and several lieutenants were elected to supply vacancies."

October 4: "Had an interview with General Tilghman this morning — and he expressed great dissatisfaction because my Regiment did not elect any of his Kentucky friends. I have come to the conclusion after mature deliberation that he is a humbug."

October 7: "The Regiment was paid off, and some clothing distributed. The men said that after General Tilghman's speech — they expected better things. An order was issued today to have our tents struck and ready to go to Jackson. The news from Corinth is unfavorable today."[7]

10. The Exchange Cartel, and Iuka and Corinth

In April 1862 at Shiloh, Tennessee, 62,000 Federal troops battled 40,000 Confederates protecting the rail center at Corinth. Total carnage for both sides was a staggering 23,000 killed, wounded, missing, and captured. Among the dead was notable general Sidney Johnston, who, while leading his army, was shot in the leg and bled to death in the saddle before he realized the wound was lethal. Placed in command of the huge Confederate Department No. 2 by Jefferson Davis, he had had no success whatsoever in stemming the Federal tide into Kentucky and Tennessee in 1862. General Grant said in his memoirs: "Johnston was a bold strategist in his planning but vacillating and undecided in his actions."[8]

Union General Halleck took personal command of the huge Federal army, deciding to consolidate their gains. Rather than push into Mississippi pursuing the retreating rebels, he began to dissipate the Federal forces for other engagements, including guarding the many railroad lines leading into Corinth. The Confederates, realizing the importance of winning back Corinth, reviewed their position, knowing full well Corinth had been weakened. Now encamped in northern Mississippi at Holly Springs, fifty miles west of Corinth, was General Earl Van Dorn, with the Army of the West.

Earl Van Dorn, the 42-year-old great-nephew of Andrew Jackson, was an eminent cavalier and one of the Confederacy's most promising generals. After graduating from West Point in 1842, he fought in the Mexican and Seminole Wars. Named brigadier general of Mississippi troops at the beginning of the war, he was put in command of the forts below New Orleans. In April 1861, he was given command of the Department of Texas when Ben McCulloch seized U.S. property and received the surrender of Federal troops. Promoted rapidly to brigadier and major general, Van Dorn was ordered to Virginia, where he led a division near Manassas. In early 1862, he was sent to command in Arkansas, where he led an attack at Pea Ridge. Joining Beauregard at Corinth just after the Battle of Shiloh, Van Dorn prepared to retake Corinth. Joining and strengthening the rebel forces was General Sterling Price, who had come across the Mississippi River with Arkansas troops.

Price was a 43-year-old farmer, lawyer, congressman, ex-governor of Arkansas, and leader of the Missouri State Guard. Recruiting and training about 5,000 men, he fought at Wilson's Creek. He officially joined the Confederacy on March 6, 1862, when he was appointed a

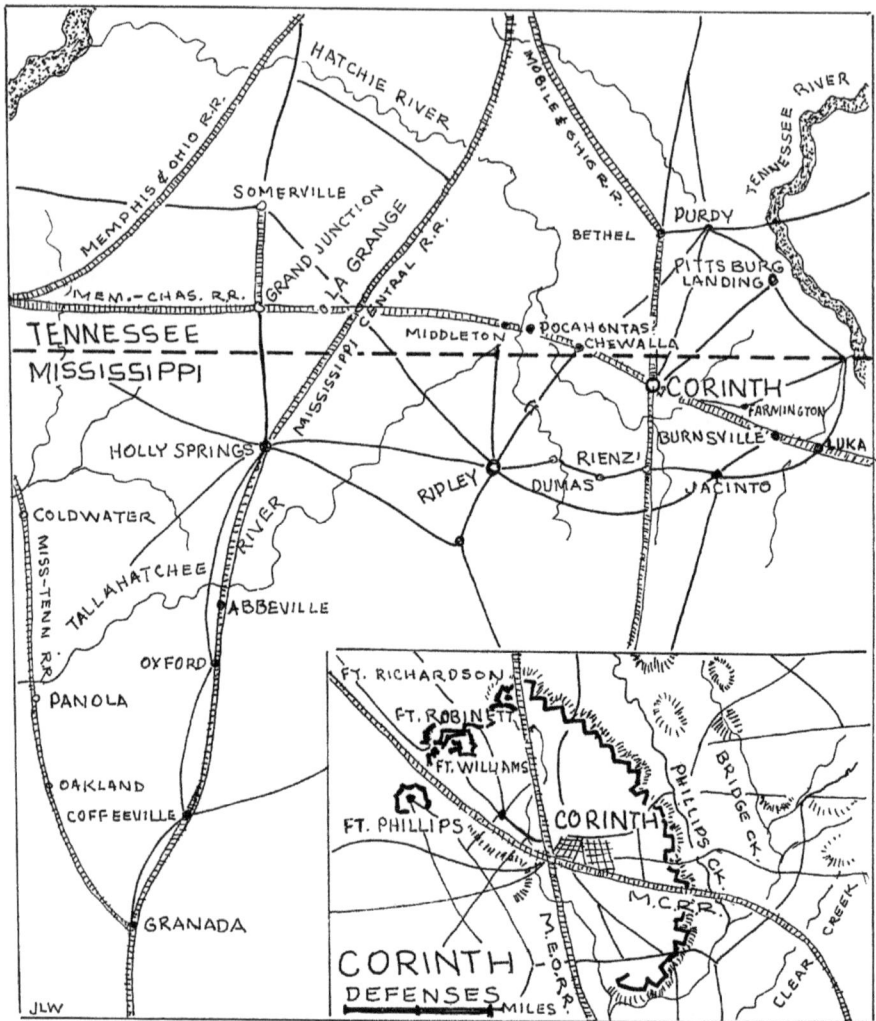

Battle for Corinth, Mississippi, for control of the railroads.

major general, C.S.A. His small army was bivouacked at Tupelo, Mississippi, forty miles south of Corinth and fifty miles southeast of Earl Van Dorn's butternut soldiers.

In early August, Van Dorn broached the idea of a combined attack on Corinth with Price, and they reached a verbal agreement. For whatever reason, the impatient Price, not waiting to join with Van Dorn on the combined movement, marched north and attacked Iuka, west of

Corinth, in an attempt to block the Federals' movement towards the middle of Tennessee. Grant, knowing Price was nowhere near Van Dorn, attacked Price's spirited Arkansas Army on September 19. After an all-day battle, again with heavy losses, Price saw it was a hopeless situation and removed his battle-weary men from Iuka, barely making his escape westward to Ripley, Mississippi, now about thirty miles from Van Dorn at Holly Springs.

Van Dorn's army succeeded in joining with Price on September 28, with a combined strength of 22,000 men. The consolidation of commands had an inspiriting effect on the troops; they now felt that they were in sufficient force to make effective headway against the Yankees. Because of his rank, Van Dorn became the senior officer. The two corps would be led respectively by Generals Mansfield Lovell and Sterling Price.[9] Their goal was still Corinth, and it would be a plume in Van Dorn's hat to retake the valued railroad center.

Coping with an erratic railroad and quartermaster system, Tilghman equipped the paroled POWs at Clinton as quickly as possible. In Van Dorn's and Price's eyes, Tilghman was to match the restructured POWs with their officers and companies and when properly exchanged, send them out to corps of the Army of the West. Both commanders wanted fresh troops. They knew the returned POWs were piqued at being incarcerated for the past five months, would fight like angry hornets, and would incite any new volunteers to do likewise, less they all end up back in a Federal prison pen.

Pleas from Generals Van Dorn and Price, stressing urgency in getting the paroled troopers exchanged and forwarded, fell upon the deaf ears of Tilghman, who, being honest, kept to the letter of the Cartel Agreement. "Though I was urged frequently by Generals Van Dorn and Price to send forward the troops allotted to their several commands, I was forbidden to do so by my orders until the Exchange was ratified."[10]

On September 22, Tilghman sent a part of the first 2,000 exchanged soldiers to Sterling "Pap" Price at Ponchatoula, Mississippi, which helped fill Price's ranks, depleted from his recent disaster at Iuka.

General Tilghman did not join Van Dorn or Price at Ripley; he remained at Clinton with 8,000 paroled POWs, awaiting the exchange rosters. He would not participate in the coming advance on Corinth. The flamboyant Van Dorn, throwing caution to the wind, ordered a combined movement of the Army of the West forward towards Corinth, without the benefit of Tilghman's 8,000 replacements encamped at Clinton. General Price categorically opposed Van Dorn's movement and said so. He agreed that the taking of Corinth warranted more than the usual hazard of battle, yet was of the opinion that the hazard could have been much reduced had they delayed the attack a few days until Tilghman's exchanged forces could be forwarded. "Without their added numbers, Price failed to see how the Confederates could hold Corinth, much less exploit its capture."[11]

Regardless of the objections, the elegant Van Dorn began the plan formulated by the two generals. He marched from Ripley to Pocahontas on the M & C Railroad and threatened Bolivar, Tennessee, in hopes of diverting the Federal troops from his true goal. Then he turned suddenly and made a beeline for Corinth, hoping to attack before the Federal troops were aroused and could concentrate their forces. On October 3, 1862, General Lovell's corps was placed in line of battle south of the railroad in the following order: Villepigue's brigade on the right with cavalry flankers; Bowen in the center; Rust on the left with his flank resting on the railroad. Price's corps was deployed on the north side of the railroad. Corinth was two-thirds surrounded by Union outer lines of entrenchments, including four small forts to protect the two main railroad lines: Fort Phillips, south of the M & C Railroad; Forts Williams, Robinett, and Richardson, north of M & C Railroad, west of the Mobile & Ohio line.

Raising the chilling "rebel yell," the charging butternuts made a dash for the outer works, Lovell's forces driving the Federals into Fort Phillips. Lovell was met by rapid fire from the small fort's artillery, but managed to gain ground until within several hundred yards, when the bluecoats abandoned their fort. In possession of the fort and the outer line of defense south of the railroad, Lovell's division rested and remained motionless from the heat of the day.

The ever-colorful "Pap" Price rode on the north side of the M & C Railroad at the head of his corps, accompanied by his mounted headquarters band, which paused now and then to encourage the troops with a popular tune such as "Listen to the Mockingbirds."[12] "With a wave of his hand, 'Old Woodpecker,' as the boys in blue sometimes called Price, said, 'Boys, if they are many, we will take them, and if they are but few, we will take them the quicker.'"[13] Price, with his gallant corps of followers, engaged the Federals in and around Corinth, as he pushed the Federals back from position to position, finally winning the day.

The next day, the grandiose General Van Dorn arrayed his entire army in full view of the surrounded earthworks and the Federal brigades inside. Retaining no reserves, Van Dorn began his advance on the town in unison with Price and Lovell's corps, or so he thought. The Indian summer day became a heat wave by noon, the temperature reaching 90 degrees. The men began falling out with heat exhaustion. Worst of all, Grant's reinforcements began arriving, and Price was compelled to yield the ground he had gained the day before. Price said his troops were too much fatigued from the heat, too hungry and thirsty to risk a final attack on the enemy.[14] While Price's command was making a desperate effort to hold the line, for some unknown reason Lovell's division remained inactive all day. The battle was short but violent, with decisive losses for both sides. The Federals had rallied because they had been heavily reinforced and met Price's movement with firmness. By this time, the Army of the West was wrecked with staggering casualties. Van Dorn's forces lost 2,470 killed or wounded, with 1,763 missing. Grant's men fared no better, losing over 2,500 men.

Fearing additional Federal reinforcements by rail, Van Dorn ordered a general withdrawal. Villepigue's brigade was marched out and formed across the line of withdrawal. Through their ranks passed the retreating Confederates, weary and downcast, plodding slowly in the heat to the rear, moving towards Chewalla, where they halted at nightfall. But the battle was not over. At Chewalla, a courier brought a dispatch to Van Dorn indicating that the Federal force at Bolivar was moving south with 9,000 rested troops. The Hatchie River bridges were in danger of being blockaded by them, which meant Van Dorn could lose his wagon train and much of his army could be trapped. It was only by the skin of his teeth and extra hard fighting by Colonel Wirt Davis's cavalry and Colonel Hawkins's 1st Texas Legion that the army extracted itself out of this tight situation. The rebels' withdrawal became a full-blown retrograde as the Federal cavalry became very aggressive in their pursuit. Never stopping, Van Dorn's strung-out forces passed through Ripley and ended their forced march back in Holly Springs, avoiding capture.

A concerned President Davis, not wanting a repeat of the command disaster experienced at Fort Donelson, decided he needed better cooperation among these cavalier generals in the West. On September 30, he ordered Major General J. C. Pemberton to move west from his assignment in South Carolina and assume command of the Department of Mississippi and East Louisiana. When President Davis learned of the latest brouhaha at Corinth among the generals, he promoted the latecomer, Pemberton, to Lieutenant General in command,[15] thus crushing Van Dorn's hopes of further advancement. Van Dorn was put in command of the field forces and the paroled prisoners waiting to be exchanged at Clinton.

The aftermath of this shake-up put Tilghman in an awkward position with his own army. Would supplying Van Dorn's and Sterling Price's requests for reinforcements have turned the tide of their lost battle? Who would ever know if he released the men a few days *before* the exchange forms were filled out? What could the Yankees have done to him? The Cartel Agreement specified: Prisoners of war will be paroled and delivered at some point within the lines. A receipted list must be taken in duplicate, one copy sent to the adjutant general in order to effect an exchange. An impatient Van Dorn had to go it without waiting for these exchanged forces, and it cost him dearly. The smoke from the Battle of Corinth had hardly passed when Tilghman received ratification of the exchange and the men could be forwarded. Without losing any time, Tilghman sent forward, as fast as the railroad transportation could be found, over 7,800 men, the last of the forces reaching Holly Springs on October 14. With his duties completed, Tilghman and his staff left Jackson, making the 200-mile rail journey north to Holly Springs, joining Van Dorn, and receiving a new assignment with the army.

On arriving, Tilghman found the disaster of Corinth hanging like a heavy cloud over the dejected and scattered brigades. The only positive note was the arrival and assimilation of his replacement forces to fill the depleted companies. Special Order No. 54, Holly Springs, October 16, 1862, detailed some of the changes: "All the cavalry of the army will report immediately to Col. W. H. Jackson, who is hereby announced as chief of cavalry. This army will hereafter be known as Army of West Tennessee, and will be divided into two army corps, to be commanded respectively by Major Generals Lovell and Price." Special Order No. 53, of same date: "Brigadier General Tilghman will report to Major General Lovell, all officers and soldiers belonging to the different regiments and

The rebel flea. "You put your finger on him, and he isn't there" (*Harper's Weekly*).

battalions, of exchanged prisoners, will at once join their proper commands."[16] "You put your finger on him, and he isn't there."

General Grant had 45,000 Federal troops in western Tennessee, in and around Memphis. After the Union's victory at Corinth, their columns began making an appearance in northern Mississippi. Accordingly, General Pemberton ordered Van Dorn's army out of Holly Springs. Taking the stage road, the Confederates moved south towards Abbeville, Mississippi, where entrenchments had been constructed on the south bank of the Tallahatchie River; Tilghman's division was placed at the mouth of the Tippah River.

The people of Mississippi had not thought it would come to this or believed they would see the day that those "damn Yankees" would set foot in their state. But here they were. The alarmed citizens, believing the Confederate army was abandoning them — which they were — panicked and fled with the soldiers, carrying every bit of moveable personal property, slaves, and livestock. They clogged the road so that Van Dorn's brigades lost valuable time in moving to Abbeville.

Once the army was encamped at Abbeville, the loss of Corinth, with its heavy casualties, began to be discussed by the officers and soldiers. The blame had to be placed on someone. The early scapegoat was of course General Lovell, who seemed to stay put in his fort with his forces. His unpardonable sin was being born in the north; generally the nicest things he was being accused of were imbecility and incompetence, although the less generous men were thinking more in terms of cowardice and treachery. As things moved forward, Lovell slowly removed himself from the hook, as other information was factored into the battle.

Assuming Lovell's unfortunate position was General Van Dorn, the commander; he became the object of ridicule. The camp rumor was that he was negligent for his part in the battle. Some of the accusations: he was without proper maps of the area; he refused the services of available artillery; he went into battle without proper food for his men; he needlessly delayed the attack; he permitted the enemy to run reinforcement trains; and that he was guilty of cruel treatment of officers and men. Added to these charges was a personal one by General J. S. Bowen, an insulting remark that he thought Van Dorn had been drinking.

General Van Dorn earned his reputation as a daring young officer whose heroic conduct during the first year of the war was rewarded by several promotions. Alienated because of these charges, the general demanded a court of inquiry into the matter as soon as possible to clear his good name. Pemberton directed that the allegations against Van Dorn be heard November 15 at Abbeville. Officers were appointed as follows: General Price, General Tilghman, General Maury, and Captain Cummings. After having heard the charges, witnesses and testimony, every point against the cavalier was disproved, he was acquitted, and the court recommended the matter be closed.

On the unpleasant news that Federal forces had landed on the eastern shore of the Mississippi, opposite Helena, Arkansas, and that Grant was beginning a march to Vicksburg, General Pemberton ordered the defensive south bank entrenchments along the Tallahatchie River to be vacated with a general withdrawal of the Confederate army, southward towards Oxford, Mississippi. It was now December.

The Union 13th Corps' cavalry commander, Colonel Lyle Dickey, was ordered to pursue the retreating rebels as they crossed the Tallahatchie. Colonels Lee and Hatch headed up two cavalry columns that dogged the retreating rebels. Pressing forward on the stage road, they began skirmishing with Colonel Jackson's cavalry, which made a strong stand one mile north of Oxford, Mississippi. The 7th Kansas Cavalry made a mounted charge but was checked by heavy Confederate fire. The entire Federal regiment deployed and dismounted, and using revolving rifles and carbines, they made an attack on Van Dorn's rear guard, driving the stubborn rebels through and beyond Oxford.[17] The Federals continued to advance rapidly, resulting in another sharp cavalry fight at Water Valley. Again the rebels were outnumbered and roughly handled.

As Grant's commanders moved to secure the fruits of their recent victories, Mississippians began feeling the full evil of the war as the foraging bluecoats entered the state. Foragers were sent out daily by military authorities on both sides; it was just another term for stealing property such as food, grain, horses, mules, cattle, and maybe a raid on the henhouse and barn, if one had time. A Confederate soldier who showed a keen interest in pilfering at Bowling Green said, "According to the military education I was receiving, it did not appear to be so very wicked as my conscience was inclined to make me out to be."[18] Presently the 7th Kansas Cavalry was accused of Jayhawking — i.e., poaching and ransacking. These knights of the road were credited with many atrocities.[19]

Colonel Dickey's Union forces secured Oxford and began occupying Water Valley. Nevertheless, the Union cavalry continued to harass the slow-moving Confederate rear guard, as Grant sent Colonel Dickey encouragement to press the southerners as far as possible. Dickey's men crossed the Otuckalfa River south of Water Valley the morning of December 5, pressing down the stage road that served as the main north-south route from Water Valley to Coffeeville. They hit Van Dorn's skirmishers at 2:00 P.M., fanned out, forming a broad front, and moved within a mile north of Coffeeville. Generals Lovell and Tilghman commanded the defense. The Battle of Coffeeville, as the fight was called, commenced on Red Hill near Velma Station. The two West Pointers decided to take advantage of the opportunity presented, i.e., laying a trap for the overconfident Union cavalry headed by the Kansas Jayhawkers, who enjoyed the reputation of being the most expert plunderers connected with Grant's army. They came forward with "a rush and a yell" expecting to take the town by coup d'état and have the pillaging to themselves.[20]

11

The Skirmish at Coffeeville, Mississippi

"This action was fought under peculiar difficulties. The road was narrow and extremely muddy, lined nearly all the way on both sides by a dense and almost impenetrable growth of oak trees and underbrush running over a broken and impracticable country or through river bottoms of a miry character. It was impossible to see the enemy's position or note his strength till we were upon him. It was equally difficult to show a strong front or properly dispose of the wagons and ambulances and the horses of the dismounted men. In this pursuit, over muddy road and through almost incessant rains, in a country destitute of forage for horses and without rations for men, the enemy was followed four successive days, skirmishing daily and almost hourly, and chased as far as Coffeeville, a distance of about 50 miles." So wrote Colonel T. Lyle Dickey, Chief of U.S. Cavalry, regarding the pursuit of Van Dorn's rear guard.[1]

At the same time, Confederate General Lovell observed it was impossible for Lee's cavalry to see the rebels or their strength because the muddy stage road was narrow, lined along the way on both sides by a dense growth of oak trees and underbrush.[2] Lovell sent Tilghman back up the stage road to form a screened front upon the road at Red Hill. Tilghman posted his infantry in timber on a ridge running perpendicular to the road, and behind his infantry he placed four pieces of artillery. General Tilghman described the skirmish at Coffeeville.

At about 2:30 o'clock on Friday afternoon, 5th instant, while engaged in the town of Coffeeville with the various duties of my command, I learned that the enemy, emboldened by their successes heretofore, had pushed their advance within one mile of the town, and that, having commenced skirmishing with our rear guard of cavalry, Major-General Lovell, commanding First Corps, had gone out with a portion of my division to check them. I immediately rode out with a portion of my staff and body guard to the point selected by General Lovell on which to form, and found that he had pushed forward a portion of the First Brigade, under [Brig.] Gen. [W. E.] Baldwin, on the right of the main road to Water Valley, while the Ninth Arkansas, of General Rust's division, commanded by Colonel Isaac L. Dunlop, was placed in line of battle on the left of the same road. Colonel A. P. Thompson commanding brigade, of the Second Division, had also been ordered to place the Third Kentucky Regiment, of his brigade, upon a road leading out from Coffeeville to the west of the main road spoken of, in order to watch our left flank. Upon the main road and in rear of the First Brigade, upon a small eminence, four pieces of artillery had been placed, being part of Capt. [Alcide] Bouanchaud's company of the Point Coupée Artillery, while at 300 yards to the rear of this battery two Parrott guns from Capt. [W. H.] Hedden's battery, of my own division, were placed on a still higher point and in a position not to endanger the infantry or the battery in front should occasion present itself to open upon the enemy.

Before reaching the point at which General Lovell was stationed I heard brisk cannonading, and on joining General Lovell, near where the rear battery was placed, found that it proceeded from our advanced battery, which was being replied to by a rifle gun of the enemy. I immediately reported for orders to General Lovell, who directed me to ride with him to the position held by the advanced battery. On reaching that point and finding that the enemy had obtained the exact range of our guns I retired with General Lovell to the rear battery, and was immediately ordered to open fire with the Parrott guns at short intervals. This was done, and in a few moments the fire of the enemy's battery ceased. I then asked permission of the major-general commanding to press the enemy and drive them back, and upon receiving his orders to do so, with information that General Rust had been ordered to maneuver on my right with parts of two of his brigades, rode rapidly to the front, ordering at the same time the Fourteenth Mississippi Regiment, under Maj. W. L. Doss, which had been held in reserve, to move up at double-quick and take position on the extreme right of my line. The cavalry, under Colonel [W. H.] Jackson [Seventh Tennessee Cavalry], numbering about 700, were placed at my disposal also. The proper disposition of the forces was soon made. Orders were given to General Baldwin, on the right, and to Col. A. P. Thompson, of the Second Division, who had assumed the direction of the Ninth Arkansas of his own brigade, to deploy the right companies from each regiment as skirmishers 100 paces in front of

11. The Skirmish at Coffeeville, Mississippi

the main line; a greater distance was not deemed prudent, as the woods were very dense and the enemy known to be in close proximity. The cavalry was formed in the main road and ordered to move with caution in rear of the main line.

The line of skirmishers being formed and everything prepared, orders were given to the men to hold their fire until within 50 yards, to move with caution until the enemy was reached, but then to press them with all their energy. The command forward was given and both skirmishers and the main line moved. The line had not advanced 200 yards before the enemy opened on our left a brisk fire. This was answered first by a yell along our whole line, the men moving rapidly and with great enthusiasm until they were within good range, when the Ninth Arkansas, directed by Colonel A. P. Thompson, and the Eighth Kentucky, under Col. H. B. Lyon, opened fire in return. Very soon the fire extended towards our right, along the Twenty-third Mississippi, under Lieut. Col. Moses McCarley, and the Twenty-sixth Mississippi, under Maj. T. F. Parker. The order to press the enemy was fully carried out. They were not allowed time to breathe, and though making two gallant stands in the first mile they were driven from their positions without our men faltering for a moment. The tactics of the enemy did them great credit. Their whole force consisted of mounted infantry armed with Colt's, Smith's, and Sharp's most approved weapons, with two pieces of artillery. The country over which they had to pass was an alternate wood and field. On being driven to the edge of a field they mounted and retreated across it, dismounting and sending their horses to the rear. They had all the advantage of position, being covered by the woodland while our men advanced across the open field. At these points the fire of the enemy was terrific, but nothing could stop the onward movement, and our men moved forward without slackening their pace in the least.

Having driven the enemy for more than a mile it occurred to me that should the troops of General [Albert] Rust's command not have moved to their left far enough to guard my right flank, I might run some risk of being outflanked. To guard against this I detached Lieut. [J. G.] Barbour, commanding my body guard, with a portion of his men, with orders to move at full speed to my extreme right and take position with his men well extended and watch my right flank. No sooner had he reached the point and commenced moving up with our main line than he was fired upon by the enemy. Lieutenant Barbour immediately sent a courier informing me of the fact, when I ordered the Fourteenth Mississippi, under Maj. [W. L.] Doss, to move at double-quick by the right flank until he reached the point occupied by Lieutenant Barbour, then to assume his original front and press them again.

During all this time the enemy were uninterruptedly driven from every position and forced back to a point three miles from Coffeville, when on reaching a commanding position they opened fire from their artillery, again supported by the severest fire of musketry we had yet encountered. The heaviest fire was encountered by the Ninth Arkansas and the Eighth Kentucky Regiments. Their efforts were, however, useless; nothing could check the advance of our men, and the position was carried without a moment's delay just at dark.

It occurred to me a few moments before this that a dash of our cavalry might have secured the piece of artillery in its last position, but it would have involved a heavy loss of life, not warranted under the circumstances, and I did not give the order.

Having already driven the enemy much farther than was ordered by a message from General Lovell, I gave the order to halt and cease firing, very much to the chagrin of both officers and men, who, notwithstanding the severe duties and deprivations of the last week, seemed to forget everything but the desire showed by all to repay the injuries suffered by them during their long and barbarous imprisonment at the North.

The Fourteenth Mississippi, Major Doss commanding, towards the close became too far separated from the main command, but was abundantly able to take care of itself, and drove back the enemy in their front, killing and wounding a number, among them Lieutenant-Colonel [William] McCullough, who was shot dead within twenty paces of our line. This regiment also captured 17 prisoners, with all their horses, arms, and accouterments.

The loss on our part, as stated in my note to Major-General Lovell of the 6th inst., is known to be accurately as follows: Killed 7; wounded, 43. That of the enemy 34 killed, among them Lieutenant-Colonel McCullough and a second lieutenant, who gave his name as [Thomas J.] Woodburn, of the Third Missouri [Seventh Kansas], just before expiring. The wounded of the enemy could not be accurately ascertained, inasmuch as all who were not too badly wounded were removed on horseback as fast as they fell. Estimating their wounded by the number killed in the same ratio as that known to exist on our part, the wounded may be given at 234, which from the number seen in the act of being removed is under rather than over the actual loss. Sixteen of their severely wounded fell into our hands. Thirty-five prisoners, with 17 horses, and all their arms and accoutrements were captured. Among the prisoners were one captain and several non-commissioned officers. The wounded on both sides were removed at once to Coffeeville and every care taken of them. The dead were buried next morning. The body of the Federal lieutenant was decently buried; marked on the head-stone, so that it could be recognized. The body of Lieutenant-Colonel McCullough was not secured. The command returned to its first position near Coffeeville and bivouacked in line of battle.

The whole affair was a complete success and taught the enemy a lesson I am sure they will not soon forget. The troops behaved in the most gallant manner. Officers and men emulated each other. All did their duty nobly.

I take especial pleasure in mentioning the names of Brig. Gen. W. E.

Baldwin, of my own division, and Col. A. P. Thompson, commanding a brigade in General Rust's division. These officers, in command on my right and left, displayed the greatest good judgment and gallantry.

The brunt of the battle was borne by the Ninth Arkansas, Colonel I. L. Dunlop; Eighth Kentucky, Col. H. B. Lyon; the Twenty-third Mississippi, Lieutenant-Colonel McCarley; and the Twenty-sixth Mississippi, under Maj. T. F. Parker. I have seldom seen greater good judgment and impetuous gallantry shown by any officers or men.

The cavalry, under Col. Jackson, maintained the most perfect order and were always in position to answer any summons.

The batteries engaged rendered the most efficient service up to the time of my ordering the advance. The first shot fired from the Parrott guns of Captain Hedden's battery, under the direction of Capt. [Jacob] Culbertson, chief of artillery of my division, wounded Colonel Mizner and killed his orderly and three men. These facts were related by a noncommissioned officer among the prisoners.

My thanks are especially due to those members of my personal staff who were present. Maj. Watts, inspector-general; Major Halliday, chief commissary; Lieuts. George Moorman and [Lloyd] Tilghman [Jr.], aides-de-camp, rendered most efficient and valuable service.

I notice with great pleasure also Lieut. Barbour, commanding my body guard together with Lieutenant Lundy of that company. These officers and their men rendered me great aid. The timely service of Lieutenant Barbour on my right wing may have saved us possibly from serious injury.

The whole force engaged on our side may be stated as not exceeding 1,300 men, while the enemy is known to have had not less than five regiments, numbering not less than 3,500 men.

Inclosed I have the honor to submit a correct list of the killed and wounded on our side.

I regret the absence of Capt. Powhatan Ellis [Jr.], chief of staff during the action. He was engaged at my headquarters on important business, and I was thus deprived of his always valuable services.

The same may be said of others of my staff who were absent on duty at various points.

Respectfully, your obedient servant,
LLOYD TILGHMAN,
Comdg. First Division, First Corps, Army of West Tennessee[3]

It is noteworthy to learn that his son, Lieutenant Lloyd Tilghman Jr., was traveling with the general as aide-de-camp. Otherwise, the retreat by the Confederates in the first week of December was a costly one, as outlined by Colonel Dickey, chief of Union cavalry.

In the expedition we captured 750 prisoners and near 200 horses and mules; also five railroad cars, four wagons loaded with supplies, $7,000 of

Confederate money in the hands of a Rebel quartermaster; compelled the enemy to burn several hundred tents and to abandon and destroy several hundred stand of small-arms: saved from destruction all of the railroad bridges on the route and most of the trestle work, and obtained a correct map of the country through the assistance of the assistant topographical engineer who accompanied me.

We lost 10 killed, 63 wounded, and 41 captured. Of the enemy at least 70 were killed, 250 wounded, and 750 taken prisoners. His loss in stragglers and deserters on the retreat is probably 600 or 700 more.

I transmit herewith a list of the casualties, which is respectfully submitted.

I am, sir, very respectfully, your obedient servant,

T. LYLE DICKEY,
Colonel and Chief of Cavalry,
Commanding Cavalry Division[4]

The renowned Van Dorn passed the engagement off with a two-line report: "Enemy came up to within two miles of town this evening. Infantry attacked them and drove them back two miles. Firing just ceased. Night put a stop to pursuit. He will be careful how he comes up again."[5] There is no mention of the booty his army lost over the last seven days. On December 7, General Lovell was relieved of his corps to face a court of inquiry about the fall of New Orleans in April while under his command. Later he was absolved of the charge. General Van Dorn was moved sideways, to 1st Corps Commander of the Cavalry; and the army was renamed The Army of Mississippi and East Louisiana, with General Pemberton as commander.[6]

Back at Oxford, the 7th Kansas Cavalry was given the duty of guarding the nearly 1,000 Confederate prisoners and stragglers who had gathered during the past days. The 7th Kansas had laid in a bountiful supply of tobacco at the expense of Oxford merchants. Discovering their prisoners were desperate for a "chaw," the Jayhawk soldiers began to pitch whole plugs of tobacco to the suffering Johnnies. Despondency disappeared, and three cheers for the Jayhawkers were given in gusto by the captive rebels.[7] In all theaters tobacco was consumed in great quantities by both sides; cigars, pipe tobacco, chewing tobacco, snuff — a poor man's tranquilizer in times of fear and melancholy — were bartered between the blue and the gray at day's end.

Grant was not just pursuing a retreating Confederate army; he was also trying to get to Vicksburg by going over land through Mississippi.[8]

In this last month of the second year of the war, it was impossible to deny that Anna E. Carroll's military strategy had been correct. It was December and Grant's forces were moving in northern Mississippi, advancing towards the rear of Vicksburg, while General Sherman was already proceeding down the Mississippi River with an invasion force to attack Vicksburg. It looked like a pincer movement. But the stubborn Confederate army refused to collapse, contesting each mile with the Federal invaders. Moving south overland, the Federals had to rely on the railroad for their supplies; with each mile away from their supply base they grew weaker and the defending Confederates grew stronger. Grant's supply line, a one-track railroad extending 180 miles, was vulnerable to the whims of the roaming rebel cavalry. After Van Dorn departed Holly Springs, Grant made the town his forward supply base. This base was 50 miles from the engagements at Coffeeville.

General Jackson, with the Confederate cavalry, held the country between Coffeeville and Grenada. The main part of the jaded Confederate army, with its refugees tagging along, crossed the rain-swollen Yalobusha River at Grenada, Mississippi, and took up defensive positions along the south bank of the Yalobusha, where Tilghman and his brigades joined them. The main body of the Federal army was encamped near Water Valley, with advance outposts in the vicinity of Coffeeville. No other advance was attempted, and during the next two or three weeks in December, the most perfect quiet prevailed between the lines.[9]

"The Yankees seemed to have no rear, for strong detachments were posted all along the railroad as far as southern scouts had gone, and were known to extend as far north as Holly Springs, 50 miles away. General Grant was accumulating an immense depot of supplies at Holly Springs; was repairing the railroad south of that place; and hastening every preparation necessary for a continuation of his advance. To arrest his progress was a matter of vital importance, otherwise the whole interior of Mississippi, its capital at Jackson, Vicksburg, and its railroad would fall into Federal possession. The Confederate force in front of Grant was insufficient to take on 80,000 Federals, with any hope of success."[10]

"A plan was suggested by Col. Griffith of the Texas Cavalry Brigade, to Lieutenant General Pemberton that Pemberton organize into a division three mounted brigades then in north Mississippi, and that he send this formidable force against Grant's supply depot at Holly Springs. At

Pemberton's request, General Bragg ordered Brigadier General Forrest to distract Grant by striking the Mobile & Ohio Railroad, the Federal supply line running from Columbus, Kentucky, south through Jackson, Tennessee."[11]

Whether by design or luck, a form of cooperative Confederate offense strategy was being played out by Generals Pemberton and Forrest these last two weeks of the year. Their Christmas cheer to the boys in blue, so far from their beloved homes, would be to disrupt Grant's supply line of food, clothing, gifts, mail, sutler's supplies, ammunition, grain, and whatever else they carried on that endless railroad.

On December 11, Forrest, with a magnificent combined cavalry force of 2,500 horsemen and 10 cannon, left Columbia, Tennessee, and began to operate northward against Grant's rail line in western Tennessee. With so many cavalrymen on the move in the countryside, it did not take long for Grant to be apprised of Forrest's advance. To counterattack, Grant ordered a concentration of troops at Jackson, Tennessee, calling other horseback infantry from garrisons at Columbus, Forts Heiman, Henry and Donelson (which they occupied), Bolivar, Corinth, and even Oxford to intercept Forrest's movement. This substantially reduced Grant's cavalry strength protecting the Holly Springs depot.

On December 15, General Pemberton ordered his main body of Confederate horsemen in Grant's front to cross south of the Yalobusha River and form into three brigades made up of Colonel Griffith's Texas Cavalry; Colonel William Hick Jackson's Tennesseans; and Colonel Robert McCulloch's Mississippians. This group of 2,500 rebel marauders would be led by the versatile Van Dorn, whose goal was to pilfer and plunder his old base of operations, Grant's forward supply depot at Holly Springs.

Van Dorn's corps was poorly mounted and badly armed with shotguns, squirrel guns, Bowie knives, and captured Yankee weapons mounted on whatever animals (horses and mules) they could find or steal. This herd of Confederates headed northeast towards Ripley, thundering along at a great rate of speed, and cut west to Holly Springs, where, on December 20, they captured Grant's huge supply depot with a minimum of effort. "At dark we were ordered to move forward in perfect silence; at midnight, the head of the column was a mile from Holly Springs. After passing the pickets, the column of horsemen, without abating its speed, struck the Federal camp in Holly Springs like a thunderbolt. The sleeping Federals were aroused by the wild Rebel cheer and rushed out of their tents; the scene of a regiment, with night garments fluttering to the breeze, trying to dodge an avalanche of horsemen, was truly laughable. There was no resistance. While 1,500 prisoners were taken, the Confederate raiders plundered warehouses, cut telegraph lines, and tore up track. By 8:00 A.M., Van Dorn was in possession of the town."[12]

The raiders found tons of medical, quartermaster, ordnance, and commissary stores, which were put to the torch. The raiders helped themselves to boots, hats, saddles, food, arms; sugar, coffee, crackers, cheese, and sardines were powered into sacks and tied behind saddles. In ten hours Van Dorn's patriots destroyed $1.5 million of supplies and burned several buildings, including a new 2,000-bed hospital.[13] At sunset the work of destruction had been completed, the prisoners paroled, the magazine exploded, and the command moved out of town.

The long trek back to Grenada was treacherous; they had to dodge the enraged pursuing Union cavalry, who were trying to catch up to the raiders. But they were too late. Van Dorn's spectacular round trip was 400 miles long and took two weeks to complete. Van Dorn's army, with limited striking force and little bloodshed, accomplished more to stop Grant's Mississippi adventure in the last two weeks of the year than the combined Confederate army had done in the previous three months. And there was more. Van Dorn learned that at the other end of Grant's supply pipeline, Forrest's cavalry had shut down the Mobile & Ohio Railroad in western Tennessee for the past ten days, not only disrupting communications, but also tearing up railroad track into Kentucky.[14] The command arrived at Grenada about the 1st of January.

For the year 1862, General Grant's advance movement of Federal armies was from Forts Henry and Donelson, up the Tennessee River to Corinth, as he attempted to invade the heart of Dixie by land. On his western flank was the Mississippi River. Here Grant was faced with formidable Confederate fortifications at locations the Confederates were sure would maintain their control of the river. The eastern bank of the river, bounded by lofty plains stretching for miles, terminated at river's edge with precipitous bluffs 80 to 200 feet above the muddy river water. The Confederates reasoned, "They afford [no] foothold for any army approaching by land, and were unassailable by the navy gunboats on the river. A ship's guns could not be elevated sufficiently to inflict fatal damage on such summits, while the defenders could return a plunging fire from above."[16]

Despite these defensive forts, the Federal army and navy had splendid early victories in the north at Columbus, Kentucky; Fort Pillow, and then Memphis, Tennessee; and more recently in the southern part of the river at New Orleans and Baton Rouge, Louisiana. Naturally the rebels always claimed a chain of events, or some other excuse, why these strongholds were surrendered, then quickly moved down or up the river to the next fortification. By autumn, 1862, the Confederate part of the Mississippi water route had shrunk to the area from the city of Vicksburg south 130 miles to Port Hudson, Louisiana. Now the Yankee invaders began to squeeze the river defenses from both ends.

The northern terminus of this seemingly impregnable river link was the city of Vicksburg, crowning the bluffs at a height of 200 feet above water and saturated with all types of cannon on the Mississippi side of the river. Eleven miles south on high bluffs was Grand Gulf, armed and regarded as an outwork of the Vicksburg defense. One hundred miles below Grand Gulf was Port Hudson, Louisiana. Armed with 20 heavy siege cannon on 80-foot bluffs, they guarded four small landside forts, furnishing an additional 30 pieces of field artillery. This formidable bastion was on the western bank of the Mississippi, an anchor of defense that would deny the invading Yankees from Baton Rouge any chance of joining their blue-coated troops in north Mississippi.

In addition to the transportation and commerce value of keeping the river open for the southerners, it was also the line of communication for the southern armies, something the northerners did not have at present. In addition, the Red River, a small stream that empties into the Mississippi above Port Hudson, was the water crossroad to western states and Mexican ports. It was the highway by which the states of Texas, Louisiana, and Arkansas were connected with central and eastern portions of the Confederacy and their railroads. It was the entrance to an inexhaustible granary of the western states, furnishing cattle, foodstuff, horses, mules, and imports of rifles, cannon, and ammunition brought in by blockade-runners and ships of other nations at neutral seaports in Texas and Mexico. Cotton was traded for gold and soon went west on the Red River.

It was the communication center for the rest of the outer world. Vicksburg and Port Hudson posts both drew their supplies from western Louisiana and Texas by way of the Red River.

"Between these two points the Mississippi River was entirely in rebel hands. Farragut's fleet at New Orleans could not pass above Port Hudson, nor could Davis's fleet at Helena, Arkansas, pass below Vicksburg, without incurring great danger in running by the batteries on the cliffs. No Union army could land on the eastern bank of the river at any point without severing itself from every source whence supplies could reach it. The guns of Port Hudson closed the way to all supplies coming up the river, and the guns of Vicksburg bluffs frowned off all attempts to come downriver. The Red River, the great avenue between east and west, was jealously guarded by the Confederates."[17]

If the Yankees wanted a victory in the western theater, they would have to adopt a course of action to smash this barrier to enter the gateway of victory. This meant more manpower. "In the month of November, 1862, Major-General N. P. Banks, Federal army, sailed from New York City with a force of between 15,000 and 20,000 men. His instructions were to proceed to New Orleans, relieve General B. F. Butler, and unite the forces brought with him with those already serving on the Gulf, then advance up the Mississippi against Port Hudson, in cooperation with Grant's operations against Vicksburg in the north."[18]

As General Grant was taking inventory of his losses at Holly Springs, General Sherman's troops on the Mississippi attacked Vicksburg on Christmas Eve. General S. D. Lee, with less than 3,000 butternut soldiers, repelled Sherman's bluecoats and sent them packing back up the river shortly after the New Year. This was the Battle of Chickasaw Bayou. The raids of Van Dorn and Forrest, and Lee's successful defense of Vicksburg, without any doubt had immediate and far-reaching repercussions upon the Federals' high command decision to abandon the invasion of northern Mississippi by land. Grant's army was ordered back to Memphis; General Grant was ordered to join Sherman's forces and Admiral Porter's operations. The 1863 campaign would be fought on the Mississippi River and its environs leading to Vicksburg.

12

Grenada: Winter Quarters, 1863

At Grenada in December of 1862, soldiers rested and exchanged tales of past battles, while gala dances again became a part of the war's second holiday season. Colonel Rus Stirman, commanding the 2nd Brigade, was quite the ladies' man. Rus was enjoying himself as he went to a ball at Carrollton, 22 miles south of Grenada. The dance was given in a very large college room and was filled with gentlemen and ladies. "I fell in love of course with a Miss Wolf," he wrote his sister. "I will describe her as well as I can, as I saw her by candle light. She has laughing black eyes, dark hair, rosey cheeks, and OH the sweetest ruby lips, at least they tasted that way to me as I helped her into her father's carriage, and bid her good bye with promises to call to see her.... The old man owns four thousand acres of land, eighty-seven negroes, and plenty of stock." This was neither the first or last time Rus Stirman fell in love. The month before at Holly Springs, he wrote: "I have a sweetheart. OH what a pretty face and curls," and at Mobile, Alabama, two months before this, Rus met "a Yankee girl named Nelie. OH, but she was sweet, she moves like a Queen, ... got lots of money and no poor kin."[1]

Elsewhere in camp, the Richmond authorities, hoping to stem wholesale unrest among the independently minded generals and recognizing the increasing gravity of the command situation, decided it might be helpful if President Davis visited the Mississippi theater to see for himself what the situation entailed and to raise morale. Sacrificing his holiday for the cause, President Davis, traveling incognito, made the 900-mile journey on half a dozen railroads. He arrived at Jackson accompanied by General Joseph E. Johnston, the new commander of the Department of the Confederate West, a geographical department rather than a command. Johnston's circle of power would oversee General Braxton Bragg's Army of Tennessee, General E. Kirby Smith's Department of East Tennessee, and Lieutenant General Pemberton's Department of Mississippi and East Louisiana. Johnston's headquarters would be located at Chattanooga, Tennessee.

The presidential party visited with Pemberton at Vicksburg and later with some of his forces near Grenada on Christmas Eve. General Loring, in command of Van Dorn's forces while he was on his Holly Springs raid, wrote: "I was in command a few days of the army at which the President and Joe Johnston were present. The army presented a fine appearance." President Davis returned to Jackson on Christmas Day, and on the 27th, information was received that because of Van Dorn's Holly Springs raid, General Grant was retiring to Memphis, Tennessee. As the Confederates celebrated Van Dorn's stunning victory, command changes were posted. Major General W. W. Loring, who had arrived from West Virginia in early December at Coffeeville, was assigned commander of Van Dorn's 1st Division and would be second in command to Pemberton.[2]

General Tilghman took command of the 1st Brigade, hitherto under General W. E. Baldwin, and reported to Loring. Rounding out the division was General A. Rust, who served with Loring at Cheat Mountain, West Virginia, and Colonel T. N. Waul's Texas Legion of Infantry, Artillery and Cavalry.[3] The Loring-Tilghman relationship would be a good one — Tilghman, the distinguished general from West Point, and Loring, the nondescript combative commander.

Forty-four-year-old Loring had become the youngest second lieutenant in the Florida militia during the Seminole War. Later a practicing lawyer in St. Augustine, Florida, he was elected representative to the Florida Territorial Legislature and later, State Legislature. In the Mexican War he was captain of Mounted Riflemen, and his left arm was severed at the Battle of Chapultepec. He never attended West Point because his home state was a territory when he was a young man. Thereafter he fulfilled extensive service with the Mounted Riflemen in the territories of Oregon and Washington, and in the U.S. Army in Texas, New Mexico, and Arizona. Despite his disability, he was appointed a full colonel, not brevet, in the Federal army, before switching allegiance to the Confederate cause. After the Loring-Jackson debacle at Romney, West Virginia, in the winter of 1861, he had a splendid run in West Virginia, capturing Charleston in the fall of 1862. Disgusted with mountain duty, he requested field duty in another active theater of war.

Northern-born Pemberton, age 48, class of 1837 USMA and of Philadelphia Quaker ancestry, was not of landed gentry, nor qualified as a cavalier from the plantation. He had limited wartime duty in the Seminole War and border duty in the Mexican War and the Utah Expedition against the Mormons. He served his entire U.S. Army tour with the artillery. He resigned in April of 1861 and journeyed to his wife's native state of Virginia, where he joined the state forces as a lieutenant colonel. Promoted rapidly in the C.S.A., he was placed in command of the 4th Military District, Department of South Carolina, Georgia, and Florida. Due to his counseling of the abandonment of Fort Sumter and the building of Fort Wagner as the basis of defense, the South Carolina citizens who disliked him requested the "Yankee" be replaced. In November he was assigned to the command of Mississippi and East Louisiana, to guard Port Hudson and Vicksburg on the Mississippi River. Pemberton had great ability and experience and was very loyal to the cause, but suffered under conflicting instructions from his superiors, which he always obeyed, time and again, which placed him in situations that could not be resolved. Of course he was blamed for these coming defeats; he was the commander.[4]

In January of 1863, Loring sent Tilghman to Jackson on temporary duty to handle the exchange of Federal prisoners who had been captured by the Confederates from the December engagements and imprisoned there. In the prison were over 700 bluecoats, including 20 officers.[5]

Tilghman showed little compassion towards the Federal captives, especially for those of the 7th Kansas Cavalry. He was intent on punishing the hard-bitten Kansas boys for their Jayhawking habits. U.S. Colonel Lee denounced Tilghman for his treatment and said bitterly that some of his officers were held in close confinement on hard fare. "I desire to call attention to one fact. There are among these prisoners three men of the Seventh Kansas Cavalry. Tilghman ordered them in irons, they are chained together, hand and foot, by heavy irons. This is only because they are connected with this regiment."[6] These three prisoners had been captured near Memphis on January 23.[7]

Colonel Lee took his complaint to General Grant. "Is there any method of righting this wrong or of retaliation? If our policy will permit it, I will capture three Confederate officers within the fortnight and put them in irons in the camp of the Seventh Kansas, and then open up a correspondence with General Tilghman."[8] General Grant advised Colonel Lee that if he was perfectly satisfied that some of his men were being punished, as described by him, by rebel authorities, he might serve in the same manner an equal number of the enemy, and then open a correspondence with Tilghman as he proposed.[9] If any retribution was served by Colonel Lee, it was not recorded in the Official Records. At this time prisoners were being exchanged within ten days.

On January 20, the flamboyant General Van Dorn was appointed permanent commander of Pemberton's army cavalry in the Mississippi Valley. Soon thereafter, Braxton Bragg in Tennessee requested from Pemberton the loan of Van Dorn's cavalry force of 4,500 horsemen for the coming Tullahoma campaign he was planning. Pemberton acquiesced to Bragg's request in the spirit of cooperation, and perhaps maybe to be rid of Van Dorn because of his scandalous private life in Mississippi. This was a terrible mistake made by the Quaker, one he regretted later. In effect, he had given away a fighting general, Van Dorn, plus his most effective defensive land fighting force to date. He was left with next to nothing of an effective cavalry to cover the entire state of Mississippi, a situation too complicated to be handled even by Pemberton.

While Grant and Sherman were developing their strategy to reduce Vicksburg, old vindictive Pemberton found time to alienate his officers. The latest casualty would be no less than General Tilghman, resulting in another court of inquiry.

Back in November when the Confederate army was making a hasty move from Abbeville, Mississippi, there was not sufficient transportation belonging to General Tilghman's division to haul the soldiers' wet and muddy tents. In a verbal order from Major General Lovell, Tilghman was told to burn and abandon the tents, which General Tilghman did.

Pemberton, upon learning of this, requested a court of inquiry for the purpose of investigating the circumstance attending the burning of the tents.

On February 1, 1863, a court of inquiry was assembled at Grenada, Mississippi. The point in question was the interpretation of Pemberton's order, which on November 30 read in part "... required stores that could not be transported to be destroyed."[10]

At the inquiry it was brought out that there was not sufficient transportation belonging to Tilghman's division to haul the tents and that they were then burned and destroyed in compliance with a verbal order issued by Major General Lovell, i.e., "to throw out sufficient tents, as they were wet and heavy, to enable wagons to pass over the bad roads and keep up with the train."[11]

The court of inquiry findings were that "Brig. Gen. Tilghman was fully exonerated from all censure in relation to the burning and destroying of the tents and they recommended that no further proceedings be had in relation thereto against him."[12]

General Tilghman was cleared in the eyes of the court, but not in Pemberton's mind. It did not appear to Pemberton that the transportation of the tents was impracticable and their destruction consequently necessary.

After this court of inquiry there was a coolness in Pemberton's dealings with Tilghman throughout the winter and spring campaigns. And it is puzzling.

Both had northern ties. In fact, at this time Tilghman's mother was living in Philadelphia, which was Pemberton's hometown. Pemberton, the Quaker from Pennsylvania, served his cadetship at West Point at the same time as Tilghman. "These future generals were schooled and spanned the years together at the Point."[13]

Even more binding in spirit was the fact that "the most distinguished ancestor of Pemberton's wife-to-be, Martha Thompson, was Elbridge Gerry, a signer of the Declaration of Independence."[14] General Tilghman was the great-grandson of Matthew Tilghman, who was the president of the Revolutionary Convention of Maryland and a member of the Continental Congress.

These considerations and the fact that they both served in the Mexican War should have created an amicable relationship between the two generals. But they did not.

One thing that plagued Pemberton's career was his lack of cooperation and mutual understanding of his officers and men. Pemberton remained aloof from Lloyd Tilghman until the Battle of Champion Hill; here the relationship burst open in all of its ugliness.

From the beginning of hostilities, the Confederates had occupied and defended an assortment of river forts on the long, winding Mississippi River. Beginning at Columbus, Kentucky, which Polk was ordered to abandon, one by one these river forts were either captured or abandoned by the Confederates. As mentioned before, by January 1863 the Federal forces controlled the entire vital river except for a stretch from Vicksburg to Port Hudson, Louisiana, a distance of almost 200 miles.

The northern anchor was the river port Vicksburg, with its crowning bluffs so high that the invading ships' guns could not be elevated sufficiently to inflict any fatal aim. Through the planning and great efforts of Generals Van Dorn and Pemberton, cannon — by the dozen for several miles on the bluff overlooking the winding river — guarded Vicksburg and controlled the river traffic. The task of taking Vicksburg would be an arduous one for the Federal fleet and army. Twenty-five miles below, along the river, was another well armed bluff called Grand Gulf, another guardian of the Mississippi.

Anchoring these two northern strategic locations some 150 miles farther down the river was Port Hudson and its strongly garrisoned fort. North of Port Hudson was the great Red River, which empties into the Mississippi from Louisiana. This river was the last east-to-west waterway by which the Trans-Mississippi connected with the Confederacy, a valuable supply line over which arms and munitions from abroad were transported from the Mexican and Texas seaports.

Filled with cypress swamps, much of the Mississippi River was nothing but a network of bayous and streams as crooked as the river itself. The riverbanks being interspersed with dense forests and creeping vines, it was next to impossible for a naval force to make a successful landing of Federal troops.

Grant's Union juggernaut was positioned north of Vicksburg, preparing to assault one of its last river obstacles to get below Vicksburg without having to travel the heavily guarded river. First, the Federals embarked on trying to cut a series of canals to bypass fortified

Vicksburg. The strategy was to dig a mile-long, nine-foot-wide canal through the bayous on the Louisiana side, opposite Vicksburg. As many as 3,500 soldiers toiled away at excavating these ditches in the swamps. The duty inflicted incredible hardship and suffering on the young bluecoats. Snakebites, foul water, and wretched sanitary facilities led to diarrhea and fever, which took their toll on the invaders. This idea became a failure, as the rebels established a battery of heavy guns opposite the mouth of the manmade canal, nullifying this plan.

Next, an attempt was made to cut a canal at Duckport Landing, again on the Louisiana side, to connect a winding route through the bayous; later a 400-mile route from Lake Providence, Louisiana, through the swamps was started and then stopped. Again, disappointment for the Federals as the fickle Mississippi River either receded or flooded and negated these schemes to get south of Vicksburg. Frustrated, Generals Grant and Sherman switched from ditch digging to an amphibious mode of war; the engineers of the canals would have to give way to officers and sailors of the Union navy.

Five miles below Helena, Arkansas, on the eastern bank of the Mississippi River was the sealed Yazoo Pass. Used earlier in the century as the shortest route to Memphis, the pass was now sealed in order to protect the fertile fields of the rich bottomlands of the delta, which were lower than the surface of the river by eight feet. To safeguard these fields from periodic flooding from the river, a levee 18 feet high and 100 feet thick had been constructed across the mouth of the Yazoo Pass that led into Moon Lake. If this pass could be reopened, it would permit access to Moon Lake from the Mississippi for the Federal navy squadron.

13

The Yazoo Pass Expedition

This new strategy would have the U.S. Navy enter the Yazoo Pass from the Mississippi with a flotilla of gunboats, steamers, and transports. Sailing to the end of the lake, they could enter into the Coldwater River. Going south, this stream entered into the Tallahatchie River, which, when united with the Yalobusha River, became the headwaters of the Yazoo River. It continued south to Yazoo City and eventually came out at Haines Bluff, the northern approach to Vicksburg. This was the 200-mile mission being proposed by the Union hierarchy.

Quite quickly, Confederate informants brought to Pemberton's attention this new experiment being prepared by the Federals. On January 21, Pemberton ordered Loring, at winter quarters in Grenada, to send a party of civil engineers and overseers with 200 Negroes up the Tallahatchie and Coldwater Rivers to locate, and then fortify, a Confederate position that would stop Grant's newest expedition. The detachment proceeded all the way to the Yazoo Pass, where the overseers and Negroes were landed on both sides of Moon Lake, and the Negroes commenced felling the huge trees leading into the pass to obstruct it.[1]

The Confederate forces under Loring were organized as follows:

Commanding Confederate Forces, Maj. Gen. William W. Loring
  1st Brigade, Brig. Gen. Lloyd Tilghman
  54th Alabama Infantry, Col. A. Baker
  8th Kentucky Infantry, Col. H. B. Lyon

20th Mississippi Infantry, Col. D. R. Russell
23d Mississippi Infantry, Col. J. M. Wells
26th Mississippi Infantry, Col. A. E. Reynolds
Company C, 14th Mississippi Artillery Battalion (4 guns),
Capt. J. Culbertson

On February 3, Union pioneers, operating from the Mississippi River side of the pass, cut two ditches through the embankment. Sappers then buried a 50-pound can of gunpowder under the earthen dike and exploded it, opening a gaping 40-yard ditch into Moon Lake. It took four days for the rush of water into Moon Lake to subside, and the pass deep enough for the passage of some U.S. Navy tugs and light draft gunboats. As they entered the breach they encountered the obstacles of fallen trees, and at

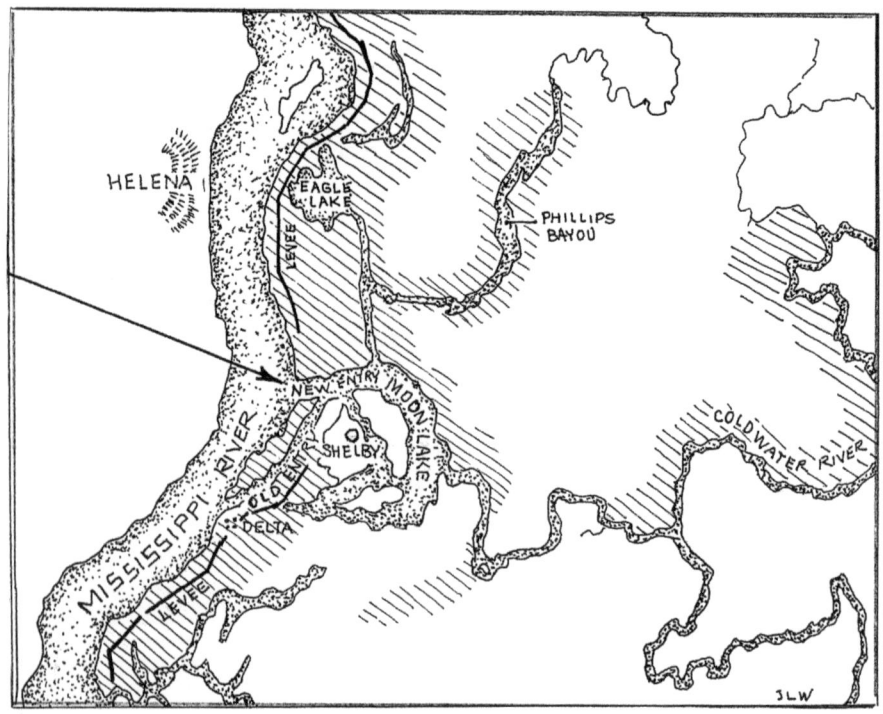

Grant's Yazoo Pass expedition. On February 3, 1863, Union pioneers operating on the Mississippi River buried a 50-pound can of gunpowder under the earthen dike and exploded it, opening a gaping 40-yard ditch, the Yazoo Pass.

certain places the depth was inadequate for the boats. They slowly moved towards the cut into the Coldwater River, taking three days to make the twelve-mile trip. Confederate Navy Lieutenant F. E. Shepperd's dispatch on February 14 said: "The enemy have driven us off the works on the Pass, and are coming through. I have done my best, worked under their noses till their pickets came in 100 yards of me."[2] Here, and elsewhere in the fight for command of the Mississippi, the Negroes were very instrumental in performing unconventional service for the Confederacy.

"Old Blizzards" Major General William Wing Loring, C.S.A. (1818–1886).

On February 17, General Pemberton shifted Generals Loring and Tilghman to Yazoo City to prepare for the Federal advance. Loring journeyed up the Yazoo River to Greenwood. Upon landing, he was conducted by Major M. Merriwether to an area two and a half miles north of the town, where fortifications were being constructed at Beck's Ferry landing. Here gangs of soldiers and impressed Negroes had started work on another inland fort, which Loring approved. The site for fortifying was a neck of high land looping the two rivers, the Yazoo on one side and the Tallahatchie on the approaching side. Located on the Clayton Bayou, the site was named Fort Pemberton by the Confederates, while the Federals referred to it as Fort Greenwood.

The fort would become a typical Mississippi cotton-bale fortification, constructed under the direction of Captain Powhatan Robinson of the Confederate Engineers. Robinson ordered a boat up the Tallahatchie River to Dr. Curtis's plantation, where a load of cotton bales was obtained to be used to build the breastworks, while a similar boat of cotton bales was obtained from the Purnell plantation downriver.

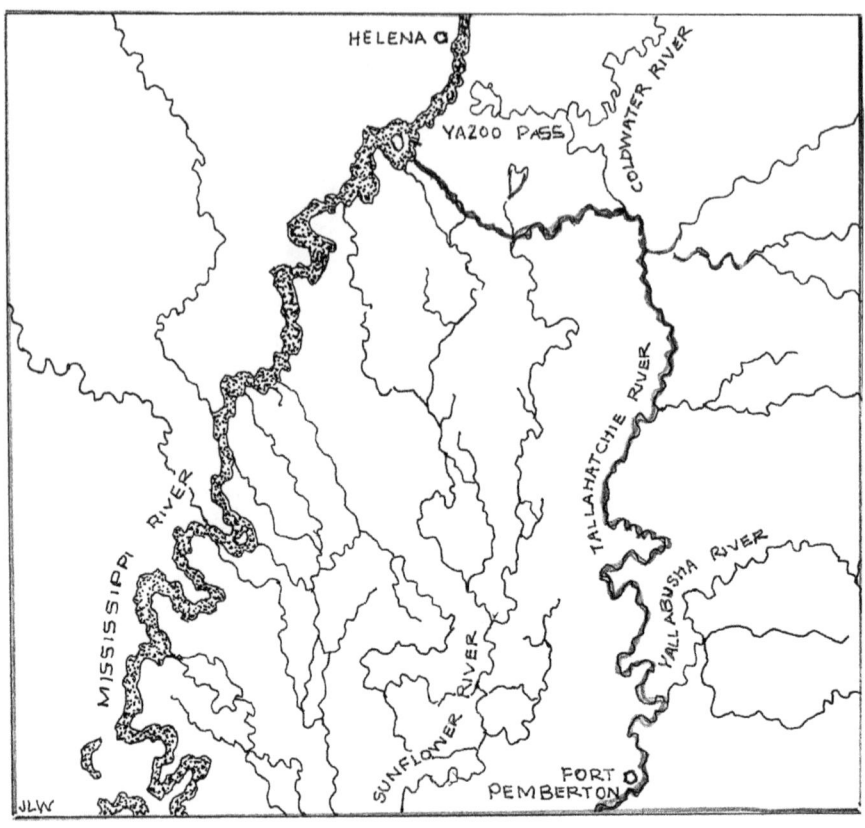

Union route to Fort Pemberton: A 250 mile river junket.

Arriving at the site, the 400-pound cotton bales were partly sunken, and the breastworks were made by putting from three to five bales of cotton on top of one another and four to five bales wide, joined together with sheet iron. After this, five to six feet of earth were thrown on the bales, finishing off a formidable breastwork.

The parapets of the stronghold were built of logs, mud and cotton bales, covered with rawhide so the enemy shells would bounce off. The flank of the defense rested on both sides of the water barriers; they zigzagged to the right on the Tallahatchie, and zigzagged to the left of the Yazoo. Once the shelling began, the cotton bales would be watered down to prevent them from burning from the Federal shells, which often consisted of red-hot cannonballs that were heated on the gunboats.

Captain J. D. Myrick was placed in charge of the seven guns mounted en barbette. The guns were emplaced in partially sunken redans 35 feet long, with gun platforms one foot below the surface emplaced to command either river. Within the fort were three well protected magazines. General Tilghman sent a regiment of infantry and a field battery to the fort and then ordered Colonel McCulloch and his cavalry force to the vicinity of the Coldwater River to harass the Federal boats from the banks of the river at such points as might be practicable.[3]

Pemberton transferred troops from Grenada to Fort Pemberton. Additional forces from Haines Landing, Snyder's Mill, and on the Yazoo River above Vicksburg were rapidly transferred to the fort. The garrison was composed of about 2,000 men in all, including Waul's Texas Legion, the 2nd Texas Infantry, the 20th Mississippi Infantry, the Pointe Coupee Artillery, and Loring's Cannoneers.[4] If driven from the fort, Loring promised to backtrack throughout the length of the Yazoo Valley. Consequently, he directed that an additional fortification be constructed on the right bank of the Yazoo, south of Fort Pemberton; these earthworks were designated "Camp Loring."[5]

With a view to obstructing the Tallahatchie and Coldwater Rivers, Loring proceeded up the Tallahatchie for 70 miles, where he learned of the breakthrough by the Yankees. Loring returned to the fort on February 24 and assigned Thomas Weldon, a civil engineer and shipbuilder from Yazoo City who was acquainted with the locality, to supervise the obstruction of the Tallahatchie River.[6]

By the beginning of March, news that the Union task force was en route down the Coldwater caused the soldiers to redouble their efforts to put the fort into a defensible condition. Loring took no chances as he ordered the placing of a wooden raft across the river. But the raft being only partially completed at the approach of the enemy, he ordered that the famous *Star of the West* be scuttled in the channel immediately behind the raft.

USS *Star of the West*

This large side-wheeler sailed with cargo and reinforcements from New York on January 5, 1861, bound for Fort Sumter in Charleston, South Carolina. The vessel reached the entrance to Charleston Harbor on January 8, and the next day began its passage towards Fort Sumter, but was fired upon by Confederate batteries on Morris Island, forcing her back out to sea. These opening shots were the first overt acts of war. The side-wheeler served the Union navy until captured by Confederates at Indianola, Texas, in April, 1861. Renamed the *St. Philip*[7] in the Confederate navy, the vessel was used as a receiving ship at New Orleans. A year later, Commander D. G. Farragut, with a fleet of Union wooden and mortar boats, succeeded in passing rebel forts protecting New Orleans, forcing the *St. Philip* and other vessels to flee up the Mississippi River to Vicksburg.

The vessel was towed up to the head of the Yazoo and then into the Tallahatchie, to the site at Fort Pemberton. Seven days before, Lieutenant A. A. Stoddard had his men drill about 250 holes in the hull of the vessel below the water line, plugging them with crude oak bungs. When

The *Star of the West (Frank Leslie's Illustrated Magazine).*

the order to sink the *Star* was given, she was eased into position abreast of the fort and moored broadside to the current. Cables were attached to trees on each bank of the Tallahatchie. When Stoddard gave the word, the crew quickly knocked out the plugs and abandoned ship. The *Star* sank to the muddy bottom of the river, thus blocking the channel and becoming an integral part of the outer defense at Greenwood.

Tilghman was informed on March 1 that some of the Federal boats had gone back to Helena, Arkansas, to bring down the fleet to pass through the breach at Yazoo Pass, now known to the Federals as Grant's Pass.[8] The following day, Tilghman learned that the Federals had two large ironclads, the *Chillicothe* and *DeKalb*, two rams, and six light-draught gunboats that had passed through Grant's Pass on to Moon Lake and were ready to enter the cut into the Coldwater.[9] The message "The tug has passed into the Coldwater and returned; intention is to bring gunboats through evident" was next wired to Tilghman.[10]

In addition to the gunboats, 5,000 Federal forces were on Moon Lake on twelve transports. They were transporting Brigadier General L. F. Ross, with a division of General J. A. McClernand's corps from Helena, and the 12th and 17th Missouri of Sherman's corps.[11] Lieutenant Commander W. Smith, in charge of the Union flotilla, was becoming distressed. Moving with the river's current, the ten-boat task force, plus the twelve transports, took three and a half days to move over Moon Lake to the Coldwater. This 250-mile water junket was going to take longer than planned. However, once in the Coldwater River, Smith found that the heavy March rains brought strong currents, and the convoy found it difficult to maneuver the abrupt turns in the winding river; steering the ironclads in swift currents was very difficult. The riverbanks and lowlands were under water and the dense and tangled growth formed barriers on the river, delaying the convoy. At one spot, large trees reaching from bank to bank had been felled by the Confederate engineers and Negroes. The soldiers, in parties of 500 work details, debarked from the transports and worked like beavers in chopping the boughs and hauling the massive tree trunks out of the river so the transports could pass.[12] With the weather warming, there appeared the buffalo gnats, the scourge of Mississippi River living; they swarmed and drove the soldiers and horses into a frenzy from their poisonous bites.

Life aboard these Union transports, mostly on converted side-wheeler steamboats, was often likened by the boys in blue to that of an early slave ship. Jam-packed, shoulder-to-shoulder, they shared the ship with horses, mules, rifles, wagons, camp equipment, ammunition, and food, but no running water. At rest stops, the soldiers would pour ashore to relieve themselves, to pillage and plunder any fresh food they could find, such as chickens, turkeys, geese, pigs, and fresh vegetables from a nearby farm or plantation. Disease, sickness, and death prevailed. The bodies of the unfortunate soldiers who died ended up buried on the shore in unmarked graves at the next stop along the river

14

The Siege of Fort Pemberton

Cavalry scouts informed Tilghman on March 6 that the vanguard of the Union convoy was twelve miles below the confluence of the Coldwater and the Tallahatchie. "The Yankee boats are here; four of them are lying at E. V. Dickens's place, and two went below and landed at George McRaie's place."[1] Colonel McCulloch's cavalry continued to shadow the Federal convoy as it moved down the Tallahatchie. On the 10th, he wrecked the steamer *Parallet* and a barge in the river that was loaded with 3,000 bales of confiscated cotton. He set them on fire, leaving them to drift into the path of the gunboats in an effort to delay and harass the invaders as much as possible.[2] Despite McCulloch's efforts, when the Federals tied up alongside the riverbank that night, they were now only thirty-two miles above the fort. General Tilghman was ordered to take the balance of his command from Jackson and proceed to Yazoo City headquarters as rapidly as possible.[3] Arriving at Yazoo City, Tilghman requested more ammunition be sent up to Fort Pemberton in preparation for the coming siege.[4]

Two of Tilghman's communications dated March 11, 1863, show his concerns about the developing situation:

Grenada, *March* 11, 1863.

Lieutenant-General PEMBERTON:

Yours received. Am prepared. [R.] McCulloch's cavalry ordered to fall back as enemy advances to cross to south bank of Yalabusha. If Fort Pemberton is attacked, near Dugan's Ferry, order so far only embraces McCulloch's command. What do you wish as to irregular cavalry, now above

Tallahatchee River, in Panola and De Soto? Still hold one regiment ready at Dugan's [Ferry], by order of General Loring. Force here available, 942 infantry, exclusive of militia. Very short of ammunition.

LLOYD TILGHMAN.

HEADQUARTERS, Fort Pemberton, *March* 11, 1863
Lieut. Gen. J. C. PEMBERTON:

A perfectly reliable spy, who succeeded in escaping and returning to-day, gives the following information:

Two iron-clads (one of them a ram) and seven other gunboats, including one mortar-boat, and twenty-seven transports filled with men (of the number could not form correct idea), comprise what he saw of this fleet, commanded by Generals Walker and Slack and Commodore Hall. Their avowed intention is to pass Yazoo City, with a view to operate in rear of Vicksburg. Seemed to be fully apprised of our strength in Yazoo City.

W. W. LORING.
LLOYD TILGHMAN.

The Confederates inside the fort compound were not surprised at the appearance of the gunboats on March 11. They had followed the steady approach of the expedition for the last eight to ten miles as it came downstream with curling, black smoke rising high above the vast canopy of foliage shrouding the winding river. As fast as the current permitted, the large gunboat *Chillicothe* advanced, wishing to inspect the fort and its defenses, including the newly sunk *Star of the West*, and to obtain the range of the fort for their ship's cannon. As the *Chillicothe* came within range, the heavy cannon of Fort Pemberton greeted the U.S. tars with a five-gun "salute." Two shells struck hard on the turret and portside of the *Chillicothe*. Within minutes the gunboat reversed itself, moving back upriver out of harm's way until her black hulk, except for her bow, was hidden behind the trees in the bend and out of cannon range.

Federal scouts on the riverbanks reported that the rebels were seen driving their cattle and carrying gear from the fort. This convinced their officers that Loring was preparing to abandon the works. To verify this rumor, the *Chillicothe*, followed by the ironclad *Baron DeKalb* and the ram *Lioness*, floated downriver to investigate. At 4:15 P.M., the Confederate cannon reopened fire, and within seven minutes the ironclads had enough and backed out of range. Loring, an old frontier fighter, had tricked them, and they knew it.[6] In this encounter, four sailors were

14. The Seige of Fort Pemberton

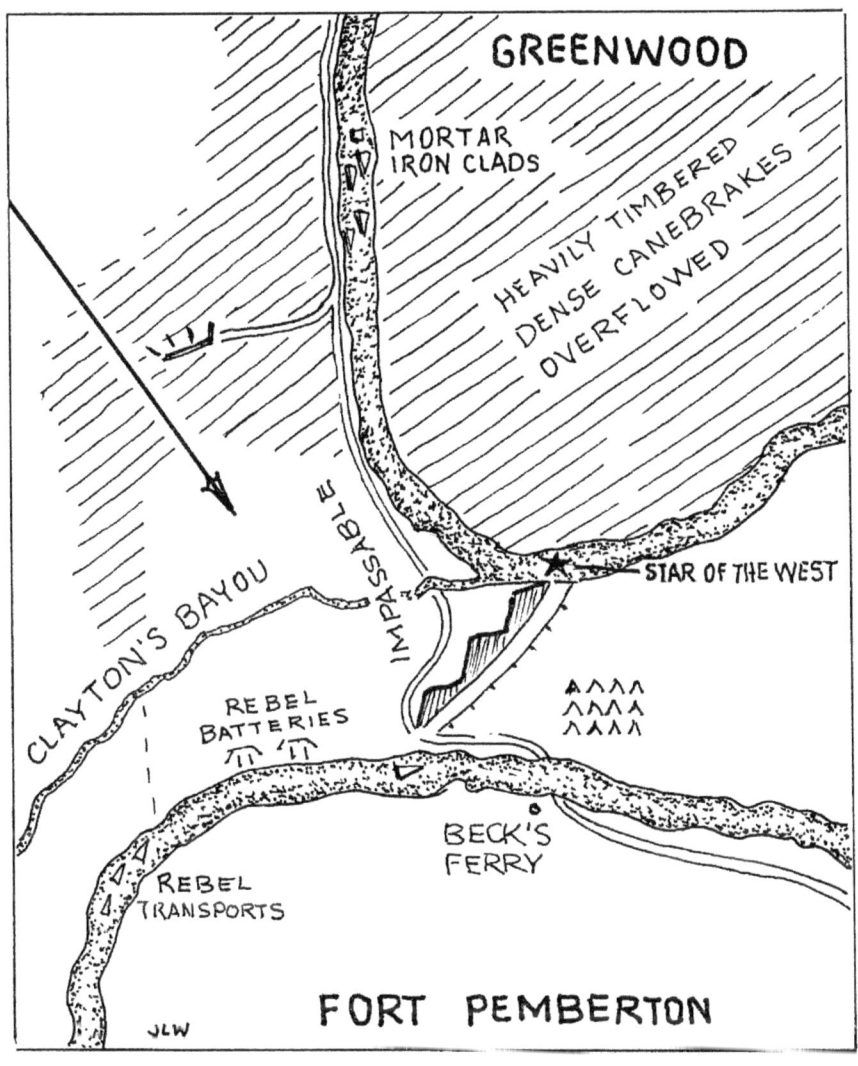

Fort Pemberton at Greenwood, Mississippi: "Cotton bales and fortitude."

killed and nine wounded on board. The heavy guns in the fort had done good service in holding the Federals at bay.

At the same time some of the Federal transports tied up at Shell Mound plantation on the right bank of the river. General L. F. Ross ordered his Indiana troops to disembark and feel out the rebel position.

But the flooded countryside prevented the Hoosiers from making much of an approach on Colonel Waul's Texans, who were in place in their main line of resistance. Frustrated and soaking wet, the bluejackets retired back onto the transports. Towards dark, the Yankees managed to land a fatigue party on the edge of the woods, about 700 yards from the fort. Here they constructed a makeshift cotton-bale battery; since the Federals had no siege guns with them, one of the 30-pound Parrotts, a rifled, muzzle-loading cannon from the Union *Rattler*, was landed and moved into the emplacement. On the 12th a second Parrott was landed, as well as a 12-pounder howitzer.[7] During this interval on the 12th, the sailors toiled away, reinforcing with bales of cotton the bows and bulwarks of the *Chillicothe*, the *Baron DeKalb*, and the mortar boat, transforming them into cotton-clad gunboats.

On the morning of the 13th, the guns of Fort Pemberton began the day's fight. By 11:25 A.M., the Federals on the water and in the land batteries returned fire on the Confederate fortifications. The *Chillicothe* remained in position until 1:03 P.M. when, after firing 54 11-inch projectiles, she withdrew to fill shells and cut fuses. While thus engaged, the ironclad was hit by 38 projectiles; six sailors were wounded, and cotton bales were ignited, but these were then extinguished. The *DeKalb* held her position and fire on the fort at 15-minute intervals. She in turn was struck six times, suffering three dead and three wounded. The 13-inch mortar vessel had lofted 49 shells into the fort during the day, exhausting its supply of 200-pound shells.[8] The cumbersome gunboats found it slow sailing through the narrow, tree-lined stretch of river. Unable to maneuver or turn about, they became sitting ducks for the Confederates, causing them to take a terrible pounding from the fort artillery. Their return fire on the fort accomplished little, as their projectiles bounced off the resilient parapet of cotton bales and earth, inflicting minor damage on the fortification.

"It was on top of these cotton bales, throughout the heaviest fighting of the day, that one-armed General Loring pranced back and forth, shouting and cursing purple oaths, his spittle flying, encouraging his men, 'Give them blizzards, boys! Give them blizzards!' And blizzards of shot and shell the Confederates gave the Yankees until they retreated back up the muddy river. Loring's future nickname, 'Old Blizzards,' was thus earned in battle."[9] Throughout the night of the 13th, Loring and Tilghman kept the men busy repairing the fort's damaged parapets. The Federal ironclads, badly crippled and needing repair, were also running out of ammunition.

The main Federal force, awaiting debarkation upriver, found the banks still overflowing; thus they were unable to land any men. The best the navy could do on the 14th was to fire the twin Parrotts of their land battery for a thirty-minute shower of shells. This same day the Confederates' eight-inch naval gun arrived by steamer from Yazoo City, and under cover of darkness on the 15th the gun was placed in the battery.

Loring repeatedly begged for more ammunition, and several of his reports stated that if he did not have enough, he would lose the engagement. This ammunition shortage kept the Confederates from opening fire on the Yanks while they were constructing their land battery. Finally Tilghman came up to the fort from Yazoo City and wired Pemberton that the ammunition for the heavy guns had just arrived.[10]

The Federals resumed their attack on the 16th. It was decided that the ironclads would close rapidly on the fort and smother the defenders under a storm of grape. But "close quarters"—the time-honored principle of gunboat warfare—did not succeed. As the *Chillicothe* closed within 1,100 yards of the fort, the Rebel gunners registered eight hits within 15 minutes, sealing both gun ports so that neither could be opened. Both the *Chillicothe* and *DeKalb* retired while the land battery pounded the Confederate fortifications. Federal sharpshooters advanced to within 450 yards of the Confederate rifle pits, but they failed to reach their targets, owing to dense woods, cane, and river overflow.

Loring and Tilghman were then informed that the steamboats carrying Union General I. F. Quinby's men, who had been ordered by General Grant to Moon Lake, had entered Grant's Pass. To slow this advance down the Coldwater, Southern sympathizers operating along the riverbanks were to build fire rafts and attempt to burn the Federal transports.

After Commander Watson Smith's humiliating failure to defeat the rebels at Fort Pemberton, he turned over his command to Commander J. P. Foster. The new naval chieftain called a council of war among the officers of his boats to decide what course of action the expedition should follow, and they later decided to remain in the vicinity of the fort until the ranking Quinby arrived. From the 16th to the 20th, the Federal infantry vainly scoured the area in an effort to discover a feasible approach by land to the fort. The sunken *Star of the West* ensured that it would be no easy task to clear the river.

Foster finally agreed to an immediate retreat. As the task force withdrew with the intention of returning to the Mississippi River, they encountered General Quinby and his division of six transports heading to the fort on March 21, forty miles below the confluence of the Coldwater and Tallahatchie. Quinby, the ranking officer under orders, deemed it best to order the force back to Fort Pemberton. After much difficulty, the boats were turned about and headed back downstream. On the 23rd the *Chillicothe* appeared and the Confederates detonated a torpedo near her bow, requiring the boat to withdraw upriver.

The aggressive Quinby established headquarters in a farmhouse and believed his men would be able to reach the Yalobusha below the fort by building a pontoon bridge, allowing a force to land south of Fort Pemberton and attack the fort from the rear. Quickly the rebels threw up new fieldworks that covered the reach of the Tallahatchie where Quinby intended to cross the river.[11]

During the Yankees' brief absence, the fort was greatly strengthened by secondary strong points that had been thrown up, and the number of defenders had been augmented by the arrival of General W. S. Featherston and Brigadier General J. C. Moore's brigades. By April 1, the fort's command exceeded 7,000 officers and men, as Major General D. H. Maury arrived from Vicksburg with his command, assigned to the Confederate left wing. On the second the fort shelled Quinby's farmhouse headquarters; his guns hardly replied, while the Federal pioneers were laboring to construct advance batteries.

Tilghman's brigade joined on the right. Using a Masonic county map of Mississippi,[12] Tilghman drew a diagram showing the position of the farmhouse where Quinby had his headquarters in the dense forest. Tilghman trained his guns by a compass while Generals Maury and Tilghman's staffs, the 37th Mississippi Infantry, the 1st Mississippi Sharpshooters, and the 2nd Texas Infantry made a reconnaissance of the position.[13] Maury could scarcely find dry land enough on which to form a line of battle for his force. Fires were ignited along the way, providing smoke so the men and mules might stand in them for some measure of protection from the swarming buffalo gnats. Maury claimed, "I lost 24 mules one night from their poisonous bites."[14] Nevertheless, at an appointed signal, Tilghman opened up with his artillery fire; the infantry and sharpshooters went to work surprising the crowded camp of Federals, scattering them in all directions as they scrambled onto their transports for protection.

Completely dejected from the beating they were taking from the fort's garrison, Quinby loaded his infantry, tents, guns, equipment, mules, and horses on board the transports. Backing up and turning one at a time, they withdrew up the river back towards Moon Lake and Grant's Pass. The two-month siege and expedition was another failure for Grant. Ordered by Loring to "hit them on their way out," detachments from the 26th Mississippi, Waul's 2nd Texas, and General J. Z. George's Mississippi State Militia posted along the Tallahatchie above the fort fired upon the retreating boats from ambush positions along the banks of the rivers.

Much of the western theater of war resembled Indian warfare; we read of skirmishing, ambushing, and sharpshooters scattering the enemy. Most of the time, the method of standing up and marching towards a designated target was abandoned because of trees, ravines, rocks, streams, rivers, earthworks, forts, and even gunboats. With this arm's length warfare, the sniper and sharpshooter were utilized by both sides and recognized as psychological weapons. Firing any rifle they chose from any position they preferred, snipers were attached to regular regiments for special deployment at a field general's order in a specific action. The 1st Arkansas Cavalry Battalion, under the command of 23-year-old Colonel Rus Stirman, was designated as Stirman's Sharpshooters — "the requirements are that no man is admitted to the regiment who does not shoot at six hundred feet, ten consecutive shots at an average of five inches from the bull's eye."[15]

Armed with Sharps rifles, Whitworth rifles, sporting arms, and custom-made, privately owned target weapons (some weighing over thirty pounds), northern and southern marksmen performed efficient service with demoralizing effects and undoubtedly killed more men than given credit for in and out of battle.[16] Oral history supplies the tidbit that neither side would fire upon a squatting form.

After the siege of Fort Pemberton, it was determined that Camp Loring, roughly a mile and a half south of the cotton bale fort, would be made into an encampment because there was still a strong Federal presence of troops arriving in the area. Colonel T. A. Mellon's 3rd Mississippi Infantry arrived, and the men diligently pitched in to transform the plantation area into a Confederate outpost, while Fort Pemberton on the river was dismantled to open up the river for traffic.[17]

Newspaper headlines and editorials constantly inquired about General Grant's movements in the western theater. A newspaper in Helena, Arkansas, offered these headlines on March 28, 1863:

THE YAZOO EXPEDITION

The Truth Concerning the Yazoo
Expedition — Gen. C. C. Washburn's
Energetic Opening of the Yazoo Pass —
Unwarrantable Delays of the Naval Force —
Criminal Negligence of the Naval
Commander — Eight Days Lost in
Consequence — Rebel Fort Built in this
Time — The Expedition Brought to a
Standstill — The Greatest Opportunity of the
Movement against Vicksburg Thrown
Away — Where the Blame Rests.

Grant made five unsuccessful attempts to reach Vicksburg, which consumed four months and numerous casualties. Despite the costly loss of manpower and time, he was slowly moving south towards Vicksburg, and though he was playing a cat-and-mouse game with Pemberton, he finally had the Confederate forces separated over a wide radius of miles, reducing the effectiveness of the rebels. Pemberton, Loring, Tilghman, and other generals were put on the defense as Grant moved units from one place to another. As the Confederates gave up control of their natural defensive posture along the Mississippi, the Federals took over the river in order to move their supplies. The Confederates, forced off the river, had to depend on haulage of all supplies by wagon over dirt roads and on three railroad trunk lines that quickly became overtaxed in attempting to supply over 60,000 troops, animals, civilians, and slaves.

15

Grierson's Raid, Port Gibson, and the Grand Gulf Collapse

On April 13 upon General Bragg's request, Pemberton ordered the brigades of Generals Rust, Buford, and Tilghman to Tullahoma, Tennessee, to bolster Bragg's army.[1]

General Grant, not discouraged by his failures over the past four months, ordered J. A. McClernand's bluejackets to open a road for his army from Milliken's Bend on the Louisiana side of the river to a point on the western bank of the river south of Vicksburg. At the same time, Grant committed Admiral Porter to run past the Vicksburg batteries with his flotilla of boats and then rendezvous with McClernand.

On April 16, a Federal procession of ironclads, cotton-clads, and barges loaded with ammunition and rations for McClernand swept past the Vicksburg defenses under the cover of darkness and arrived safely below the town. Flush with confidence, the navy continued to outrage Vicksburg defenders by sailing 12 barges and six transports downriver. Although almost every vessel was hit repeatedly by the cannon along the river, this did not stop the Yankee invaders. Admiral Porter succeeded in joining McClernand's forces on the west bank at a little village named Hard Times.

Why General Pemberton paid little attention to Federal activities across the river from Vicksburg is puzzling, since Major I. F. Harrison's Confederate cavalry had been skirmishing with McClernand's vanguard since the last day of March. Pemberton seemed undeterred by the warning from General J. S. Bowen of the enemy drive southward from Milliken's Bend.

Additional reports from Bowen continued to reach Pemberton's headquarters in Jackson on the 10th and 11th of April, telling of continued clashes between the bluejackets and Colonel F. M. Cockrell's Missourians on the Louisiana side of the Mississippi. When the hookup of Federal land forces and navy occurred at Hard Times, Pemberton abruptly countermanded his orders to Tilghman and the other brigades; Tilghman, encamped along the Mississippi Central Railroad, was directed to move his forces to Jackson.[2]

Grant devised a scheme of action and strategy to further divert Pemberton's attention from his beachhead at Hard Times. This time he called for help from his large cavalry force; he proposed a series of combined cavalry raids all over northern Mississippi that he hoped would distract Pemberton even more, forcing him to scatter his infantry reserves encamped north of Vicksburg. Cavalry rides "around the enemy" were common during the war, each side bragging how they did this and that with some success, such as Van Dorn at Holly Springs in December. The one now ordered by Grant was a gigantic affair that would, to its end, excite the whole state of Mississippi.

At dawn on April 17, Colonel B. H. Grierson, with 1,700 Federal cavalrymen and six two-pounder cannons, rode out of La Grange, near Memphis, Tennessee, and proceeded south towards Pontotoc, Mississippi. Here one regiment of horsemen went to the right, the other to the left, and Colonel Grierson, with his own regiment, moved towards the Jackson Railroad near Meridian. At Starkville on the 22nd, 500 bluejackets left Grierson's main column, riding east towards Macon and Enterprise, thus effecting another division in hopes of confusing the rebels.[3]

As Grierson's men moved south, Pemberton dispatched messages all over Mississippi hoping to prevent the escape of the cavalrymen, no matter which direction they took. So began the rapid draining away to the east of Pemberton's reserve strength, in pursuit of less than 1,000 elusive Federal cavalrymen, while Grant, across the Mississippi River, was preparing to strike him hard on the east with a force of 30,000. Grant's strategy was working, while General Pemberton, without the eyes and ears of Van Dorn's cavalry (gone to General Bragg), was hurting badly for communications.

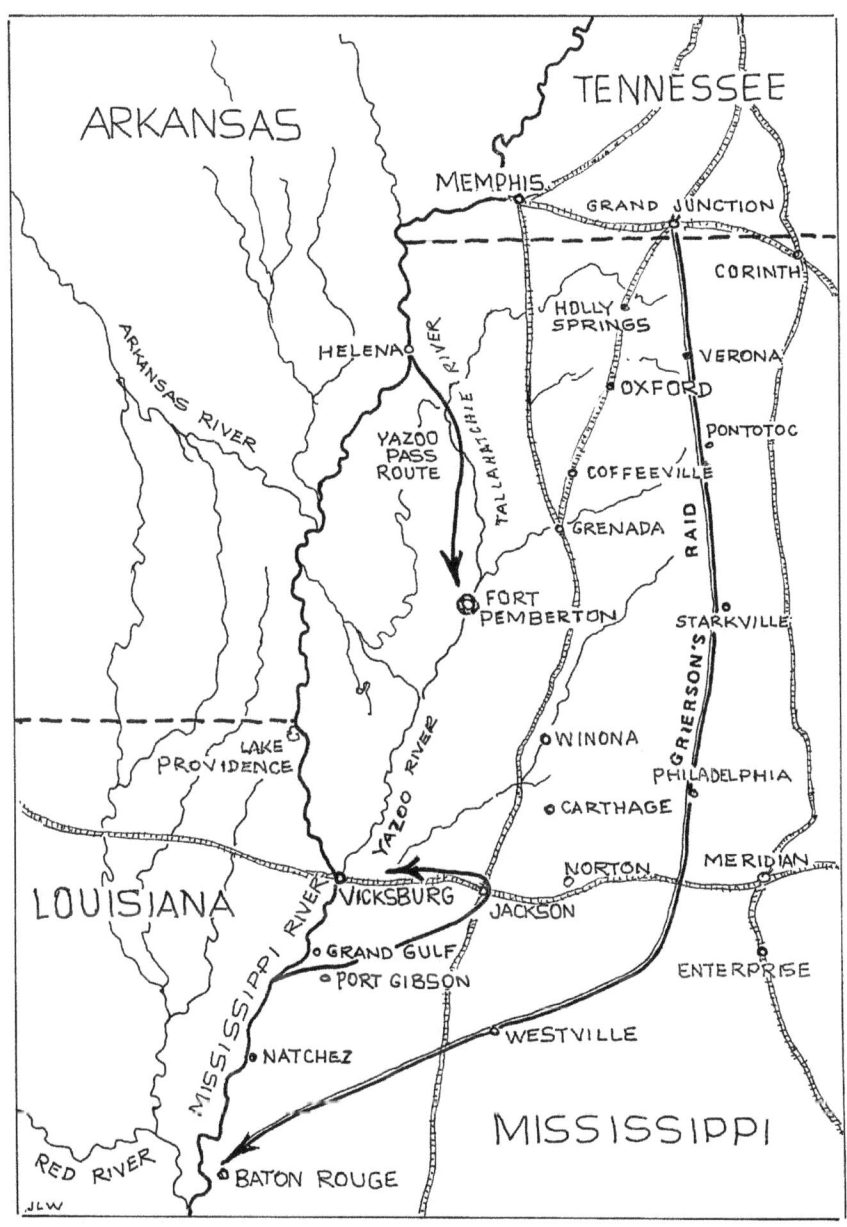

Grierson's riad. In one of the most brilliant Union cavalry exploits, Col. Benjamin H. Grierson's horsemen rode through the heart of the Mississippi — six hundred miles in 16 days — to divert Gen. Pemberton's attention from Grant's movement towards Vicksburg. In futile efforts to halt Grierson's escapades, Pemberton wore down and scattered his strategic forces.

Pemberton, not realizing at the time there was more than one column of Federal cavalry, devised a multi-jawed trap for Colonel Grierson that he thought would close in and capture the invader. He dispatched Loring to Meridian to command all troops in the vicinity, to try to contain Grierson's movement. Likewise, Colonel J. Adams, with three infantry regiments, was sent to Morton to prevent Grierson from making a move on the capital at Jackson. Next he ordered Tilghman, who had moved to Canton, to have his force put in readiness to move to Winona, 60 miles north of Canton, to block any retreat by Grierson towards the northwest.[4]

Pemberton was fairly confident he now had the Yankee cavalry cornered. To tighten the noose, Pemberton ordered Tilghman to send one-half of his command to Carthage. On April 24, Tilghman wired Pemberton: "Messenger from Carthage again reports a regiment of cavalry approaching that place. I have started Fifty-fourth Alabama and section of artillery, with orders to move rapidly. I have Eighth Kentucky, about 100 strong, and a section. Might effect something if I had more force. Please send it if practicable. I need a few cavalry."[5] On the 25th, a courier from Carthage reported to Tilghman that 700 Union cavalry were at Philadelphia the day before. This was southeast of Starkville, which meant the Union force had slipped Pemberton's trap. On this same day, Loring informed Pemberton that the enemy was raiding the Mobile & Ohio Railroad at Enterprise, demanding the surrender of the town. "Enemy appeared here at 1 o'clock and demanded the town. They were represented as 1,500 strong. Col. Goodwin was here with the Thirty-fifth Alabama, who defied them. We are now on the road pursuing them. They are on the road to Paulding; think they will endeavor to go back and make their way to Baton Rouge." Old Blizzards Loring, who by now was pretty well disgusted with the wild goose chase, closed his wire with: "I have no hope of catching them on foot."[6]

Since the Confederates were unable to defend every railroad station on the road with infantry, Grierson's columns struck at will in breaking up the railroad and cutting the telegraph. Moving southward, the young warriors smashed the vital Southern Railroad at Newton, then rejoined Colonel Forbes's brigade at the crossing of the Pearl River and reentered Union lines on May 2 at Baton Rouge, Louisiana. Traveling 600 miles in 16 days and living off the land, Grierson's fast-moving mounts had

15. Grierson's Raid, Port Gibson, and the Grand Gulf Collapse

simultaneously cut through the center of the state and wreaked havoc on Confederate communications, destroying vital military material and spreading the Confederate brigades all over the state. In his futile attempt to destroy or trap Colonel Grierson, Pemberton had worn down his weary and scattered strategic reserves. Colonel Grierson was rewarded for his raid, being promoted to brigadier general on June 3.[7]

The Union strategy of deception and diversion continued. Sherman's forces moved northeast of Vicksburg on April 29 and 30, heading up the Yazoo River to make a demonstration against Confederate works at Haines Bluff and Drumgauld's Bluff, diverting the attention of General C. L. Stevenson, who was defending Vicksburg. On dry roads, McClernand's army marched south on the Louisiana side of the river, and by the 28th his advance corps reached the hamlet of Hard Times, Louisiana. He was now south of Vicksburg, opposite Grand Gulf, waiting for the balance of his land forces. As soon as the Federal flotilla arrived, the Union men began ferrying across the Mississippi River to Bruinsburg, six miles away on the eastern shore. The largest amphibious invasion since the Mexican War was beginning. A worried Pemberton wired General Joe Johnston at Tullahoma. Johnston replied by wire: "If Grant's army lands on this side of the river, the safety of Mississippi depends on beating it. For that object you should unite your whole force."[8]

Pemberton repeatedly requested General Bragg at Tullahoma to return Van Dorn's cavalry to him, but was repeatedly turned down.[9] Pemberton turned to General Taylor across the river in Louisiana for reinforcements, but only a token force of cavalry ever appeared.

When it seemed probable that the Yankees would succeed in opening a navigable canal or cut a road across the peninsula opposite Vicksburg, avoiding the batteries established there, Pemberton directed that Grand Gulf on the river south of Vicksburg should be occupied and as many heavy guns placed in position as could be without weakening the defenses of Vicksburg too much. Grand Gulf was not selected as a position for defense but for the protection of the mouth of the Big Black River, the back door to Vicksburg. The necessary works were constructed by General J. S. Bowen. The army's sustenance came necessarily from Vicksburg, 40 miles away and connected by a dirt road, or Jackson, 45 miles away.[10]

Up to this time Grant's intentions had been to secure Grand Gulf as a base for his supplies, detach McClernand's corps downriver to General N. P. Banks, and cooperate with him in reduction and capture of Port Hudson. Grant heard from Banks, who at the time was on the Red River acting in concert with Farragut's and Porter's fleet to control the entrance to the Mississippi. If he waited for General Banks's cooperation, Grant knew he would lose a month's time, in which Grant was sure Pemberton would strengthen his defenses around Grand Gulf. Banks, unable to communicate directly on a day-to-day basis, knew nothing of the northern army's movement. There was no telegraph as yet; for the Yanks, communication was pretty much a one-man express by land or a slow trip by boat on the Mississippi. A round-trip message could take several weeks, providing the messenger could stay clear of rebel home guard and spies. Under these conditions, all cooperation between Banks and Grant was virtually impossible; it was inevitable that Banks could not assist Grant at Vicksburg. Moreover, Pemberton was faced with a split department. General Franklin Gardner at Port Hudson, Louisiana, with 7,000 Confederates, was rendered useless to Pemberton at Vicksburg. He could not draw on their strength since they would shortly be under siege by Banks's forces as they moved north towards Vicksburg. Pemberton's situation to a great degree resembled that of the late General Sidney Johnston in that the land area of the department was too much for one commander.

Against the advice of his subordinates and in violation of his orders to join Banks at Port Hudson, Grant decided to cut loose from his supply base at Grand Gulf, to feed his troops on what they could carry in their haversacks and what they might pilfer along the way. Unencumbered by heavy supply wagons and moving with all possible speed to keep the rebel troops separated as much as possible, Grant began his move in the direction of the state capital, Jackson. At the capital, Governor John Pettus began moving the state archives. Staff, state records, and all valuable stores were sent to northeastern Mississippi to establish the state government in exile at Columbus, Mississippi.

On the 30th, a desperate Bowen at Grand Gulf, situated in the thick of the Federal invasion, was faced with two Union corps coming ashore at Bruinsburg and marching overland towards Port Gibson, a crossroad village ten miles east of the Big Black. He dashed off a wire to Pemberton to hurry up some reinforcements. On short notice, General E. D.

15. Grierson's Raid, Port Gibson, and the Grand Gulf Collapse

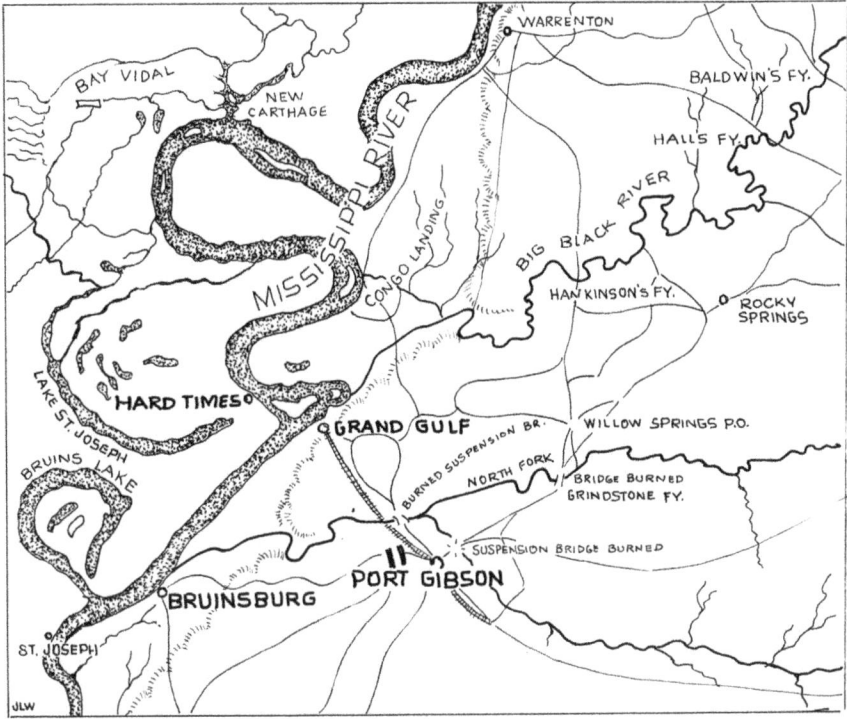

Grand Gulf and Port Gibson. Two forts — Fort Wade and Fort Cobun — guarded Grand Gulf. The Union invaders moved down the west bank of the Mississippi River, crossed over to Bruinsburg, and moved on Port Gibson. The battle for Vicksburg was beginning.

Tracy's forces tramped out of their camp at Warrenton and marched 27 hours nonstop to join Bowen. Likewise, General W. E. Baldwin's brigade, north of Vicksburg, marched all the way to Port Gibson over a dirt road to join the other assembling rebel forces.

After establishing their beachhead at Bruinsburg, McClernand's 13th Corps came ashore closely followed by the divisions of J. B. McPherson and J. A. Logan, presenting a Federal front of 22,000 bluecoats moving on Port Gibson. On May 1, after an afternoon of severe fighting, Bowen had to withdraw from the field and give ground to McClernand's overwhelming forces. In the battle, General Tracy was one of 272 casualties sustained by his 1,500-man brigade. He "fell near the front line, pierced through the breast, and instantly died without uttering a word."[11]

In the same time frame, Pemberton ordered Tilghman to take his field battery and troops via railroad to the Big Black River Bridge at Vicksburg and assume command of the troops in the vicinity. On his arrival, Tilghman wired Pemberton that he had an effective aggregate of 1,550 men.[12] Then a bevy of orders to Loring from Pemberton: "You will proceed at once to Port Gibson with Tilghman's two regiments, your troops from Jackson to come via Vicksburg. You will take command of operations there. General Tilghman will be placed in command of Tracy's brigade, and his own regiments there."[13] Loring ordered Tilghman's two regiments and field battery to be withdrawn from Big Black Bridge and as rapidly as possible to move to Grindstone Ford, and hold at all hazards, to prevent the Federals from flanking Bowen's force.[14] More orders to Tilghman from Pemberton: "Hurry on your two regiments as rapidly as possible; wait yourself for Loring ... take no artillery and send your two regiments with greatest dispatch to Grand Gulf by the dirt road. Loring will bring the Pointe Coupee Artillery from Jackson." Next a countermand: "Do not march by Grand Gulf, but go the most direct route to Port Gibson."[15]

A dutiful Pemberton wired Richmond: "Unless very large reinforcements are sent here, I think Port Hudson and Grand Gulf should be evacuated. I will require at least 6,000 cavalry to prevent heavy raids and to keep railroad communications on which our supplies depend."[16] The Richmond authorities promised heavy reinforcements would be sent from General Beauregard's department; the Creole could spare only two brigades, totaling 5,000 men. General Joe Johnston sent word that Forrest was moving west with his cavalry.[17] With the overused and patched southern railroad system of lines, reinforcements coming from the east would take at least two weeks or longer. In the interim Pemberton had to begin switching infantry units from one location to another in hopes of containing the Federal advance so that he could hold Vicksburg until the reinforcements arrived.

General Bowen continued an attempt to maintain his position below Bayou Pierre. On May 2 he was relieved to see Generals Loring and Tilghman come riding into camp. His hope was for sufficient Confederate forces to defend the area. This thought came to naught when he discovered the two generals brought only an additional 3,500 butternuts. At midnight, Bowen, with the approval of the other generals, issued marching orders to quickly abandon their positions and begin a retrograde to the Hankinson Ferry crossing of the Big Black. Once everything of military value in Grand Gulf had been destroyed, the Confederates were on the road, now under the command of Loring. The long column of weary rebels reached the flatboat bridge on the 3rd of May, began crossing Big Black, and by midafternoon the soldiers, animals, baggage, ammunition, and supply train had crossed the river. A formidable rear guard of Tilghman, A. E. Reynolds, and F. M. Cockrell's units harassed the advancing Federal cavalry. Once everyone was over the Big Black, Loring wired Pemberton: "The troops are prostrated by constant marching and want of sleep."[18] The Confederates were west of the river, moving towards Mount Alban, then Bovina. By 10:00 P.M., the rear of the vanguard passed through Mount Alban, followed by Tilghman and the rear guard five to six miles behind the main column. Earlier, Tilghman's brigade held the Federals in check on the road from Grindstone Ford to Hankinson's Ferry.[19]

Admiral Porter's gunboats took possession of Grand Gulf on May 3, opening the Big Black to the Union navy. Loring reported to Pemberton that the enemy was now at Hankinson's Ferry with pontoons, preparing to cross the river. Grant, knowing that Confederate reinforcements were being assembled at Jackson, avoided the error of moving straight on to Vicksburg without first defeating the Confederate forces in the field that could come to Pemberton's assistance; thus his move on Jackson, separating the wings of Pemberton's forces. Grant established his base of supplies at Grand Gulf while the Federal forces remained three days in bivouac at Willow Springs and Hankinson's Ferry, awaiting the arrival of General Sherman's corps from north of Vicksburg, via the Mississippi River.

Loring's forces and large supply train withdrew from their proximity to the Hankinson's Ferry on May 4, establishing headquarters three miles south of Mount Alban on the Baldwin Ferry-Mount Alban Road, west of the Big Black River, with headquarters at N. B. Lanier's plantation.[20] Loring's line of defense at this time fronted on the Big Black and was scattered over a six-mile distance from Baldwin's Ferry, where Tilghman was anchored, to General C. L. Stevenson's line on Hall's Ferry Road. In between were 6,500 fatigued rebels.

At the capital, General Adams and Governor John J. Pettus were doing their best to arm the city. A few days earlier, a concerned President Davis wired General Joe Johnston at Tullahoma to proceed at once to Mississippi and take chief command of the forces, giving to those in the field, as far as practicable, the encouragement and benefit of his personal direction. As soon as General Sherman crossed the river at Hard Times on May 7, the invading Federal forces numbered about 45,000 soldiers. As mentioned previously, Grant's first intention was to establish his forces on the eastern side of the Mississippi and detach a corps south to cooperate with General Banks in Louisiana in reducing the Confederate bastion at Port Hudson.

The center Union wing, under Sherman, headed for Bolton Station; the right wing, under General "Birdseye" McPherson, was directed towards the village of Raymond; and the left wing, under McClernand, began marching up the eastern bank of the Big Black, threatening Tilghman and Loring at Edward Depot. Tilghman reported he saw plainly about 60 Federal cavalrymen on the opposite bank of the Big Black, moving towards Edwards Ferry. "The man at the ferry says the enemy stated their number to be 4,000 to 5,000, all cavalry, bound for Edwards Depot."[21]

Yankee General McClernand's corps, 11 miles west of the village of Raymond, made contact with Loring's outposts guarding the crossings of Fourteen Mile Creek. Sharp skirmishing ensued as the Federals drove Loring's picket back across the creek. Generals Loring and Tilghman were now confronting Major General John A. McClernand, a political appointee whose military career had become a thorn in the side of General Grant's Vicksburg expedition.[22]

President Lincoln, in order to spur support for his war effort throughout the Midwest, appointed McClernand a general for his recruiting abilities. Given charge of a division, McClernand took part in the advance against General Tilghman at Fort Henry, but his infantry arrived too late to assist the naval force in its victory. Marching overland, his division moved against Fort Donelson, where he launched a premature attack that General Grant criticized as reckless.[23] Despite the censure, McClernand credited himself with the Fort Donelson victory.[24]

Later he recruited forces in Illinois, Indiana, and Iowa for planned operations against Vicksburg, Mississippi, a plan approved by President Lincoln.[25] As his new recruits arrived at Memphis, Tennessee, General

Grant appropriated them for General Sherman's sortie on Vicksburg, which went poorly. McClernand reclaimed his corps, leading them up the Mississippi River and a victory at Arkansas Post, Arkansas, in January 1863. A sour General Grant labeled the advance as a wild goose chase, only to learn that General Sherman had approved the planned attack.[26]

Thereafter there was little love or cooperation from McClernand, as he had no use for West Pointers such as Grant, Sherman, or McPherson.[27] Upon returning from Arkansas, General Grant claimed control of the Federal army, placing the outraged McClernand in command of one of the three army corps. The general's 15 minutes of fame occurred at Arkansas Post, and misfortune or General Grant seemed to find him for the balance of the war.

For the present, General Grant ordered McClernand to disengage his advance and contain Tilghman's and Loring's brigades along the Big Black, hoping to confuse Pemberton as to the whereabouts of the bluejackets.

16

Champion Hill

Rather than march north on Vicksburg, Grant directed his army in a northeasterly direction in order to cut the rail line that connected the hill city, Vicksburg, with Jackson, and cut the Confederate garrison off from supplies and reinforcements. In a 17-day period which is often referred to as the "blitzkrieg of the Vicksburg campaign," Grant's army marched more than 200 miles and overcame Confederate resistance in five battles. The first battle had occurred at Port Gibson and Grand Gulf in early May, the second at Raymond on May 12, and the third on May 14 when the Union army captured Jackson, the capital of Mississippi. Not wishing to waste combat troops on occupation, Grant and Sherman neutralized Jackson with the torch, then turned west toward the objective — Vicksburg.

En route from Jackson to Vicksburg, his force inflicted devastating casualties on the Confederate army commanded by Lieutenant General John C. Pemberton at the Battle of Champion Hill on May 16. On the following day, May 17, Grant soundly defeated Confederate forces in a battle at the Big Black River Bridge, hurling Pemberton's army into the defenses of Vicksburg.[1]

General Pemberton moved his headquarters to Vicksburg. It was a safe place to be, defended by a continuous line of trenches and rifle pits that formed a huge semicircle around Vicksburg. The flanks rested on the Mississippi River, above and below the city, and had nine major forts with 172 big guns. Major Samuel Lockett, chief engineer of the department, was responsible for its improved image.

President Davis warned Pemberton not to be trapped in Vicksburg and not to permit a siege. The problem Pemberton was facing was the same problem as at Fort Donelson — too many autonomous generals.

16. Champion Hill

Besides orders from President Davis and General Bragg, there was General Joe Johnston and his strategy, plus ideas from his roster of generals: W. W. Loring, Lloyd Tilghman, Abraham Buford, Winfield S. Featherston, Carter L. Stevenson, Seth M. Barton, Stephen D. Lee, Alfred Cumming, John S. Bowen, Martin E. Green, John Gregg, W. H. T. Walker, and others at Port Hudson, Louisiana. Pemberton's claim to fame was about to be tested.

> Headquarters Loring's Division
> Near Lanier's, Baldwin's Ferry Road.   May 9, 1863
>
> Major R. W. Memminger,
> Assistant Adjutant-General:
> ... The enemy are reported fortifying positions along the road leading to the railroad and toward Jackson. They will not attempt to pass the Big Black or move upon the railroad until this is done. Is it not, then, our policy to take the offensive before they can make themselves secure and move either way as it may suit them? ... I believe if a well-concerted plan be adopted, we can drive the enemy into the Mississippi, if it is done in time. They don't expect anything of the kind; they think we are on the defensive.
>
> W. W. LORING[2]

General McClernand informed Grant on May 11 that Loring was preparing to throw a force on their rear. On May 12, a sharp skirmish ensued between Loring's forces and McClernand's 13th Corps. Accordingly, Grant ordered McClernand to disengage his force along Fourteen Mile Creek.

Simultaneously on May 12, Union General McPherson's advance skirmish line, moving towards Jackson, encountered 5,000 grayclads in a strong position at the village of Raymond. Pemberton was apprised of the situation: "A courier just in from Raymond talked with General Gregg on the battlefield. His troops are falling back before greatly superior numbers; General Walker is within four miles of Gregg with 1,000 men and will join him."[3] Gregg and Walker, after a furious battle with Logan's division, fell back towards Jackson in hopes of finding General Joe Johnston there with promised reinforcements from the east. At the Battle of Raymond, the journey ended for Colonel Randal W. McGavock, as he was killed on May 12.

The respected Joe Johnston had been ordered west to counsel Pemberton. Departing Tullahoma, he arrived by railroad 50 miles east of

Jackson on May 13, where he received word that elements of Grant's forces were moving rapidly towards Jackson. Upon his arrival at Jackson, General Gregg told him that just 6,000 Confederates were available to defend the capital city. Johnston then wired his famous message to President Davis at Richmond: "I arrived this evening finding the enemy in force between this place and General Pemberton, cutting off our communication. I am too late!"[4]

Out of necessity Johnston decided to retreat from the capital before any pressure would be put on him to do battle, leaving Gregg behind to defend the city until the evacuation was completed. Though Gregg's and Walker's forces put up a stubborn fight during a pouring rainstorm; the Federals finally entered the city. This was the second Confederate state capital to fall since the war began, Nashville having gone in 1862. Gregg's and Walker's forces retreated on the Canton road, joining Johnston, who was ten miles north of the burning capital. Ironically, Confederate troops were on the rails to the east, and within a fortnight Johnston would have had over 20,000 reinforcements under his command. As Johnston said, he was too late to help Pemberton.

Grant's military offensive was swift and concerted as he next faced his columns west and headed for Vicksburg, leaving Sherman to burn the bridges, factories, arsenals, and government buildings in Jackson. The red-bearded Sherman did not dally in Jackson more than a day. Once the city was fired, he followed Grant to the west and camped his bummers at the town of Clinton.

General Grant's invading army, now across the Mississippi, equaled 44,000 bluecoats supported by thousands of horses, mules, and hundreds of wagons. Sherman questioned Grant about establishing a supply base for the proposed campaign. General Grant indicated that he did not contemplate supplying the army with full rations from Grand Gulf; instead, each man would be provided with two days' supply of hard bread, coffee, and salt, and the Mississippi countryside would furnish the beef, chickens, bacon, molasses, eggs, and feed for the horses and mules.

After the first two days, Yankee foraging parties became prevalent as they raided farmhouses, barns, and stripped the fields. Within a fortnight the inhabitants were devoid of their food, horses, cattle, chickens — all stolen. The city of Vicksburg went on rations in order to survive the invasion and occupation.

It was here that General Sherman learned the lesson he would apply for the next two years: live off the enemy's farms while leaving the roads and paths open for the weapons of destruction — the Federal army, its caissons, and cavalry. This policy fostered the habit of retreating Confederate forces to burn anything of value — food, barns, government buildings — in order to deny these to the Federal invaders. This sword was swung by both sides, to the detriment of the helpless inhabitants.

After Grierson's Raid and the loss of the railroad and telegraph at Jackson, Pemberton fell upon hard times, isolated and denied valuable military information. The absence of cavalry now became critical; the need for communication and cooperation between Pemberton and Johnston would be necessary for survival.

General Johnston, assembling troops near Canton, out of necessity composed written orders to Pemberton outlining plans for a proposed joint offensive upon Sherman's corps encamped at Clinton. His message: "It is important to reestablish communications. If practicable, come up on Sherman's rear at once. The troops here could cooperate; all the strength you can quickly assemble should be brought."[5] This message was made out in triplicate and handed to Captain William. S. Yerger and two other couriers. The hope was that one of them would get through to Pemberton's headquarters. Captain Yerger, by moving around McPherson's flank, delivered these instructions to Pemberton on May 14, at 9:00 A.M. At about the same time, one of the duplicates of Johnston's orders was delivered to Union General McPherson. One of the trusted southern couriers was a traitor.

In the past ten days, it had been growing unclear who was in command of the Confederate department. Newly arrived Johnston and President Davis repeatedly warned Pemberton not to surrender Vicksburg at any price, advising him not to permit a siege of the city by Federal forces. Leaving 10,000 troops in the Vicksburg vicinity, Pemberton had moved from Bovina to Edwards Depot to assume command of his field forces, when he received Johnston's order to move on Sherman bivouacked at Clinton. Pemberton sent off dispatches to his generals, alerting them to have the army ready to move forward at a moment's notice.

After these orders were dispatched, Pemberton began to have second thoughts regarding Johnston's wisdom. On reaching Edwards Depot he decided to suspend his orders of a movement forward to Clinton. He then called a council of war, expressing his negative view of the situation. Loring offered a counterproposal of "divide and conquer." The strategy envisioned a Confederate advance along the Raymond road as far as Mrs. Ellison's place. Here the army would turn south and strike the Port Gibson road, Grant's line of communication at Dillon's plantation, and the united Confederate forces would then be in a position to overwhelm and destroy Smith's isolated division at Dillon's before Federal troops, which had advanced on Jackson, could turn around and come to Smith's aid.[6] Pemberton, who wanted to sit tight and await the Federal attack, reluctantly yielded to those clamoring for battle. The badgered general adopted the plan and rejected Johnston's orders, which he considered suicidal. He then sent a messenger to Johnston informing his superior of the change of plans.

General Grant had five and a half totaling about 44,000 troops, all within ten miles of the railroad between Bolton and Edwards Station. All were within a few hours' march of each other and were located between the two principal Confederate detachments, greatly outnumbering each of them, although no more numerous than all of the Confederate detachments if combined.

On the morning of May 15, the Confederate field army consisted of three divisions totaling 23,000 in strength. There were close to 11,000 Confederates in Vicksburg. Johnston was moving north, away from Jackson, with 12,000 men. Some of them had just been defeated in two engagements and some of them were just arriving from the east as replacements. Thus, nearly 44,000 Confederate troops, divided into three detachments, were scattered ineffectively over a territory 50 miles long and 20 miles wide. Despite this, a resolute Pemberton ordered his forces forward.

Those forces were organized as follows:

Loring's Division, Maj. Gen. William W. Loring

1st Brigade, Brig. Gen. Lloyd Tilghman, Col. A. E. Reynolds
1st Confederate Infantry Battalion, Lt. Col. G. H. Forney
6th Mississippi Infantry, Col. R. Lowry
23d Mississippi Infantry, Col. J. M. Wells
26th Mississippi Infantry, Col. A. E. Reynolds, Maj. T. F. Perker
Company C, 14th Mississippi Artillery Battalion (4 guns), Lt. J. Culbertson
Company G, 1st Mississippi Light Artillery Reg (6 guns), Capt. J. J. Cowan

2d Brigade, Brig. Gen. Abraham Buford
27th Alabama Infantry, Col. J. Jackson
35th Alabama Infantry, Col. E. Goodwin
54th Alabama Infantry, Col. A. Baker (W)
55th Alabama Infantry, Col. J. Snodgrass
9th Arkansas Infantry, Col. I. L. Dunlop
3d Kentucky Infantry, (4 Cos.), Maj. J. H. Bowman
7th Kentucky Infantry, Col. E. Crossland
12th Louisiana Infantry, Col. T. M. Scott
Companies A and C, Pointe Coupée Artillery
(8 guns), Capt. A. Bouanchaud

3d Brigade, Brig. Gen. Winfield S. Featherston
3d Mississippi Infantry, Col. T. A. Mellon
22d Mississippi Infantry, Col. F. Schaller
31st Mississippi Infantry, Col. J. A. Orr
33d Mississippi Infantry, Col. D. W. Hurst
1st Mississippi Sharpshooter Battalion, Maj. W. A. Rayburn
Company D, 1st Mississippi Light Artillery Reg (4 guns), Capt. J. L. Wofford

In marching order of the Confederate field army, the artillery and ambulances followed in the rear of each brigade of men; the ordnance wagons followed in the rear of the division, while the supply wagons followed in the rear of the train. Thousands of horses and mules were employed to pull the entire train, which was two and a half miles long. Colonel Adams's cavalry formed the advance guard and rode out at least one mile ahead of the snakelike column. Following Adams was Loring's division with Tilghman; next Bowen's division constituted the center. Stevenson's division constituted the rear of the column.

Geography determined how people traveled: roads, foot and horse trails, Indian paths, all with endless zig and zag. Vicksburg was the end of such a collection of roads, paths, railroads, and rivers. This day the Confederate army would experience the vicissitude of misfortune—tomorrow, the dilemma of entrapment.

Continuing spring rains had made Baker's Creek impassable by the ordinary ford on the main Raymond road where the country bridge had been washed away. The long, winding Confederate columns had to detour onto the Clinton road, where there was a good bridge for crossing Baker's Creek. Once over, the long snaking columns of men, beasts, wagons, and ambulances traveled a mile and a half to Champion Hill,

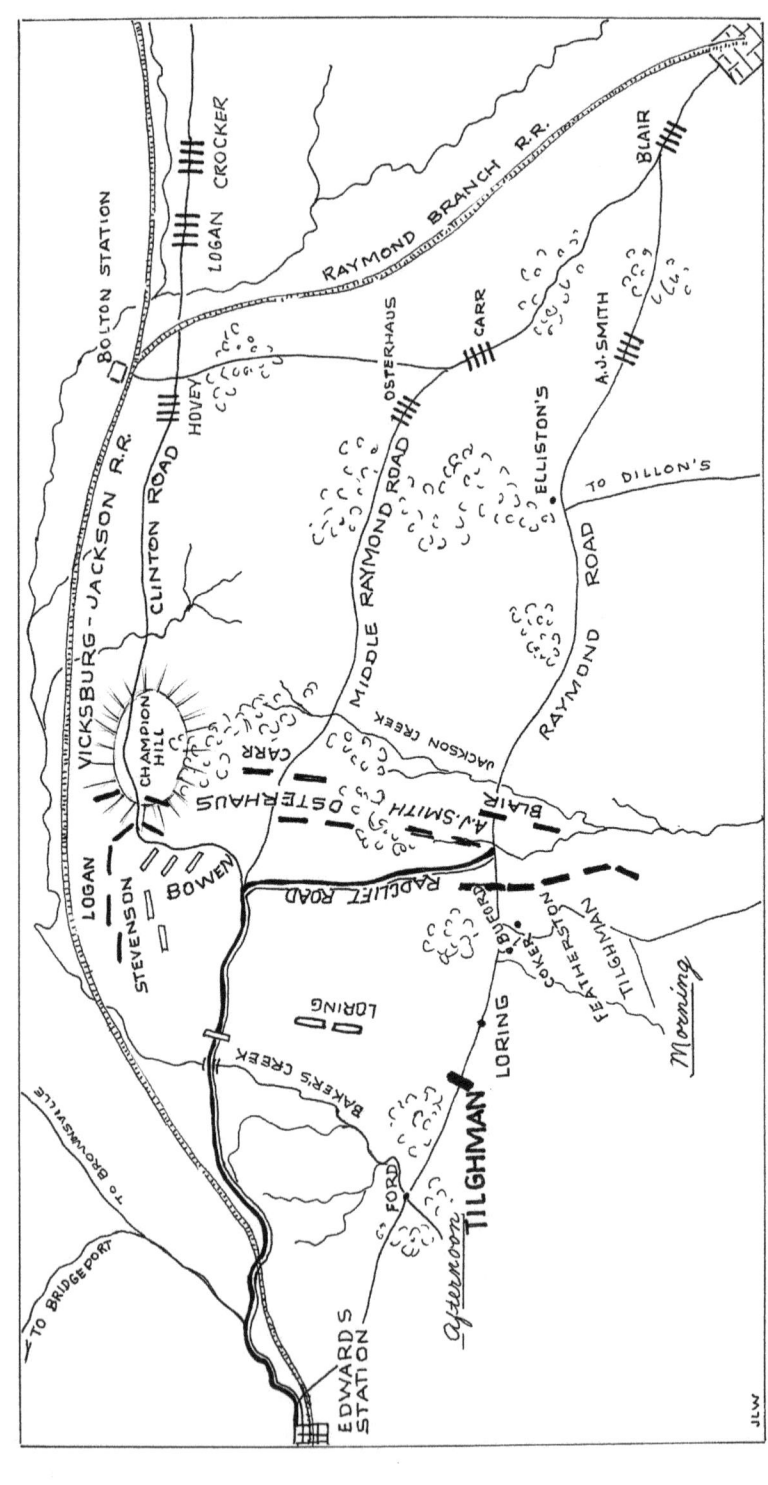

then over a portion of the plantation of Sid and Mary Champion. The Champions had constructed their home slightly northeast of the prominence of the hill; an important early road connecting the state capital, Jackson, and the river-city, Vicksburg, passed by the foot of the hill. Here the army turned right on Radclift Road, a neighborhood road, so as to strike back towards the main Raymond road. This was a narrow, dirt country road hedged on either side by dense woods.

The serpentine procession of men, animals, and wagons continued on the Radclift Road until the front end of the train, led by Loring and Tilghman, came back to the main Raymond road, where they turned left and continued to the Ellison house. There the Loring and Tilghman forces bivouacked for the night of the 15th.[7] At the same time, Grant's bluecoats were in close supporting distance of one another, between Bolton and Raymond. They were also bivouacked for the night.

During the day, Pemberton's messenger managed to get around tight Federal pickets and arrive at Johnston's headquarters at Canton with Pemberton's message. Johnston was distressed at Pemberton's change of mind, as his plan moved his forces away from Clinton, thereby increasing the distance between the two Confederate commands. Johnston repeated his order, "Your dispatch of yesterday received, your plan impracticable. The only mode by which we can unite is by your moving directly to Clinton." At 6:30 A.M. on May 16, Pemberton received this order from Johnston, reiterating his command to move north of the railroad so that he could form a junction of the two forces. He further told Pemberton his move southward against Grant would have to be abandoned.

Pemberton realized from the slow and poor movement of the previous day that the Loring plan had degenerated and decided he would obey Johnston's latest order. Without consulting his council of generals, Pemberton at once gave instructions to reverse the march and to turn around and get back across Baker's Creek. This change of orders early on the 16th brought on wholesale confusion among the brigades. The tail of the army, resting partially on the Clinton road, now would become the head of the army, while the head of the army resting on the Raymond road, the Loring and Tilghman forces, would become the tail of the army. It would require a day to reverse the army on this narrow road. Pemberton's field

Opposite: **Confederate line of march—Champion Hill, May 16, 1863.**

army was boxed into a frightful predicament. By sunrise it became evident that some Confederate forces had come into close proximity with the advancing Federal forces, and the bluecoats on the Raymond road had begun skirmishing with Loring's advance mounted infantry at the Ellison place. There would be no marching to join Johnston.

Prior to Pemberton's countermarch orders, Tilghman unexpectedly received orders from Pemberton's headquarters early that morning, relieving him of his command and directing the senior colonel of the brigade to take command. An exact or plausible reason has never been found for this order, except that throughout the spring Tilghman had the misfortune to incur the displeasure of General Pemberton.

There had been an episode the evening before, at Loring's headquarters at the Ellison house. Lieutenant Drennen of General Featherston's staff wrote to his wife: "I sat down under a tree and listened to Generals Loring, Tilghman and Featherston engage in quite an animated conversation, the principal topic being General Pemberton and the affairs of the country in general. They all said harsh, ill-natured things, made ill-tempered jests in regard to Genrl. Pemberton and when an order came from him, the courier who brought it was not out of hearing, before they made light of it and ridiculed the plan he proposed."[8]

Lieutenant Merrin wrote: "Here was a pretty kettle of fish. The whole army right close up, face to face, with Grant's army, twice or three times as strong, and our officers are all in a stew!" He continued: "General Loring who acted as a breakwater between the two on past occasions, now again cut the Gordian knot. This one-armed general rode squarely up to the pompous Pemberton and in language more forcible than elegant, more caustic than clever, informed Pemberton that unless he then and there revoked the order of the day before in reference to Tilghman, that he might dispense with his [Loring's] service for the day's battle. Then and there an order was hastily written by Pemberton on the pommel of his saddle, restoring General Tilghman to his command."[9]

Mary Champion, her four children, and a handful of loyal ex-slaves had remained on the land while Sid had volunteered for Confederate service with the 28th Regiment Mississippi Cavalry. There had been an unusual increase in military activity in the area for the past several days, and she had to act quickly as two great, opposing armies converged on each other with the Champion place square in the middle of it all.

Throughout the predawn darkness of May 16 she hurriedly gathered and packed those one-of-a-kind articles that families accumulate over the years. There was very little space in the wagon and carriage and no time to save everything. She was up at daylight getting her carriage and wagon loaded for the trip to her father's house in Madison County. As she was departing, a Union officer rode up and ordered her to leave due to the impending battle. He could have saved his breath, for she was already whipping her team. The conveyances groaned under the weight of their cargoes as the small group of refugees headed eastward. When she reached Bolton, some four miles distant, she could already hear cannon fire.[10]

The battle line at Champion Hill lacked any evidence of a connected line of defense. No earthen levy had been erected or trenches dug; only a smattering of unsurveyed ravines and bushes separated the tides of the blue and the gray. On May 16, over 65,000 soldiers from the Union and Confederate armies converged on and inhabited a two-and-a-half-mile stretch of countryside outside Edwards Depot. The Battle of Champion Hill was imminent.

Pemberton had begun the retrograde movement back towards Edwards Depot when Colonel Adams reported that his pickets were skirmishing with the Federals off the Raymond road, some distance in front of Tilghman's forces.[11] It was early morning when Colonel Goodwin rode to the front to confer with Colonel Adams about the strength of the bluejackets. Here he found "the Federal cavalry drawn up in an open field, at intervals of 40 to 50 yards and slowly advancing, driving in the Confederate vedettes. Behind the cavalry a long battle line of Yankee infantry moving to the right."[12] This was McClernand's 17th Army Corps, which had been ordered by Grant the day before to move forward cautiously, "feeling out the enemy, but not to bring on an engagement unless he felt entirely able to contend with him."[13]

The sound of small arms and artillery fire on the Raymond road sent Pemberton and his staff scurrying and their units jockeying into a defensive posture. Pemberton initially moved Carter L. Stevenson's division to protect the left flank at the vital crossroads near Champion Hill; John S. Bowen's division positioned the center of the line, and Loring and Tilghman took the right flank on Raymond Road.[14]

Loring rode forward, reconnoitered the front himself, and ordered the Confederate line of battle be changed to a high hill on a continuous ridge some 600 yards in the rear of the line that was now established. This became known as the Coker House ridge of defense. Upon this ridge, Tilghman's artillery was advantageously posted on both sides of the Raymond road. The field to the front was entirely open as far as Mrs. Ellison's house. This new line of resistance offered the Confederates a stronger position, permitting coverage of the plantation road that could be utilized by Pemberton to shift troops from one threatened sector to another. The position fronted eastward.[15] The U.S. 10th Division, spearheaded by General Burbridge's 1st Brigade, advanced down the Raymond road and was brought up short when the vanguard reached Jackson's Creek, discovering the bridge had been destroyed by Goodwin's men. Efforts by the Union pioneers to repair the bridge were frustrated as Tilghman's artillery became active with his smoothbores, which had a range of 1,200 yards. General Burbridge's eyewitness account reveals: "I pushed my brigade rapidly ahead until the skirmishers began to find it a hot contest, as we rose to the crest of the hill the Rebels poured in a most terrific fire of shot, shell, grape, and canister. My sharpshooters kept the enemy annoyed, forcing them to abandon some of their guns. After a lively artillery duel for an hour or more, the attack was relinquished."[16] Grant again admonished McClernand to move cautiously; thus there was no advance by the Union forces posted on the Middle and Raymond roads.

Elsewhere at the Federal front that was forming, Sergeant Samuel H. M. Byers, Company B, 5th Regiment Iowa Infantry, penned: "The morning of the 16th my regiment was up and getting breakfast long before daylight. The breakfast consisted of some wet dough cooked on the ends of ramrods; nothing more. Troops were hurrying past our bivouac by daylight. Once I went out to the roadside to look about a bit. It was scarcely more than early daylight, yet cannon could occasionally be heard in the far distance, something like low thunder. As I stood watching some batteries hurrying along I noticed a general and his staff gallop through the woods, parallel with the road. They were leaping logs, brush, or whatever came in their way. It was General Grant, hurrying to the front. Shortly came the orders 'Fall in!,' and we too were hurrying along the road toward Champion Hill."[17]

The battle at Baker's Creek, another name for the Battle of Champion Hill, came together quickly. As the demonstrations of the Union army became more active, Pemberton ordered his division commanders to form in a makeshift line of battle on the crossroad from the Raymond road to the Clinton road. Shortly, the country road was likened to a one-and-a-half-mile string of fireworks; it was ignited early by Tilghman's artillery and soon spread across the countryside to the Clinton road. It let go with one big bang at 10:00 A.M. after Generals Stevenson and Stephen Lee discovered three Federal divisions were moving rapidly towards them at Champion Hill. Disaster was in the making.

Pemberton was uneasy about the swollen Baker's Creek to the rear of his forces, especially with the Raymond road bridge washed out. During the morning hours, he sent instructions to Tilghman to collect all the spades and picks he could commandeer, move some soldiers down the Raymond road to the creek, and cut down the banks of the ford, making it possible to cross over Baker's Creek. Later, Major Lockett got a pioneer company to throw up a temporary bridge across the creek.[18]

By 11:00 A.M. the engagement became a general battle raged with increasing fury as Stevenson's men were driven back with great slaughter at Champion Hill. As the engagement intensified, Pemberton ordered General Bowen, who was commanding the middle of the defense line, to send one of his brigades at once to the support of Stevenson. Neither Bowen nor Loring wished to weaken their position lest the front cave in, but Bowen complied with Pemberton's order. Bowen's departure left Loring and Tilghman alone on the Coker House ridge of defense that fooled no one, with Yankee brigades in sight. When the summons came from Pemberton for Loring to follow Bowen, Loring declined, stating it would be suicidal to move and permit McClernand to begin his offense. But he did close the gap somewhat by moving General Abe Buford and his 2nd Brigade towards Bowen.[19]

Subsequently, after much badgering from Pemberton's subordinate officers with verbal orders to move, Loring, at wits' end, took General Featherston's brigade with him, leaving Tilghman's single brigade alone on the Raymond road to cover the right and center of the original Confederate line, a position previously held by five brigades.[20]

Tilghman's brigade began following Loring's lead to the left, when they were met by Major Lockett, who had been directed by Pemberton to inform General Tilghman "that the position he occupied was one of vast importance in securing a Confederate retreat, and that he must hold the Raymond road at all hazard."[21] At this order, Tilghman halted his command and, facing about, returned to the Raymond road, taking a new position on a ridge some six hundred yards in rear of his first position, just in front of the crossroad known as Cotton Hill. Here, Captain Cowan's battery, 1st Mississippi Light Artillery, and Colonel Wither's regiment of artillery, straddled the same road.

As the afternoon battle continued, the pressure upon Stevenson's and Bowen's forces at the northeast end of the battle line mounted, and when Logan added the weight of his division to the Yanks' cause, the line at Champion Hill became unsupportable. A private of the 3rd Mississippi Regiment reported, "We made it to Champion Hill, with the rest of the division followin' close behind with General Lorin' leadin' from his mount. The old seasoned trooper we called 'im 'Old Gizzards,' and he rode stiff and proud like someone out of a crusader's army in the old days."[22] As southern forces attempted a breakout through the encircling Union army, the roar of thousands of muskets and artillery fire filled the air. The same private tells us in detail, "Then we saw 'em runnin' back to our main line. Then they came, in the thousands. Over their heads came the shells blastin' all about us. The Blue line wuz seen comin' from the south. They wuz coming a double quick, bayonets fixed. We unload at their cavalry and infantry, sendin' 'em rollin' back on their first charge. They kept coming for more 'n hour."[23]

Pemberton, with heightened anticipation and awareness of the circumstances, and uncertainty of continuing the battle, called for a general retreat towards Vicksburg. At this order, bedlam broke out as the soldiers looked for ways to cross Baker's Creek. Acute fear became contagious. Some went over the Clinton road bridge and others swam across. By midafternoon the Jackson Road crossing was closed, leaving the Confederates on Loring's end of the line the Raymond road makeshift bridge as the last avenue of escape. About 3:00 P.M., Loring began withdrawing his division from the battlefield. He rode up to Captain Cowan's battery, which had come to the field at Baker's Creek with Tilghman's brigade, and said, "I intend to save my Division, as I have been cut off by the defeat of General Stevenson. I want your Battery to hold this position until sundown, fall back, and follow my line of retreat."[24] Old Blizzards was not going to follow Pemberton into Vicksburg; instead he found another way out of the dilemma.

General Grant ordered McClernand's fresh forces to take charge of the pursuit. Many things happened coincidentally or in succession. Union General Carr's division, taking the advance along with Lindsey's and Burbridge's brigades, took possession of the ridge Tilghman had abandoned on his move towards Loring, who was now occupying the Coker House position. Irishman Pat White and his Chicago Mercantile Battery went into position with six 10-pound Parrott guns; Cowan had four six-pound guns, and two 10-pound howitzers. The Federal battery began firing accurately, assaulting Tilghman's and Cowan's batteries that were defending the lone Confederate escape route over Baker's Creek. By inspiration and personal courage, Tilghman's and Cowan's batteries, in a woefully undermanned position on Cotton Hill, kept the Federals from charging, while the Raymond road filled up with men in gray fleeing for their freedom, with horses, artillery, and ambulances moving in every direction. After the war, White recalled, "It was one of the hottest artillery fights I was ever in. I was deaf and dazed from the bursting of shells; I could hardly hear myself give an order and one of my ears bled."[25]

A soldier relates, "Tilghman came to our position in an open field on foot at about 5:20 that evening. He was in a particularly good humor, wearing a new fatigue uniform. He ordered his son, Lloyd Tilghman, Jr. who was one of his aides-de-camp, to go with a squad of men and drive some Federal sharpshooters from a gin house on the left of the Raymond road who were annoying Wither's cannoneers."[26]

Cowan's officers were mounted, with Captain Cowan himself on a large gray horse making him a conspicuous target for the sharpshooters. Tilghman said in a pleasant manner, "I think you and your lieutenants had better dismount. They are shooting pretty close to us, and I do not know whether they are shooting at your large gray horse or my new uniform." The officers promptly obeyed and dismounted. Shell from Federal battery passed close to Tilghman while the gun was being reloaded.

Tilghman then went to one of the 12-pound Napoleons and remarked to the gunner, "I think you are shooting rather too high," and sighted the gun himself. Stepping back, he returned to a little knoll within a few feet of the gun, stood erect, and put his field glasses to his eyes, watching for the effect of the shot from the gun, when suddenly, in the fury of the battle, Tilghman suddenly careened and collapsed to the ground. A piece of an incoming exploding Parrott shell had struck Tilghman in the upper part of his stomach. The three-inch piece of solid metal passed through him, nearly cutting him in half. As he lay unconscious, soldiers raced to find his son, who was brought back to his fallen father.[27] With grief and lamentations, the son cast himself on his dying father. The soldiers who witnessed this distressing scene shed tears of sympathy for the bereaved son and of sorrow for this fallen hero, the chivalrous and beloved Tilghman. While the order "Fire rapidly at will" was given, Tilghman was carried to the shade of a tree, lived about three hours, and died in the arms of his faithful adjutant general, Powhatan Ellis. Four of his men with a litter carried off his body from the field of battle, taking it to Vicksburg for burial in the Searles City Cemetery.[28]

It was now dusk. Loring came riding down the lines of stragglers to encourage them, saying that they had been sold, but he would be damned if they should be delivered, calling on all to follow him, and taking them out of this dilemma.

Loring turned eastward and marched his men through woods and fields, arriving the next morning at Crystal Springs, a railroad station 30 miles south of Jackson. He had saved a good portion of the Confederate army from being trapped in Vicksburg. When learning of Tilghman's death, the old veteran said, "He was directed to hold the Raymond road at all hazard. It was [in] the execution of this important trust, which could not have been confided to a fitter man, that the lamented general bravely lost his life."[29] If General Tilghman had not been killed, he would have gone out with General Loring to fight another day.

General Pemberton's remaining scattered forces were forced back to Big Black Bridge; General Pemberton, for the first time in his long military career, found himself in charge of a routed army. The next day he gave orders for the army to fall back into Vicksburg fortress.

At the time Vicksburg was under siege, a similar crisis took place downriver at Port Hudson, Louisiana, at the other end of the Rebels' blockade. During the autumn of 1862, the Port Hudson garrison, like Vicksburg, was reinforced by exchanged Confederate prisoners from Forts Henry, Donelson, and Island Ten. Among these POWs was cousin Oswald Tilghman, acting adjutant in Captain Weller's company, Tennessee Light Artillery.

Major General Nathaniel P. Banks's bluecoats moved north from the Red River campaign, besieged Port Hudson in May and June, with little success, resulting in a stalemate similar to Vicksburg. Both fortifications, besieged daily by the invaders for six weeks, successfully defended every inch of their strongholds. The ultimate end for Port Hudson and Vicksburg was not Yankee guns or cannon, but starvation.

Captain Richard McClung, 15th Arkansas, relates: "We ate all the meat and bread in the fort — prepared an old railroad engine to grind corn and peas — ate all beef— ate all mules — all dogs — all of the rats around us. We were surviving on peas and parched corn when surrendered."[30]

Misfortune was everywhere. In the east, General Robert E. Lee was retreating from Gettysburg. The fame of Lieutenant General John C. Pemberton, the Philadelphia Quaker, crashed as he surrendered his command in sorrow and disgrace. Pemberton finished out the war as an obscure colonel of artillery, commanding the artillery defenses of the Confederate capital.

At Port Hudson, Major General Franklin Gardner, he too of Northern birth (New York City), was denied any claim to fame because no one remembered his name after the war. He ended up in service of the Department of East Louisiana.[31] Cousin Oswald Tilghman, also surrendered, was now a prisoner of war. He was shipped with other prisoners to Johnston's Island, Sandusky, Ohio, and incarcerated for the next 23 months, until the end of the war.[32]

Fame — her foes enough would fame thee in their hate.[33]

An abbreviated summary of this important campaign is supplied by U.S. Grant in his report. "The result of this campaign has been the defeat of the enemy in five battles outside of Vicksburg; the occupation of Jackson, the capital of the state of Mississippi, and the capture of Vicksburg July 4, and its garrison and munitions of war; a loss to the enemy of 37,000 prisoners, among who were 15 general officers; at least 10,000 killed and wounded, and among the killed Generals Tracy, Tilghman, and Green, and hundreds and perhaps thousands of stragglers who went missing and can never be collected and reorganized. Arms and munitions of war for an army of 60,000 men have fallen into our hands, besides a large amount of other public property, consisting of railroads, locomotives, cars, steamboats, cotton, and much was destroyed to prevent our capturing it."[34]

17

In the Midst of Life There Is Death

Ah! Fearless on many a day for us
They stood in front of the fray for us
And held the foeman at bay for us
And tears should fall
Fore'er o'er all
Who fell while wearing the gray for us.[1]

"Poor Tilghman," lamented Lieutenant Drennan. "Three hours before I had sat and listened to him talking and jesting—full of life and gaiety—and now he has gone to that place from whence no traveler returns." Loring's condolence for his loyal friend: "It is befitting that I should speak of the death of gallant and accomplished Lloyd Tilghman. Quick and bold in execution of his plans, he fell in the midst of his brigade that loved him well, after repelling a powerful enemy in deadly fight, struck by a cannon shot. The brigade wept over the dying hero, alike beautiful as it was touching."[2]

Colonel Reynolds, who succeeded to the command of Tilghman's brigade, paid this high tribute to the general's memory: "As a man, a soldier, and a general, he had few superiors. Always at his post, he devoted himself, day and night, to the interests of his command. Upon the battlefield, collected and observant, he commanded the respect and entire confidence of every officer and soldier under him, and the only censure ever cast upon him was that he always exposed himself too recklessly."[3]

17. In the Midst of Life There Is Death

President Jefferson Davis had these remarks about General Tilghman:

Martyrdom has generally been considered, and with reason, a fruit of the sanctity of the cause in which the martyr died. You know how many examples your army furnished of men who piously served and piously died from wounds received in battle. The proofs of martyrdom, if I were to attempt to enumerate, would exceed your time and my strength on this occasion. Yet I am not willing to pass by as silent memory some of those examples of heroism, of patriotism, of devotion to country which the Army of Tennessee furnished. The Greek who held the pass, the Roma who for a time held the bridge have been immortalized in rhyme and story. But neither of those more heroically, more patriotically, more singly served his country than did Tilghman at Fort Henry, when approached by a large army, an army which rendered the permanent defense of the fort impossible, with a handful of devoted followers went into the fort and continued the defense until his brigade could retire in safety to Fort Donelson; then when that work was finished, when it was impossible any longer to make a defense, when the wounded and dying lay all around him, he, with the surviving remnant of his little band, terminated the struggle and suffered in a manner thousands of you who have been prisoners of war know how to estimate. All peace and honor to his ashes, for he was among those, not the most unhappy, who went hence before our bitterest trials came upon us.[4]

General Tilghman's 18-year-old son, Lloyd Jr., who was with his father when the general died at Champion Hill, was himself killed on August 6, thrown from his horse while riding with Jackson's cavalry at Canton, Mississippi.[5] Because Mrs. Tilghman lived behind the enemy lines at Clarksville, Tennessee, Jackson requested Tecumseh Sherman to inform her of his death. Sherman replied, "I also according to the request, communicated to Mrs. General Tilghman, at Clarksville, the sad news of the death of her son, Lloyd."[6] After the war the Tilghman family moved to New York City. Augusta lived to the age of 79.

At Mobile Bay, Admiral Franklin Maury augmented his squadron with floating batteries that carried four heavy guns and could provide powerful support to the earthwork bay batteries. Maury named these eight floating batteries after Confederate officers who had died in the line of duty, including General Lloyd Tilghman, who died at the Battle of Champion Hill, Mississippi.[7]

On May 26, 1865, in New Orleans, Louisiana, General E. Kirby Smith's Trans-Mississippi Department was formally surrendered by General Simon Buckner. Buckner returned to Kentucky and in 1887 was elected governor of the state.

Later in Time

Sid Champion, of Champion Hill plantation, went to an early grave when his health broke from hardships he experienced as a Confederate soldier fighting for the cause. He died September 17, 1868.

Colonel Rus Stirman returned after the war to Fayetteville, graduated from University of Kentucky's law school in Lexington in 1869, and became mayor of Fayetteville in 1870. He married Mirium Gist (probably a woman of face, form and fortune, with black eyes and hair, as this was the type of woman with whom he fell in love so often in Mississippi), of New Castle, Kentucky. He and Mirium had ten children. They moved to Colorado in 1879 for Rus's health. He died there in 1914 at the age of 76.[8] He lived to see the first automobiles.

Frederick and Sidell Tilghman at the dedication of the monument honoring their father on the battlefield of Champion Hill (National Park Service).

Tilghman's Monuments and Homestead

When General Tilghman offered his life in defense of the cause of the South, he wrought with his own blood an epitaph that would not be forgotten as long as bronze statues last to remind all who see them of his courage and gallantry. In 1902, his two sons, Sidell and Frederick B. Tilghman, residents of New York City, came to Vicksburg to retrieve their father's remains. The general's remains were disinterred from Vicksburg and taken to New York City where they were reburied in Woodlawn Cemetery.

While on this mission, the two successful Wall Street businessmen selected a site for the erection of a Tilghman equestrian statue and also marked the site at Champion Hill where their father was mortally wounded.

Monument to Tilghman at the Vicksburg National Military Park. The inscription reads: BRIGADIER GENERAL LLOYD TILGHMAN C-S-A, Commanding First Brigade of Loring's Division. Killed May 16, 1863. Near the Close of Battle of Champion Hill, Mississippi (National Park Service).

In 1907, the two sons returned to Vicksburg and dedicated a monument on the location where their father was killed at Champion Hill.

On May 16, 1909, the same month and day that Tilghman was killed, his two sons, in cooperation with the Paducah Chapter of the United Daughters of the Confederacy, unveiled a fitting monument in Lang Park, Paducah, Kentucky, designed by sculptor Henry H. Kittson. In 1921, the cornerstone of the new Augusta Tilghman High School was laid; the new school is built on a site donated by Lloyd Tilghman's sons.

A marker presented by the Augusta Tilghman class of 1929 gives the details of Lloyd Tilghman's life: "Born in Maryland. Chief engineer, 1855–56, New Orleans and Jackson Railroad, first to enter Paducah. Joined Confederates July 5, 1861. Killed in battle near Vicksburg, Miss., May 16, 1863.[11]

In 1919, the Vicksburg National Military Park Commission proposed specifications for the erection and completion of a granite pedestal with an equestrian statue of General Lloyd Tilghman. The sculptor commissioned was F. William Sievers of Richmond, Virginia, and Frederick and Sidell Tilghman, his two sons, would pay for the monument. The monument was dedicated on May 19, 1926. Sidell Tilghman, now the only surviving son, made the presentation, and Governor Harry L. Whitfield delivered the acceptance at Vicksburg, Mississippi.

In 1977, Champion Hill Battlefield was designated a National Historic Landmark by the U.S. Department of the Interior.

Appendix: Staff of Brig. Gen. Lloyd Tilghman

Lloyd Tilghman (1816–63). Colonel, 3rd Kentucky Infantry Regiment. Appointed from Kentucky, Brigadier General, P. A. C. S., to rank from October 18, 1861. Killed at the Battle of Baker's Creek (Champion Hill), Mississippi, May 16, 1863.

Staff

Barbour, E. P., Lieutenant, A. D. C., December 4, 1861 to October 29, 1862.
Blakemore, William T., Lieutenant, A. A. G.
Culbertson, Jacob, Captain, C. A., A. A. I. G., October 27, 1862.
Dallam, Herbert S., Major, C. S., February 12, 1862.
Ellis, Powhatan, Jr., Captain, A. A. G., February 12, 1862.
Enbank, E. N., Captain, A. C. S., October 29, 1862.
Gerard, Louis, Lieutenant, _____, at Battle of Fort Donelson.
Halliday, E. W., Major, C. S., December 6, 1862.
Hayden, Charles, Captain, E. O., February 7, 1862.
Jones, H. L., Captain, A. Q. M., February 7, 1862.
Jones, J. Waytt, Major, post Q. M. at Fort Donelson, February 9, 1862; Staff, Q. M., October 29, 1862.
McLaughlin, John, Captain, A. Q. M., 10th Tennessee Infantry Regiment; Staff, A. A. G., February 7, 1862.
Miller, _____, Captain, E. O., February 7, 1862.
Moorman, George, Lieutenant, A. D. C., October 29 to December 6, 1862.
Sykes, Thomas B., Captain, A. A. G., January 8, 1863.
Tilghman, Lloyd, Jr., Lieutenant, V. A. D. C., October 29 to December 6, 1862.

Voorhies, A. H., Assistant Surgeon, 55th (Brown's) Tennessee Infantry Regiment; Staff, M. D., October 29, 1862.
Watts, W. O., Captain, C. O., October 29, 1862; Major, A. I. G., December 6, 1862.

Notes

Profile

1. Neuman, Fred G. *Paducans in History*, p. 35.
2. Hanna, A. J. *Flight into Oblivion, Diary of Tench F. Tilghman*, p. 257.
3. Boatner III, Mark M. *Encyclopedia of the American Revolution*, p. 1108, and *Confederate Military History, Maryland*, Vol. 2, pp. 419–420.

Chapter 1

1. Stewart Sifakis, *Who Was Who in the Civil War*, p. 648.
2. Mark M. Boatner III, *The Civil War Dictionary*, p. 501.
3. Patricia L. Faust, *Historical Times Illustrated Encyclopedia of the Civil War*, p. 469.
4. *Easton Gazette* Collection, MSA SC 2940, M11030, 1831–1836, Maryland State Archives, Joshua J. Mason, Archivist II.
5. Milton Meltzer, *Hunted Like a Wolf: the Story of the Seminole War*, pp. 109–110.
6. Neuman, Fred. *Paducans in History*, p. 37.
7. *Maryland Confederate Military History*, Vol. 2, p. 163.
8. Philip L. Phillips, The Tilghman Heritage Foundation, Inc.
9. J. Frost, L.L.D. *The Mexican War and Its Warriors*, p. 264.
10. Robert M. Utley, *Frontiersmen in Blue*, p. 34.
11. Ibid., p. 23.
12. Frost, p. 263.
13. Faust, p. 3.
14. Frost, pp. 9–12.
15. Charles M. Cummings, *Yankee Quaker Confederate General*, p. 93.
16. David Nevin, *The Old West, The Mexican War*, Time Life Books, p. 26.
17. Cummings, p. 96.
18. Frost, p. 52.
19. Ibid., p. 54.
20. Ibid., p. 61.
21. Ibid., p. 56.
22. John K. Herr and Edward S. Wallace. *The Story of the U.S. Cavalry*, p. 34.
23. Ibid., p. 35.
24. Frost, p. 330.
25. Utley, p. 84.
26. *Maryland Confederate Military History*, Vol. 2, p. 163.
27. Frost, p. 332.
28. William A. Degregorio, *The Complete Book of U.S. Presidents*, p. 231.

Chapter 2

1. *World Book*, Vol. 4, p. 505.
2. *World Book*, Vol. 15, p. 106.
3. *Ibid.*
4. James Willis, *Arkansas Confederates in the Western Theatre*, p. 285.
5. Patricia L. Faust, *Historical Times Illustrated Encyclopedia of the Civil War*, p. 156.
6. *Ibid.*, p. 294.
7. Mark M. Boatner III, *The Civil War Dictionary*, p. 857.
8. Stewart Sifakis, *Who Was Who in the Civil War*, p. 172.

Chapter 3

1. Clint Johnson, *Civil War Blunders*, p. 7.
2. *Ibid.*, p. 14,15.
3. Mark M. Boatner III, *The Civil War Dictionary*, p. 832.
4. Boatner III, p. 95, and Stewart Sifakis, *Who Was Who in the Civil War*, p. 85.
5. Allen Hall, *Center of Conflict* booklet.
6. John Robinson, *Paducah, 1830–1980*, p. 27.
7. William C. Davis, *The Cause Lost*, p. 14.
8. *Ibid.*, p. 13.
9. *Confederate Service Record of Gen. Tilghman*, O.R., Series 1, Vol. 4, p. 197.
10. John Fiske, *The Mississippi Valley in the Civil War*, p. 42.
11. Boatner III, p. 658.
12. O.R., Series 1, Vol. 4, p. 479.
13. *Ibid.*
14. Paducah McCracken County Convention and Visitors Bureau booklet.
15. *Encyclopedia of American Biography*, p. 193, and Sarah Ellen Blackwell, *A Military Genius, Life of Anna Ella Carroll*, providing documentary evidence to prove that Miss Carroll planned the campaign of the Federal army in Tennessee. *Encyclopedia of American Biography*, p. 125.

Chapter 4

1. Mark M. Boatner III, *The Civil War Dictionary*, p. 440.
2. James W. Raab, *W. W. Loring, Florida's Forgotten General*, p. 33.
3. O.R., Series 1, Vol. 4, p. 453.
4. *Ibid.*, p. 472.
5. *Confederate Service Record, Lloyd Tilghman.*
6. O.R., Series 1, Vol. 7, p. 699.
7. Charles M. Cummings, *Yankee Quaker Confederate General*, p. 170.
8. O.R., Series 1, Vol. 4, p. 479.
9. Thomas L. Connelly, *Army of the Heartland — The Army of Tennessee*, p. 83.
10. O.R., Series 1, Vol. 4, p. 491.
11. *Ibid.*, p. 552.
12. *Ibid.*, p. 560.
13. *Ibid.*
14. Connelly, p. 85.
15. O.R., Series 1, Vol. 7, p. 719.
16. *Confederate Military History, Tennessee*, Vol. 10, p. 367.
17. *Ibid.*
18. Fort Donelson letters. Tennessee State Library and Archives.
19. *The Civil War Dictionary*, p. 847; *Historical Times Illustrated*, p. 762; *The Civil War Day by Day: An Almanac 1861–1865*, pp. 150, 151.
20. Raymond E. Myers, *The Zollie Tree*, pp. 79, 80.

Chapter 5

1. Charles M. Cummings, *Yankee Quaker Confederate General*, p. 171.
2. *Ibid.*, p. 172.
3. *Ibid.*
4. George W. Kundal, *Confederate Engineer Training and Campaigning*, p. 270, 271.
5. Cummings, p. 173.
6. *Ibid.*, p. 170.
7. Stanley F. Horn, *Tennessee's War, 1861–1865*, p. 78.
8. *Ibid.*, p. 77.
9. O.R., Series 1, Vol. 4, p. 476.
10. *Confederate Military History, Kentucky*, p. 143.

11. *O.R.*, Series 1, Vol. 4, p. 699.
12. *Ibid.*
13. Horn, p. 80.
14. *O.R.*, Series 1, Vol. 7, p. 695.
15. *Ibid.*, p. 733.
16. *Ibid.*
17. *Ibid.*, p. 145.
18. #1 copy of correspondence, Eleanor S. Brockenbrough Library.
19. #9, *Ibid.*
20. #16, *Ibid.*
21. #19, *Ibid.*
22. *Tilghman Confederate Service Record*, Broadfoot Publishing Co.
23. *Ibid.*
24. *O.R.*, Series 1, Vol. 7, pp. 710, 735.
25. Thomas L. Connelly, *Army of the Heartland — The Army of Tennessee, 1861–1862*, p. 84.
26. *O.R.*, Series 1, Vol. 7, p. 145.
27. Kendall D. Gott, *Where the South Lost the War*, p. 54.
28. Fort Donelson letters. Tennessee State Library and Archives.
29. #12 copy of correspondence, Eleanor S. Brockenbrough Library.
30. #53, *Ibid.*
31. #18 and #24, *Ibid.*
32. #44, *Ibid.*
33. Gott, pp. 61, 62.
34. Larry J. Daniel, *Cannoneers in Gray*, p. 16.
35. *Ibid.*, p. 16.
36. *Confederate Military History, Maryland*, Vol. 2, p. 419.
37. #6, *Ibid.*, copy of correspondence, Eleanor S. Brockenbrough Library.
38. #7, *Ibid.*
39. #13, *Ibid.*
40. #17, *Ibid.*
41. *O.R.*, Series 1, Vol. 7, p. 835.
42. *Ibid.*, p. 835.
43. *Ibid.*, p. 73 and #14, Eleanor S. Brockenbrough Library.
44. *O.R.*, Series 1, Vol. 7, p. 839.
45. #20, Eleanor S. Brockenbrough Library.
46. *O.R.*, Series 1, Vol. 7, p. 148.
47. #14, Eleanor S. Brockenbrough Library.
48. #22 and #21, Eleanor S. Brockenbrough Library.
49. *Ibid.*
50. #27, Eleanor S. Brockenbrough Library.
51. #41, *Ibid.*
52. *Ibid.*
53. #39, *Ibid.*
54. #40, *Ibid.*
55. #23, *Ibid.*
56. #34, *Ibid.*
57. *O.R.*, Series 1, Vol. 7, pp. 817, 818.

Chapter 6

1. Thomas L. Connelly, *Army of the Heartland — The Army of Tennessee*, p. 85.
2. Raymond E. Myers, *The Zollie Tree*, p. 62.
3. *Ibid.*, p. 47.
4. *Ibid.*, p. 48.
5. *Historical Times Illustrated Encyclopedia of the Civil War*, p. 850.
6. Myers, p. 20.
7. *Ibid.*, p. 20.
8. *Ibid.*, p. 49.
9. *Ibid.*
10. *Ibid.*, p. 51.
11. *Ibid.*, p. 50.
12. *The Civil War Dictionary*, p. 488.
13. Myers, p. 96.
14. *Ibid.*, pp. 103–110.
15. *Ibid.*, pp. 128, 129.
16. *Ibid.*, p. 118.
17. #43, Eleanor S. Brockenbrough Library.
18. #8, *Ibid.*
19. Charles M. Cummings, *Yankee Quaker Confederate General*, p. 185.
20. #33, Eleanor S. Brockenbrough Library.
21. #30, *Ibid.*
22. #28, *Ibid.*
23. #42, *Ibid.*
24. #45, *Ibid.*
25. #47, *Ibid.*
26. Alfred Roman, *The Military Operations of General Beauregard*, Vol. 1, pp. 494, 495. [epaulment: originated from the French fencing word "épée," a long blade with no cutting edge; thus, blunted defenses.]

27. #32, Eleanor S. Brockenbrough Library.
28. *O.R.*, Series 1, Vol. 7, p. 132.
29. Crowson and Brogden, *Bloody Banners and Barefoot Boys*, pp. 1–3.
30. Castle, *Battles and Leaders of the Civil War*, Vol. 1, p. 362.
31. *Ibid*.
32. *O.R.*, Series 1, Vol. 7, p. 149.
33. Fort Donelson letters, Tennessee State Library and Archives.
34. Crowson and Brogden, p. 4.
35. Herschel Gower, *Pen and Sword, The Life and Journals of Randal W. McGavock, Colonel, C.S.A.*, p. 584.
36. Benjamin Franklin Cooling, *Forts Henry and Donelson*, p. 103.
37. *Ibid.*, 103.

Chapter 7

1. Castle, *Battles and Leaders of the Civil War*, Vol. 1, p. 362.
2. M. F. Force, *From Fort Henry to Corinth*, p. 29.
3. Castle, Vol. 1, p. 363.
4. *O.R.*, Series 1, Vol. 7, p. 151.
5. Castle, Vol. 1, p. 365.
6. Benjamin Franklin Cooling, *Forts Henry and Donelson*, p. 106.
7. Castle, Vol. 1, p. 363.
8. *Ibid.*, p. 367.
9. *Ibid.*, p. 371 and *O.R.*, Series 1, Vol. 7, p. 134.
10. *O.R.*, Series 1, Vol. 7, p. 134.
11. Cooling, p. 107.
12. Castle, Vol. 1, p. 372.
13. *Ibid.*, p. 371.
14. "The Capture of Fort Henry," *Harper's Weekly*, February 22, 1862, Vol. 6, No. p. 269.
15. Kendall D. Gott, *Where the South Lost the War*, pp. 103, 104.
16. Cooling, p. 108.
17. Gott, p. 98.
18. Cooling, p. 100.
19. Crowson and Brogden, *Bloody Banners and Barefoot Boys*, pp. 5, 6.
20. *Easton Gazette* collection, Maryland State Archives.
21. *O.R.*, Series 1, Vol. 7, p. 143.
22. *Ibid.*, p. 152.
23. Broadfoot Publishing Co., *Confederate Service Record*.
24. Cooling, p. 220.
25. *Ibid.*
26. *O.R.*, Series 1, Vol. 7, p. 136.
27. *Ibid.*
28. Cooling, *Forts Henry and Donelson*, p. 283.
29. Eleanor S. Brockenbrough Library, The Museum of the Confederacy, Richmond, Virginia.

Chapter 8

1. Joseph H. Parks, *General Leonidas Polk, The Fighting Bishop*, pp. 207, 208.
2. James Willis, *Arkansas Confederates in the Western Theatre*, p. 135.
3. Nathaniel Cheairs, Hughes Jr., and Roy P. Stonesifer, Jr., *The Life and Wars of Gideon J. Pillow*, p. 211.
4. *Ibid.*, p. 213.
5. Kendall D. Gott, *Where the South Lost the War*, p. 62.
6. Willis, Drew County Historical Society, Special Collections, Microfilm, p. 19.
7. Willis, Lexington Public Library, Special Collections, Microfilm, p. 117.
8. Gott, pp. 144, 145.
9. Henry Steele Commager, *The Blue and the Gray*, pp. 343, 344.
10. M. F. Force, *From Fort Henry to Corinth*, p. 33.
11. Herschel Gower, *Pen and Sword, The Life and Journals of Randal W. McGavock, Colonel, C.S.A.*, pp. 587, 591.
12. Willis, pp. 132, 133.
13. Mark M. Boatner III, *The Civil War Dictionary*, p. 397.
14. Willis, p. 134.
15. Robert Selph Henry, *"First with the Most" Forrest*, p. 51.
16. *O.R.*, Series 1, Vol. 7, p. 296.
17. *Ibid.*, p. 237.
18. Lieutenant Colonel Peter G. Tsouras, *Civil War Quotations*, p. 238.
19. Willis, p. 134.
20. *O.R.*, Series 1, Vol. 7, p. 364.
21. Oswald Tilghman service record.

No mention where he was taken prisoner of war.
22. *O.R.*, Series 1, Vol. 7, p. 364.
23. Nathaniel Cheairs, Hughes Jr., *General William J. Hardee, Old Reliable*, p. 91.
24. Willis, footnote, p. 138.
25. Willis, p. 137.
26. Willis, p. 139.
27. Willis, p. 137.
28. Hughes Jr., p. 91.
29. Willis, pp. 137, 138.
30. Willis, p. 329.
31. Willis, p. 142.
32. Willis, p. 143.
33. Parks, pp. 212, 213.
34. Hughes Jr., pp. 92, 93, 94.
35. Parks, p. 214.
36. Crowson and Brogden, *Bloody Banners and Barefoot Boys, A History of the 27th Regiment Alabama Infantry, C.S.A.*, pp. 1, 7.
37. *Confederate Military History, Tennessee*, Vol. 10, p. 367.
38. Hughes Jr. and Stonesifer Jr., p. 247.

Chapter 9

1. Benjamin Franklin Cooling, *Forts Henry and Donelson*, pp. 213, 216.
2. Mauriel Joslyn, *Immortal Captives*, p. 9.
3. Hershel Gower, *Pen and Sword, The Life and Journals of Randal W. McGavock, Colonel, C.S.A.*, p. 596.
4. *Ibid.*, p. 597.
5. *O.R.*, Series 1, Vol. 1, p. 169.
6. Henry Kyd Douglas, *I Rode with Stonewall*, p. 260.
7. Gower, p. 601.
8. Minor H. McLain, *The Military Prison at Fort Warren*, and Hesseltine, *Civil War Prisons*, p. 35.
9. Gower, p. 601.
10. McLain, *The Military Prison at Fort Warren*, and Hesseltine, *Civil War Prisons*, p. 35.
11. Gower, p. 602, and Cooling, *Forts Henry and Donelson*, p. 259.
12. Gerard A. Patterson, *Rebels from West Point*, pp. 4, 9.

13. Cooling, p. 221.
14. McLain, and Hesseltine, p. 42.
15. Hughes and Stonesifer, *The Life and Wars of Gideon J. Pillow*, pp. 95, 100, 247.
16. Alfred Roman, *The Military Operations of General Beauregard*, p. 229.
17. McLain, and Hesseltine, p. 43.
18. *Ibid.*, p. 34.
19. Gower, pp. 654, 656.
20. *Ibid.*, p. 656.
21. *Ibid.*, p. 657.
22. *Ibid.*, p. 656.
23. *Ibid.*
24. *Ibid.*, p. 657.
25. *Ibid.*, p. 658.
26. *Ibid.*, p. 659.
27. Stewart Sifakis, *Who Was Who in the Civil War*, p. 654.
28. Patricia L. Faust, *Historical Times Illustrated Encyclopedia of the Civil War*, p. 604.
29. Gower, p. 660.
30. Burke Davis, *The Civil War: Strange & Fascinating Facts*, p. 143.
31. *Ibid.*, p. 661.
32. Southern Historical Society Papers, Vol. 1, *Secretary of War, Charles A. Dana, Cartel*, pp. 156–159.

Chapter 10

1. Hershel Gower, *Pen and Sword, The Life and Journals of Randal W. McGavock, Colonel, C.S.A.*, p. 664.
2. *Ibid.*, pp. 668, 669
3. *Ibid.*, p. 670.
4. *Ibid.*, pp. 672, 673.
5. *Ibid.*, p. 673.
6. Nathaniel Cheairs Hughes Jr., and Roy P. Stonesifer Jr., *The Life and Wars of Gideon J. Pillow*, p. 246.
7. Gower, p. 674.
8. Mark M. Boatner III, *The Civil War Dictionary*, pp. 669, 867, and Stewart Sifakis, *Who Was Who in the Civil War*, pp. 522, 673.
9. *O.R.*, Series 1, Vol. 17, Part 2, p. 729.
10. *Ibid.*, p. 698.
11. Monroe F. Cockrell, *The Lost Account of the Battle of Corinth*, p. 28.

12. Peter Cozzens, *The Darkest Days of the War*, p. 160.
13. James Willis, *Arkansas Confederates in the Western Theatre*, p. 273.
14. Cockrell, p. 28.
15. O.R., Series I, Vol. 17, Part 2, p. 728.
16. O.R., Series I, Vol. 27, Part 1, p. 729.
17. Stephen Z. Starr, *Jennison's Jayhawkers*, p. 222.
18. Willis, p. 119.
19. Starr, p. 222.
20. *Ibid.*, p. 223.

Chapter 11

1. O.R., Series 1, Vol. 17, Part 1, p. 496.
2. *Ibid.*, p. 486.
3. *Ibid.*, pp. 503–506.
4. *Ibid.*, p. 496.
5. *Ibid.*, p. 503.
6. O.R., Series 1, Vol. 27, Part 2, p. 787.
7. Stephen Z. Starr, *Jennison's Jayhawkers*, p. 222.
8. James Willis, *Arkansas Confederates in the Western Theatre*, p. 288.
9. Southern Historical Society Papers, Vol. 6, Col. A. F. Brown, *Van Dorn's Operations in Northern Mississippi*, p. 154.
10. *Ibid.*
11. Patricia L. Faust, *Historical Times Illustrated Encyclopedia of the Civil War*, p. 365.
12. Southern Historical Society Papers, Vol. 6, Col. A. F. Brown, *Van Dorn's Operations in Northern Mississippi*, pp. 157, 158.
13. Faust, p. 366.
14. O.R., Series 1, Vol. 17, Part 2, p. 495.
15. O.R., Series 1, Vol. 17, Part 1, p. 24.
16. John Fiske, *The Mississippi Valley in the Civil War*, pp. 181, 183.
17. *Ibid.*, p. 184.
18. Francis V. Greene, *The Mississippi Campaigns of the Civil War*, pp. 209, 211.

Chapter 12

1. James Willis, *Arkansas Confederates in the Western Theatre*, p. 289.
2. O.R., Series 1, Vol. 27, Part 2, p. 846.
3. O.R., Series 1, Vol. 24, Part 3, p. 592.
4. Mark M. Boatner III, *The Civil War Dictionary*, p. 631.
5. O.R., Series 1, Vol. 24, Part III, p. 61.
6. *Ibid.*
7. Stephen Z. Starr, *Jennison's Jayhawkers*, p. 237.
8. O.R., Series 1, Vol. 24, Part 3, p. 61.
9. *Ibid.*
10. O.R., Series 1, Vol. 27, Part 2, p. 847.
11. *Ibid.*
12. *Ibid.*
13. John C. Pemberton, *Pemberton, Defender of Vicksburg*, p. 10.
14. *Ibid.*
15. O.R., Series 1, Vol. 27, Part 2, p. 847.

Chapter 13

1. W. A. Gillespie, *Confederate Veteran* magazine article, Vol. 16, p. 1908.
2. O.R., Series 1, Vol. 24, Part 3, p. 629.
3. *Ibid.*, p. 656.
4. James W. Raab, *W. W. Loring, Florida's Forgotten General*, p. 93.
5. *Ibid.*, p. 94.
6. Grady H. Howell, *For Dixie Land I'll Take My Stand*, p. 74.
7. *Battles and Leaders of the Civil War*, Vol. 1, p. 625.
8. John K. Bettersworth, *Mississippi in the Confederacy as They Saw It*, p. 108.
9. O.R., Series 1, Vol. 24, Part 1, p. 388.
10. O.R., Series 1, Vol. 24, Part 3, p. 649.
11. *Ibid.*, p. 649.
12. John Fiske, *The Mississippi Valley in the Civil War*, p. 217.

Chapter 14

1. O.R., Series 1, Vol. 24, Part 3, p. 649.
2. O.R., Series 1, Vol. 24, Part 1, p. 397.
3. Ibid., p. 412.
4. O.R., Series 1, Vol. 24, Part 3, p. 657.
5. Ibid., pp. 662, 663.
6. James W. Raab, *W. W. Loring, Florida's Forgotten General*, p. 94.
7. O.R., Series 1, Vol. 24, Part 1, p. 379.
8. O.R., Series 1, Vol. 24, Part 3, p. 667.
9. Raab, p. 96.
10. O.R., Series 1, Vol. 24, Part 3, p. 667.
11. Raab, p. 97.
12. O.R., Series 1, Vol. 24, Part 3, p. 665.
13. Dabney M. Maury, *Recollections of a Virginian*, p. 178.
14. O.R., Series 1, Vol. 24, Part 3, p. 452.
15. James Willis, *Arkansas Confederates in the Western Theatre*, p. 244.
16. Mark M. Boatner III, *The Civil War Dictionary*, p. 736, and Patricia L. Faust, *Historical Times Illustrated Encyclopedia of the Civil War*, pp. 671, 672.
17. Raab, p. 98; Dismantling of Fort Pemberton is a surmise beyond the evidence.—Author

Chapter 15

1. O.R., Series 1, Vol. 24, Part 1, p. 251.
2. Ibid., p. 257.
3. Mark M. Boatner III, *The Civil War Dictionary*, p. 359.
4. O.R., Series 1, Vol. 24, Part 3, p. 777.
5. O.R., Series 1, Vol. 24, Part 1, p. 553.
6. Ibid., p. 544.
7. Patricia L. Faust, *Historical Times Illustrated Encyclopedia of the Civil War*, p. 326.
8. O.R., Series 1, Vol. 24, Part 3, p. 808.
9. James W. Raab, *W. W. Loring, Florida's Forgotten General*, p. 105.
10. O.R., Series 1, Vol. 24, Part 1, p. 256.
11. Ezra J. Warner, *Generals in Gray*, p. 309.
12. O.R., Series 1, Vol. 24, Part 3, pp. 804, 805.
13. Ibid., pp. 816, 817.
14. O.R., Series 1, Vol. 24, Part 1, p. 258.
15. O.R., Series 1, Vol. 24, Part 3, pp. 812, 813.
16. Ibid., p. 815.
17. Ibid.
18. Ibid., p. 829.
19. O.R., Series 1, Vol. 24, Part 1, pp. 655, 669.
20. Raab, pp. 106, 108.
21. O.R., Series 1, Vol. 24, Part 3, p. 841.
22. Stewart Sifakis, *Who Was Who in the Civil War*, p. 408.
23. Ibid.
24. Boatner III, p. 525.
25. Sifakis, *Who Was Who in the Civil War*, p. 408.
26. Ibid., p. 409.
27. Ibid.

Chapter 16

1. Terrence J. Winschel, *Triumph & Defeat: The Vicksburg Campaign*, pp. 9, 10.
2. O.R., Series 1, Vol. 24, Part 3, p. 849
3. Ibid., p. 864.
4. O.R., Series 1, Vol. 24, Part 1, p. 215.
5. Ibid., p. 261.
6. Edwin C. Bearss, *Decision in Mississippi*, p. 226.
7. O.R., Series 1, Vol. 24, Part 1, p. 262.
8. William Augustus Drennan letter.
9. *Confederate Veteran* magazine, Vol. 1, No. 9, Sept. 1893, p. 285.
10. H. Grady Howell Jr., *Hill of Death, The Battle of Champion Hill*, p. 11.
11. O.R., Series 1, Vol. 24, Part 1, p. 263.

12. *O.R.*, Series 1, Vol. 24, Part 3, p. 88.
13. Francis Vinton Greene, *The Mississippi Campaigns of the Civil War*, p. 154.
14. Howell Jr., p. 11.
15. James W. Raab, *General Loring* manuscript, p. 458.
16. *O.R.*, Series 1, Vol. 24, Part 2, p. 32.
17. Howell Jr., p. 12.
18. *O.R.*, Series 1, Vol. 24, Part 2, p. 70.
19. Raab, p. 115.
20. James Willis, *Arkansas Confederates in the Western Theatre*, p. 353.
21. O.R., Series 1, Vol. 24, Part 2, p. 72.
22. Dale Greenwell, *The Third Mississippi Regiment, C.S.A.*, p. 59.
23. *Ibid.*, pp. 56, 57.
24. James G. Spencer, *Private Cowan's Battery, Regimental Files, First Mississippi*, Vicksburg National Military Park, September 18, 1910.
25. Richard Brady Williams, "Chicago's Battery Boys," CWPT's magazine *Hallowed Ground*, Vol. 5, No. 3, Fall 2004, p. 36.
26. E. T. Eggleston, *Confederate Veteran* magazine, Vol. 1, p. 296.
27. *O.R.*, Series 1, Vol. 24, Part 1, p. 151. Another variation of General Tilghman's death: "As he careened and fell he said to his son, who caught him, 'Tell your mother, God bless her.'" (L. A. Flatan, St. Louis, *Confederate Veteran* magazine, Vol. 18, No. 9, September 1910.)
28. Fred G. Neuman, *Paducah's History* pamphlet.
29. *O.R.*, Series 1, Vol. 24, Part 1, p. 265.
30. Lawrence Lee Hewitt, *Port Hudson, Confederate Bastion on the Mississippi*, p. 380.
31. Patricia L. Faust, *Historical Times Illustrated Encyclopedia of the Civil War*, p. 298
32. Lawrence Lee Hewitt, *Port Hudson, Confederate Bastion on the Mississippi*, p. 120.
33. Benjamin Jonson, English poet, author and actor (1573–1637).
34. *O.R.*, Series 1, Vol. 24, Part 1, pp. 58, 59.

Chapter 17

1. Quote of Father Abram J. Ryan, poet-priest of the Confederacy.
2. *Confederate Veteran* magazine, Vol. 18, No. 7, July 1910, p. 318.
3. *Confederate Veteran* magazine, Vol. 4, No. 10, p. 1896.
4. *Confederate Veteran* magazine, Vol. 18, No. 7, June 10, 1910, p. 319.
5. James Willis, *Arkansas Confederates in the Western Theatre*, p. 406.
6. *O.R.*, Series 1, Vol. 6, p. 234.
7. Arthur W. Bergeron Jr., *Confederate Mobile*, p. 71.
8. James Willis, *Arkansas Confederates in the Western Theatre*, p. 682.
9. Richard Owen and James Owen. *Generals at Rest*, p. 161.

Bibliography

Battle, J. H., W. H. Perrin, and G. C. Kniffin. *Kentucky: A History of the State.* Part 2. 1885.

Bearss, Edwin C. *Decision in Mississippi — Mississippi Commission on the War Between the States.* Jackson, Mississippi: 1962.

———. *The Fall of Fort Henry.* Vol. 17. Reprint: West Tennessee Historical Society, 1963.

———. *The Vicksburg Campaign.* Vols. 1, 2, and 3. Dayton, OH: Morningside House.

Bender, A. B. *New Mexico Historical Review*, Vol. 9, No. 4.

Bergeron, Arthur, Jr. *Confederate Mobile.* Baton Rouge: Louisiana State University Press, 1991.

Bettersworth, John K. *Mississippi in the Confederacy as They Saw It.* Baton Rouge: Louisiana State University Press, Kraus Reprint, 1970.

Black, Robert C. III. *The Railroads of the Confederacy.* Chapel Hill: University of North Carolina Press, 1957. Reprint, Wilmington, NC: Broadfoot, 1987.

Boatner, Mark M. III. *The Civil War Dictionary.* Rev. ed. New York: David McKay, 1987.

———. *Encyclopedia of the American Revolution.* Mechanicsburg, PA: Stackpole, 1994.

Bonekemper, Edward H. III. *How Robert E. Lee Lost the Civil War.* Fredericksburg, VA: Sergeant Kirkland Press, 1997.

Brown, D. Alexander. *Grierson's Raid.* Champaign: University of Illinois Press. Reprint, Dayton, OH: Morningside House.

Burns, Zed H. *Confederate Forts.* Natchez, MS: Southern Historical Publications, 1977.

Bush, Bryan S. *The Civil War Battles of the Western Theatre.* Paducah, KY: Rutner.

Catton, Bruce. *Never Call Retreat: The Centennial History of the Civil War.* Vol. 3. Garden City, NY: Doubleday, 1965.

Cockrell, Monroe F. *The Lost Account of the Battle of Corinth.* Wilmington, NC: Broadfoot, 1987.

Commager, Henry Steele. *The Blue and the Gray: The Story of the Civil War as Told by Participants.* New York: Bobbs-Merrill, 1950.

Connelly, Thomas Lawrence. *Army of the Heartland: The Army of Tennessee, 1861–1862.* Baton Rouge: Louisiana State University Press, 1967.

Cooling, Benjamin Franklin. *Forts Henry and Donelson: The Key to the Confederate Heartland.* Knoxville: University of Tennessee Press, 1987.

Cozzens, Peter. *The Darkest Days of the War: The Battles of Iuka and Corinth*. Chapel Hill: University of North Carolina Press, 1997.

Crowson, Noel, and John V. Brogden. *Bloody Banners and Barefoot Boys: A History of the 27th Regiment Alabama Infantry, C.S.A.* Shippensburg, PA: Burd Street, 1997.

Crute, Joseph H., Jr. *Confederate Staff Officers, 1861–1865*. Powhatan, VA: Derwent, 1982.

Cummings, Charles M. *Yankee Quaker, Confederate General: The Curious Career of Bushrod Rust Johnson*. Cranbury, NJ: Fairleigh Dickinson University Press, 1971.

Daniel, Larry J. *Cannoneers in Gray*. Tuscaloosa: University of Alabama Press, 1984.

Davis, Burke. *The Civil War: Strange and Fascinating Facts*. New York: Fairfax, 1982.

Davis, William C. *The Cause Lost, Myths and Realities of the Confederacy*. Lawrence: University Press of Kansas, 1996.

Degregorio, William A. *The Complete Book of U.S. Presidents, 4th Edition*. NJ: Wings Books, 1993.

Douglas, Henry Kyd. *I Rode with Stonewall*. Chapel Hill: 1940.

Downer, Edward T. *Johnson's Island*. Kent, OH: Kent State University Press, 1962.

Eggleston, E. T. *Confederate Veteran* magazine, Vol. 1.

Encyclopedia of the Confederacy. Macmillan Reference USA, 1993.

Faust, Patricia L., ed. *Historical Times Illustrated Encyclopedia of the Civil War*. New York: Harper & Row, 1986.

Fiske, John. *The Mississippi Valley in the Civil War*. Boston: Houghton Mifflin, 1900.

Flatan, L. S. "Tribute to General Tilghman." *Confederate Veteran* magazine, Vol. 28, No. 9., September 1910.

Force, M. F. *From Fort Henry to Corinth*. New York: Scribner's. Facsimile reprint, Harrisburg, PA: Archive Society, 1991.

Frost, J. *The Mexican War and Its Warriors*. H. Mansfield, 1850. Facsimile reprint, Bowie, MD: Heritage, 1989.

George, Henry. *History of the 3d, 7th, 8th and 12th Kentucky, C.S.A.* Melber, KY: Simmons Historical Publications.

Gillespie, W. A. *Confederate Veteran* magazine, Vol. 16, 1908.

Gott, Kendall D. *Where the South Lost the War: An Analysis of the Fort Henry–Fort Donelson Campaign*. Mechanicsburg, PA: Stackpole Books, 2003.

Gower, Herschel. *Pen and Sword: The Life and Journals of Randal W. McGavock, Colonel, C.S.A.* Tennessee Historical Commission, 1959.

Greene, Francis Vinton. *The Mississippi Campaigns of the Civil War, VIII*. New York: Scribner's, 1882.

Greenwell, Dale. *The Third Mississippi Regiment — C.S.A.* Pascagoula, MS: Lewis Printing Service, 1972.

Hall, Allen. *Center of Conflict: Civil War History Timeline, Paducah, Kentucky*. (Booklet.)

Hanna, A. J. *Flight into Oblivion*. Johnston, 1938.

Henry, Robert Selph. *"First with the Most" Forrest*. Reprint, Wilmington, NC: Broadfoot, 1987.

Herr, John K, and Edward S. Wallace. *The Story of the U.S. Cavalry, 1775–1942*. New York: Bonanza, 1953.

Hesseltine, William B. *Civil War Prisons*. Kent, OH: Kent State University Press, 1992.

Hewitt, Lawrence Lee. *Port Hudson, Confederate Bastion on the Mississippi*. Baton Rouge: Louisiana State University Press, 1987.

Holland, Richard. *Paducah History Time Line*. Paducah, Kentucky.

Horn, Stanley F. *Tennessee's War, 1861–1865*. Knoxville: University of Tennessee Press.

Howell, Grady H., Jr. *For Dixie Land I'll Take My Stand*. Madison, MS: Chickasaw Bayou, 1998.

_____. *Hill of Death: The Battle of Champion Hill*. Madison, MS: Chickasaw Bayou, 1993.

_____. *To Live and Die in Dixie: A His-*

tory of the Third Mississippi Infantry. Madison, MS: Chickasaw Bayou, 1991.

Hughes, Nathaniel Cheairs, Jr. *General William J. Hardee, Old Reliable.* Baton Rouge: Louisiana State University Press, 1965.

Hughes, Nathaniel Cheairs, Jr., and Roy P. Stonesifer, Jr. *The Life and Wars of Gideon J. Pillow.* Chapel Hill: University of North Carolina Press, 1993.

Hughes, Robert M. *General Johnston.* New York: Appleton, 1893.

Johnson, Clint. *Civil War Blunders.* Winston-Salem, NC: John F. Blair, 1997.

Joslyn, Mauriel P. *Immortal Captives.* Shippensburg, PA: White Mane, 1996.

Keegan, John. *Fields of Battle: The Wars for North America.* New York: Alfred A. Knopf, 1996.

Kinkead, Elizabeth Shelby. *History of Kentucky.* American Book, 1909.

Kundahl, George G. *Confederate Engineer with John Morris Wampler.* Knoxville: University of Tennessee Press, 2000.

Lawliss, Chuck. *The Civil War Sourcebook: A Traveler's Guide.* New York: Harmony, 1991.

Leech, Margaret. *Reveille in Washington.* New York: Carroll & Graf, 1991.

Long, E. B., and Barbara Long. *The Civil War Day by Day: An Almanac, 1861–1865.* New York: Da Capo, 1985.

Mahan, D. H. *A Complete Treatise on Field Fortification.* Wiley and Long, 1836. Reprint, New York: Greenwood, 1968.

Martin, David G. *The Vicksburg Campaign.* New York: Gallery/W. H. Smith, 1990.

Maury, Dabney M. *Recollections of a Virginian.* 2nd. ed. New York: Scribner's, 1894.

McKeely, William S. *Grant: A Biography.* New York, 1981.

McLain, Minor H. *The Military Prison at Fort Warren.* Ames: Iowa State University Press, 1962. (Offprint, 17 pp.)

Meltzer, Milton. *Hunted Like a Wolf: The Story of the Seminole War.* New York: Farrar, Straus and Giroux, 1972.

Merrius, F. W. "Career and Fate of General Lloyd Tilghman." *Confederate Veteran* magazine, Vol. 1, No. 9, September 1893.

Myers, Raymond E. *The Zollie Tree.* Louisville, KY: Filson Club, 1964.

Neuman, Fred G. *Paducans in History.* Paducah, KY: Young Printing, 1922.

Nevin, David. *The Old West, The Mexican War.* Time-Life Books, 1978.

Northrop, Henry Davenport. *Pictorial History of the United States.* J. R. Jones, 1893.

Owen, Richard, and James Owen. *Generals at Rest.* Shippensburg, PA: White Mane, 1997.

Parks, Joseph H. *General Leonidas Polk, The Fighting Bishop.* Baton Rouge: Louisiana State University Press, 1962.

Patterson, Gerard A. *Rebels from West Point.* Garden City, NY: Doubleday, 1987.

Pemberton, John C. *Pemberton, Defender of Vicksburg.* Chapel Hill: University of North Carolina Press, 1942.

Raab, James W. *W. W. Loring, Florida's Forgotten General.* Manhattan, KS: Sunflower University Press, 1997.

Robertson, John. *Paducah, 1830–1980.*

Roman, Alfred. *The Military Operations of General Beauregard.* New York: Da Capo, 1994.

Rowland, Dunbar. *Military History of Mississippi, 1803–1898. The Official & Statistical Register of the State of Mississippi,* 1908.

Sifakis, Steward. *Who Was Who in the Civil War.* New York: Facts on File, 1988.

Spencer, James G. *Private Cowan's Battery. Regimental Files, First Mississippi.* Vicksburg National Military Park, Vicksburg, Mississippi, September 18, 1910.

Starr, Stephen Z. *Jennison's Jayhawkers.* Baton Rouge: Louisiana State University Press, 1973.

The Struggle for Vicksburg. Harrisburg, PA: Eastern Acorn.

Tatum, George Lee. *Disloyalty in the Confederacy.* Chapel Hill: University of North Carolina Press, 1934.

Tilghman, Oswald. *Civil War Soldier Records.* Wilmington, NC: Broadfoot.

Tsouras, Peter G. *Civil War Quotations*. New York: Sterling, 1998.

Utley, Robert M. *Frontiersmen in Blue: The United States Army and the Indian, 1848–1865*. New York: Macmillan, 1967.

Varhola, Michael J. *Everyday Life During the Civil War*. Cincinnati, OH: Writer's Digest Books, 1999.

Warner, Ezra J. *Generals in Gray — Lives of the Confederate Commanders*. Baton Rouge: Louisiana State University Press, 1959.

Willis, James. *Arkansas Confederates in the Western Theatre*. Dayton, OH: Morningside House, 1998.

Winschel, Terrence J. *Champion Hill: A Battlefield Guide*. Jackson, MS: Jackson Civil War Roundtable.

Woodworth, Steven E. *Jefferson Davis and His Generals*. Lawrence: University Press of Kansas, 1990.

Periodicals and Collections

Battles and Leaders of the Civil War. 4 vols., Edited by Robert U. Johnson and Clarence C. Buell. New York: 1887–1888. Reprint, Secaucus, NJ: Castle.

Civil War Times Illustrated. 1961.

Confederate Military History. Edited by Clement A. Evans.

Confederate Veteran magazine. 1893–1932. Nashville, Tennessee.

Dictionary of American Biography. 20 vols. New York: 1928–1937.

Easton Gazette Collection. Maryland State Archives, Hall of Records, Annapolis, Maryland.

Mississippi Department of Archives and History, Archives & Library Division. Jackson, Mississippi. Michael Hennen Manuscript Collection.

Southern Historical Society Papers. 49 volumes, 1876–1930. Richmond, Virginia.

Tennessee State Library and Archives. Nashville, Tennessee.

The Tilghman Heritage Center, Paducah, Kentucky.

U.S. War Department, *The War of the Rebellion: Official Records of the Union and Confederate Armies*. 128 vols. 1880–1901, Washington, D.C.

U.S. Army Military History Institute, United States Army War College, Carlisle, Pennsylvania, 17013–4501.

Manuscripts and Letters

Fort Donelson Letters. Nashville: Tennessee State Library and Archives.

Lloyd Tilghman's Letters. Richmond: Museum of the Confederacy, Eleanor S. Brockenbrough Library Collection.

Lloyd Tilghman's Service Records. Wilmington, NC: Broadfoot.

William Augustus Drennan Letters. Jackson: Mississippi Department of Archives and Records.

Index

Abbeville, MS 129–130, 147
Academy Honor Code 8
Achilles' heel 48
Adams, Col. J. 170, 175, 183, 187
aide-de-camp 11
Alabama 4, 25–26, 51, 61, 74, 170
Alcorn, J. L. 39
Alton, IL 86–87, 110
American Revolution 5, 7
Anderson, Adna 47–49
Anderson, Richard A. 9
Arista, Gen. Mariano 14–15
Arkansas 25, 29, 177, 193
Arkansas Post 177
Army of the West 121, 126–127
Army of West Tennessee 128

Bailey, J. E. 107
Bailey, James E. 44–45, 55–56, 73–74, 119
Bailey's Landing 59, 72, 75
Baker's Creek 183, 185, 188–191
Baldwin, Gen. W. E. 145, 173
Baldwin Ferry Road 175, 179
Banks, Gen. N. P. 143, 172, 176, 192
Baron DeKalb 157, 160, 162–163
Bates, Edward 36
Baton Rouge, LA 170
battles and skirmishes *see* specific location
Beauregard, Gen. P. G. T. 29, 93, 104, 106, 123, 174
Beck's Ferry Landing 153
Belmont 42, 58, 98
Benjamin, Judah P. 39, 59
Big Black River 171–172, 174–177, 192
Black Hawk War 37
Bolivar, TN 127, 140
Bolton 176, 182, 185, 187

border states 4
Boston Journal 109
Bovina 175, 181
Bowen, J. S. 126, 168, 171–174, 183, 187, 189–190
Bowling Green, KY 32, 36, 39, 43–44, 46–48, 52, 54–55, 57, 59–60, 63, 75, 85, 92–93, 104, 106, 113, 121, 131
Boyd, Augusta M. 10
Boyd, Joseph L. 10
Bragg, Gen. Braxton 13, 15, 117, 140, 147, 167–168, 171, 179
Bragg, Junius N. 105
Brittan, S. B., Jr. 78–79
Brown, Gen. J. C. 117
Brown, Maj. Jacob 15
Brown, John 24, 26
Browne, Walter 10
Brownsville, TX 15
Bruinsburg, MS 171–173
Buchanan, President James 37
Buckner, Simon Bolivar 30–31, 33, 39–40, 43, 46, 54, 63, 93–94, 98, 101–103, 107, 112–113, 116–117, 119, 195
Buell, Gen. D. C. 92, 104–106
Buena Vista 16
Buford, Gen. Abe 189
Burbridge, Gen. S. G. 188
Butternuts 41
Byers, Samuel H. M. 188

Cairo, IL 34, 59, 71, 86, 110
Calhoun, John C. 23
Camp Daniel Boone 31–32, 41
Camp Dick Robinson 64
Camp Douglas 110
Camp Trousdale 64

213

campaigns of Mexican War 13
Cannon, Dr. J. P. 70, 74, 84, 107
Canterbury Manor 5
Canton 170, 180–181, 185, 195
Cape Ann Advertiser 113
Carroll, Anna E. 35–36, 139
Cartel Agreement 128
Carthage 170
Central Army of Kentucky 92, 104–105
Cerro Gordo 16
Champion Hill: strategy 178; roster of generals 179; 183; map 184; 186–190, 197–198
Champion, Sid and Mary 185–186, 196
Chapultepec 17
Charleston, SC 25
Charleston Mercury 3, 24
Charlotte Road 98, 101
Chew, Benjamin 5
Chewalla 127
Chicago Mercantile Battery 191
Chickasaw Bayou 143
Chief Justice of Pennsylvania 5
Chillicothe 157, 159–160, 162–164
Chilton, D. S. 60
Churubusco 17, 30
Cincinnati 81, 86
Cincinnati Commercial 104
Citadel 15–16
Clare, Captain 61
Clarksville, TN 31–32, 39–41, 44–45, 47–48, 58, 75, 92–94, 106–107, 120, 195
Clarksville Weekly Chronicle 93
Clayton Bayou 153
Clayton-Bulwer Treaty 20
Clinton 121, 181, 183, 185, 189–190
Cockrell, F. M. 168, 175
Coffeeville, MS 131–133; battle 134; 139
Coker House Ridge 188–190
Coldwater River 151, 153, 155, 157, 159, 164
Colombia 19, 21
Columbia, TN 140
Columbus, KY 30–31, 33–34, 39, 43–44, 46, 52, 55, 58, 63–64, 69, 75, 92, 106–107, 113, 140
Columbus, MS 172
Conestoga 51
Confederacy 6, 27, 32–33, 37, 40, 107, 112, 142
Confederate 4, 32–34, 36–37, 39–40, 42–43, 46, 54, 57–59, 76–77, 98, 109, 120–121, 123, 127, 129, 131, 139, 141–142, 149, 151, 157, 163, 166, 170–171, 174–175, 180–183, 185–189
Confederate Congress 52
Confederate forts 30, 149
Confederate recruiters 4
Confederate States of America 4, 26, 29
Confederate Western War Department 37
Constitutional Convention 5
constitutional rights 3
Continental Congress 5–6

Corinth 122–123; map 124; 125–126, 128–130, 140–141
cotton bales 154, 161
Cotton Hill 190–191
court of inquiry 54
Covington, Josephine 104
Cowan, Capt. J. 190–191
Creek Indians 9
Crittenden, Gen. T. L. 39, 65–66, 86, 92
Crystal Springs 192
Cumberland City 52, 69
Cumberland Gap 39, 46, 64
Cumberland River 30, 36, 42–44, 47–48, 51, 54–55, 58, 69–70, 83, 86, 94, 101–102, 105–107, 110
Curtis's Plantation 153

Danville 32, 60, 62
Dartmouth's Thayer School of Engineering 7
Davis, President Jefferson 6, 28, 33, 39, 41, 63, 70, 92, 127–128, 144–145, 176, 178–181, 194
Davis, Col. Wirt 127
Declaration of Independence 5
Delaware 4
Dickens, E. V. 159
Dickey, Lyle 131, 133; retreat 137; 138
Dillon 182
Dimick, Col. J. E. 112–113, 116
Dix, Gen. John A. 115
Dix-Hill Exchange 115, 120
"Dixie" 109
Dixon, Joseph 50, 96, 98
Donelson, Daniel W. 47, 49–50
Dover, TN 44, 48, 94, 96, 101, 109–110
Dover Hotel 103
Dragoons, U.S. 9
Drennen, Lt. W. A. 186
Drumgauld's Bluff 171
Duckport Landing 150
Duke of Lancaster 5
Dunbar 32, 57, 74

Easton, MD 58
Easton Gazette 8
Edwards Deport 176, 181–182, 187
Edwards Ferry 176
Ellis, Powhatan, Jr. 52, 58, 192
Ellison 182, 185–186, 188
Enterprise, MS 168, 170
exit: Fort Donelson 102

Farmington, KY 60, 62
Farragut, David G. 172
Featherston, Gen. W. S. 164, 186, 189
Federal Union 33–34, 36, 45, 54, 60–61, 63, 71, 79, 84, 96, 98, 104, 127, 130–132, 139–141, 150–154, 163, 170–173, 175,–177, 180–182, 185–189

Fillmore, President Millard 22
Florence, AL 47, 51, 83
Florida 4, 9, 25–26
Floyd, Gen. J. B. 28, 92, 94, 98, 101–102, 106–107, 113
Foote, A. M. 71, 78, 80–83, 98
Forbes, Col. W. S. 170
Forrest, Col. N. B. 33, 69, 95, 102, 140–141, 174
Fort Anderson 35
Fort Bridger 37
Fort Coburn 173
Fort Donelson 42–44, 48, 50–52, 55, 57–58, 61, 67, 73, 75, 80–81, 84–85, 92–96, 98, 101; exit 102; 103–104, 106–110, 113, 140–141, 176, 192
Fort Greenwood 153
Fort Heiman 50, 55, 57, 59–61, 63, 70–71, 73–75, 80, 84, 98, 108
Fort Henry 42–44, 48–53, 57–60, 62–63, 67, 69–71, 73–75, 77, 80–81, 84–85; report 87; 94–95, 108, 140–141, 176, 178, 192
Fort Pemberton 153, 155; siege 159; map 161; 162, 164–166
Fort Wade 173
Fort Warren, MA 45, 107, 111–114, 116
Fortress Monroe, VA 112, 116
Foster, Cmdr. J. P. 163
Foster, T. J. 61
Foster, Maj. W. B. 47–49
Fourteen Mile Creek 176, 179
Fry, Col. Speed S. 65–66

Gardner, Gen. Franklin 172, 193
Gaunt, John 5
Gee: regiment 62
George, Gen. J. Z. 165
Georgia 4, 25–26
Gilmer, Maj. J. F. 42, 44, 49–51, 53–55, 70, 80, 94, 106
Glenn, T. J. 54–55
Goodwin, Col. E. 170, 187–188
Gosport Navy Yard 29–30
Grand Gulf 171–172, 174–175, 180
Grand Gulf, MS 142
Grant, Gen. Ulysses S. 12, 34–35, 42, 59, 64, 75, 80, 82, 84, 86, 92, 95–96, 98, 103, 109, 113, 123, 125, 127, 129, 131, 138–141, 143–144, 147, 149–150, 163, 166–169, 171–172, 175–177, 179–180, 182, 185–188, 190, 193
Grant's Pass 157, 163, 165
Greeley, Horace 3, 18, 25
Green River 39, 92, 105
Greenwood 153; map 161
Gregg, Gen. John 112, 179–180
Grenada, MS 139, 141, 144, 148, 151, 155
Grierson, Col. B. H. 167–168; map 169; 170–171, 181
Griffith, Col. John S. 139–140
Grindstone Ford 174

Haines Bluff 151, 171
Halleck, Gen. H. W. 35, 110, 123
Hall's Ferry Road 175
Hamilton, James M. 56–57
Hankinson Ferry 175
Hanson, Roger W. 117
Hard Times, LA 167–168, 171, 176
Hardee, Col. J. W. 93, 104–106
Harris, Gov. Isham G. 40, 47, 50, 64, 66
Harrison, I. F. 167
Hart, Simeon 27
Hatchie River 127
Hawkins, Col. E. R. 127
Haxall's Landing 115
Haynes, Lt. Col. M. A. 52, 58–59, 68–69
Hays, Jack 15–16
Head, John W. 55–56, 58
Heiman, Col. Adolphus 49–50, 57–58, 72–73, 77, 80, 84, 86, 94, 112, 119, 122
Helena, AR 130, 150, 157, 166
Henry, Gustavus A. 48
Henry County 61
Hermitage 5
Hickman, KY 33–34, 63–64
Hill, Gen. D. H. 115
Hindman, Gen. T. C. 104–105
Hoffman, Charles Fenno 16
Holly Springs, MS 123, 127–129, 139–141, 144–145
Hooker, Joseph 10
Hopkinsville, KY 39, 41–43, 48, 50, 54, 92, 106
Houston, Sam 27
Huger Battery 6
Hughes, Col. George W. 17

Illinois 96
Illinois Central Railroad 34
Illinois River 32, 34
Impressment Act 41
Indianapolis Daily State Sentinel 104
invasion of Mexico 12
Iroquois Indians 5
Island No. 10 30, 192

Jackson, Andrew 9
Jackson, Col. H. W. 128, 131, 139–140, 195
Jackson, Lieutenant 112
Jackson, MS 121, 139, 145–146, 159, 168, 170–171, 174–175, 179–182, 185, 192–193
Jackson, TN 140
Jackson Railroad 168
Jackson Road 190
Jackson's Creek 188
Jalapa 16
James River 115
Jayhawking 131
Johnson, Gen. Bushrod R. 47–50, 67–68, 94, 103–104, 107
Johnson, Gov. George W. 52

Johnston, Gen. Albert S. 33, 37, 39–40, 42, 44, 46, 48, 50–52, 55–56, 63, 65–66, 69, 85, 92–93, 98, 101, 104–106, 113, 117, 123, 172
Johnston, Gen. J. E. 145, 171, 174, 176, 179–182, 185–186
Johnston, William Preston 117
Johnston's Island 6, 193
Jones, John 80

Kansas 7th Cavalry 131–132, 138, 146–147
Kentucky 4, 25, 29, 32–33, 37, 39–43, 46, 48, 52, 58, 60, 63–64, 107, 112, 122, 141, 170
Kentucky State Guard 25, 31

La Grange, TN 168
Lake Providence, LA 150
Lanier, N. B. 175
Lee, Robert E. 17, 193
Lee, Gen. S. D. 143, 146, 189
Lincoln, Abraham 3–4, 18, 25–26, 29, 31, 35–36, 45–46, 112, 176
Lioness 160
Lobos Island 16
Lockett, Maj. S. H. 178, 189
log huts 96
Logan, J. A. 173, 179, 190
Lord Baltimore 5
Loring, Gen. William Wing 145–146, 151, 153, 155, 160, 162–163, 165–166, 170, 174–177, 179; division 182; 183, 185–187, 189–190, 192, 194
Louisiana 4, 25–26, 167–168, 171
Louisville & Nashville Railroad 32
Louisville Daily Democrat 95
Lovell, Gen. Mansfield 126–128, 130, 132–133, 138, 147–148
Lyons, Lord 46

Mackall, Col. W. W. 43–44, 56, 58–60, 85
Macon, MS 168
Madison County 187
Magoffin, Beriah 4, 30
Magoffin, James Wiley 27, 30–31
Mahan, Dennis Hart 7–8, 49–50
Manifest Destiny 9, 21
Maryland 4–5, 25, 111–112
Mason, James M. 45–46
Mason-Dixon Line 3, 26
Masonic county map 164
Matamoros 13–15, 27
Maury, Gen. D. H. 164
McCall, Gen. C. A. 116
McClernand, Gen. John A. 84, 96, 157, 167, 171–173, 176–177, 179, 187–190
McClung, Richard L. 101, 193
McCulloch, Ben 15, 27
McCulloch, Robert "Black Bob" 140, 155, 159
McGavock, Randal W. 111–112, 114, 117, 119–122, 179
McPherson, J. B. 173, 176–177, 179, 181

McRaie, George 159
Mellon, T. A. 165
Memminger, R. W. 179
Memphis, TN 32, 47, 58, 168
Meridian, MS 168, 170
Merrin, Lt. F. W. 186
Merriwether, Maj. M. 153
Metz, France 7
Mexican War 12–13, 18, 171
Mexicans' uniforms 13–14, 16
Mexico 10, 27
Mexico City 17
Milliken's Bend 167–168
Mint Spring Bayou 92
Mississippi 4, 25–26, 33, 42, 47; railroads 118; 120, 128, 130–131, 144, 157, 164, 168, 171–172, 176, 180, 186
Mississippi Army 33
Mississippi Central Railroad 168
Mississippi River 33–34, 36, 42, 47, 59, 63, 87, 94, 143, 157, 166, 168, 175, 177–178, 180
Missouri 4, 25, 29, 32, 96, 157
Mobile & Ohio Railroad 140–141, 170
Monitor-Merrimac 60
Monterrey: Citadel 15–16
Montgomery, AL 4, 27, 29, 92
Moon Lake 150, 152, 157, 163, 165
Moore, Gov. A. B. 51
Moore, Gen. J. C. 164
Mormon rebellion 37
Morris, Robert 6
Morton, MS 170
Mount Alban 175
Murfreesboro, TN 106
Murray Road 60–62
Myrick, Capt. J. D. 155

Nashville, TN 36–37, 39–40, 42, 44, 46–48, 57, 60, 64, 66, 93–94, 98, 101–102, 104–106, 113, 180
Nelson, William 64
New Orleans 17
New York City 197
New York Standard 8
New York Tribune 3, 25
Newton 170
Nicaragua 19, 21
North and South 3
North Carolina 25, 29

Ocean Queen 114
Ohio River 34–36
"Old Blizzards" 162
"Old Woodpecker" 126
Oxford, MS 131, 138, 140

Paducah, KY 4, 22, 28, 31–36, 42, 44, 63–64, 86, 92, 110, 198
Palo Alto 15
Panama 21

Index

Panama railroading 19–22
Panther Island 59, 72, 75
Parallet 159
Paris Landing 59–60
Paulding, MS 170
Pearl River 170
Pemberton, Gen. J. C. 12, 128–129, 131, 138–140, 145–147, 149, 153, 155, 159, 163, 166, 168–172, 174–175, 177–182, 185–190, 192–193
Pennsylvania 5
personal liberty laws 24
Pettus, Gov. John. J. 172, 175
Pharr, Lieutenant 57
Philadelphia 170
Pillow, Gen. Gideon 49, 51, 92–94, 98, 101–102, 107, 113, 122
Point Isabel 14–15
Pointe Coupee 155, 174
Polk, President James K. 10, 12, 16, 18, 33
Polk, Gen. Leonidas 33–34, 36, 39, 42–44, 46, 50, 55–57, 59, 62–64, 92, 96, 106
Ponchatoula, MS 125
Pontotoc, MS 168
Port Gibson 172–174, 182
Port Hudson 6, 121, 142–143, 172, 176, 192–193
Porter, Admiral D. D. 167, 172, 175
Porter, Capt. W. D. 78
Price, Gen. Sterling 123–128
proclamation 34, 41–42
Purnell 153

Quinby, Gen. I. F. 163–165

Radclift Road 185
railroads 10, 22–23
Randolph, G. W. 117
Rattler 162
Raymond 176, 179, 182–183, 185–192
Rebel flea 129
"Rebel yell" 16
Red Hill 132–133
Red River 142–143, 172, 192
Resaca de la Palma 15
Reynolds, Col. A. E. 175, 194
Reynolds, Gen. J. F. 116
Richmond, VA 33, 39, 52, 59, 92, 116, 174, 180
Richmond Enquirer 113
Rio Grande 13, 15
Ripley, MS 125, 127, 140
Robinson, Capt. Powhatan 153
Rock of Gibraltar 42
Ross, Gen. L. F. 157, 161
Russellville 48, 52
Rust, A. 126, 145

St. Louis 36
Salt Lake City 37

Saltillo 16
Santa Anna: army 16
Saunders, Dr. H. L. 57
Scott, Gen. Winfield 10–11, 16, 27
Searles 192
secession, ordinances of 4
Second Seminole Indian War 9
Seminole Indians 9
Seward, William H. 46
Shell Mound 161
Shepperd, Lt. F. E. 153
Sherman, Gen. W. T. 35, 86–87, 139, 143, 147, 150, 171, 175–177, 180–181, 195
Shiloh 123
Shoemaker, James and Caroline 6
slaves: 23; fugitive 23–24
Slidell, John 45–46
Smith, Gen. C. F. 60–61, 84, 96, 98, 109
Smith, Gen. Edmund Kirby 195
Smith, Gen. G. W. 157, 163
Smith, Gen. M. L. 182
Snyder's Bluff 155
South Carolina 4, 25–26
Southern Railroad 170
Southgate, Elizabeth 10
Stacker, George W. 55–56
Stanton 36, 86, 114
Star of the West 155, 157, 160, 164
Starkville, MS 168, 170
States' Rights 26, 32
Stevenson, Gen. C. L. 171, 175, 187, 189–190
Stirman, Rus 144; sharpshooters 165; 196
submarine batteries 57
Sugg, Cyrus A. 55

Tallahatchie River 129, 131, 151, 153–155, 157, 159, 164–165
Taylor, Capt. Jesse 50, 77, 80–81
Taylor, Gen. Zachary 12–18, 22
Tennessee 25, 29, 31–32, 40, 42, 44, 49, 51–52, 58–59, 63–64, 107
Tennessee Provisional Army 40, 47, 49, 63–64
Tennessee River 30, 32, 34, 36, 42–43, 47, 49, 50–51, 58–59, 71–72, 80, 86, 107
Texas 4, 10, 13, 18, 25,–28, 37
Texas Rangers 15 16
Thayer, Sylvanus 7–8
Thomas, Gen. George 65, 92
Tilghman, Augusta 32, 195
Tilghman, Frederick B. 196–198
Tilghman, John Leeds 6
Tilghman, Gen. Lloyd 191–192, 194–200
Tilghman, Lloyd, Jr. 137, 191, 195
Tilghman, Matthew 5
Tilghman, Oswald 6, 58, 80, 103, 192–193
Tilghman, Dr. Richard 5
Tilghman, Richard III 5
Tilghman, Sidell 196–198
Tilghman, Tench C. 5–6

Tilghman, Tench F. 6
Tilghman, William 5
Tippah River 129
torpedoes 72
Tracy, Gen. E. D. 173–174, 193
Treaty of Guadalupe 17
Trent Affair 45
Tullahoma, TN 147, 167, 171, 176, 179
Tupelo, MS 124
Twiggs, Gen. John 10–12, 15–17, 27–28

Uncle Tom's Cabin 26
unconditional surrender 103
Union 3–4, 33–37, 40, 47, 58–59, 63, 86, 109, 120
Union Navy 58–60, 71, 75, 151, 160, 187
Union recruiters 4
U.S. Army 37, 60, 188
U.S. Army, Southern leanings 28
U.S. Cavalry 37
United States Military Academy 6–7, 37
United States volunteer forces, Mexican War: officers 12
Utah Territory 37

Van Dorn, Gen. Earl 123–126, 128–131, 133, 138–141, 147, 168, 171
Veracruz 16–17
Vicksburg, MS 131, 138–139, 142–143, 145, 150–151, 155, 167–168, 171, 173–175, 178, 180–183, 185, 190, 192–193, 198
Villepigue, J. B. 126–127
Virginia 25, 29, 63, 92, 102
Voorhies, Dr. A. H. 69

Walker, Admiral Henry 71–72, 77
Walker, Gen. W. H. T. 179–180
Wallace, Gen. Lew 84, 98
Ward, S. D. 60
Warrenton 173
Washington, DC 3
Washington, George 6
Water Valley 131, 139
Waul, Col. T. N. 145, 155, 162, 165
Weakley, S. D. 51, 71
weathermen 69–70
Weldon, Thomas 155
West Point 8–9, 17, 30, 33, 47, 49, 101, 112, 132, 148, 177
Western Department, or Frontier 38–39, 43, 55, 63, 92
White, Pat 191
Williamson, George 52
Willow Springs 175
Winona 170
Wither, Col. W. F. 190–191
Woodlawn Cemetery 197

Yalobusha River 139–140, 151, 164
"Yankee Doodle" 15, 59, 109
Yazoo City 151, 153, 155, 159, 163
Yazoo Pass 150; roster 151; map 152; 157
Yazoo River 150–151, 153, 155, 171
Yerger, Capt. William S. 181
Young, Brigham 37

Zollicoffer, Felix Kirk 46, 49, 63–66, 70, 92

www.ingramcontent.com/pod-product-compliance
Ingram Content Group UK Ltd.
Pitfield, Milton Keynes, MK11 3LW, UK
UKHW041954140426
5217IPUK00015B/790